W9-BXT-564

Archaeology

drawings and maps by SHIRLEY FELTS

of the Bible

MAGNUS MAGNUSSON

SIMON AND SCHUSTER · NEW YORK

This book is dedicated to Dr James B. Pritchard, Director of the University Museum of the University of Pennsylvania, and through him to the host of scholars, both named and unnamed, whose work is reflected in this book. The book is the outcome of many months of research and travel which I undertook on behalf of the BBC for the television documentary series of the same name that was first transmitted on BBC 2 in the late winter and spring of 1977. Wherever my colleagues and I went in the Middle East, we were given every possible facility and shown nothing but kindness by the national authorities and archaeologists of every country involved. To all those who gave so freely of their time and expertise, I would like to express my sincere gratitude. Dr Pritchard was our consultant on the film series, and has also rooted out any major errors in the manuscript of the book.

I also want to thank my good colleagues on the BBC team who did so much to make the work on the series, and the book, so enjoyable: the girls on the production team, Ann Russell, Rosalind Bentley (picture research), Amina Harris (documentary research), and Alexandra Branson, who held it all together; my producers, Paul Jordan and Antonia Benedek, who enlivened every location filming with argument and illumination; and the executive producer, David Collison, comrade of many an archaeological film for *Chronicle* in the past, whose faith in the project and judicious balancing of many competing interests made the whole thing possible.

Library of Congress Cataloging in Publication Data

Magnusson, Magnus.
    Archaeology of the Bible.

    First published in 1977 under title: BC, the
archaeology of the Bible lands.
    Bibliography: p.
    Includes index.
    1. Bible.   O.T.–Antiquities.   2. Palestine–
Antiquities.   3. Excavations (Archaeology)–Palestine.
I. Title.
BS621.M33   1978   221.9   78-9547
ISBN 0-671-24010-2

Contents

Foreword

The remarkable recovery of the past through recent archaeology has revolutionised the writing of ancient history which once was totally dependent upon what Biblical and classical writers had said. The new increment to the knowledge of the past has demanded a reassessment of the older sources and evoked widely differing opinions.

The scene of scholarly debate has long been curtained off from the general public, with the excuse that the layman cannot understand. One may believe, as I do, that the specialist has underestimated his wider public, or has found himself incapable of presenting involved arguments to a general audience. In this book these conflicting views have been brought into the open. The reader is allowed to see and hear the doubters as well as the believers, to learn of ingenious theories and their rebuttal – in fact, to face candidly some of the hard questions that have for so long perplexed scholars as they have tried to reconcile what has been handed down in the Bible with the artefacts which have come up from archaeological excavations in the lands of the Bible. At long last the intelligent onlooker has been given a chance to participate, to make up his mind about possible alternatives.

Unlike the Bible, which is an avowedly partisan book committed to one faith and concerned primarily with the fortunes of one ancient people, archaeological discoveries from the Near and Middle East provide a more objective picture of ancient peoples and their traditions. Such important and often maligned peoples as the Sumerians, Canaanites, Philistines, Assyrians and Babylonians emerge from oblivion and appear as they were or considered themselves to have been.

In this new book the interviews with archaeologists who are today making discoveries and propounding new theories are up to date. The dust has hardly settled. When it does, some enthusiasms may wane; but at least the reader is in a position to share the excitement of new discoveries and know how they are to be related – for the moment at least – to the Bible saga. He is as close as he can get to the future. The view is from front row centre.

James B. Pritchard

1
In the Beginning

'In the beginning God created the heaven and the earth. And the earth was without form, and void; and darkness was upon the face of the deep. And the Spirit of God moved upon the face of the waters.'

These are the opening words, in the Authorised Version of King James, of the most famous book in the world: the Old Testament of the Bible. I always tend to think of the Bible as a saga, because to my mind it is above all a tremendous literary epic that tries to encompass the whole range of human experience: man in relation to the universe of which he is significantly, or insignificantly, a part.

'In the beginning' – what a magnificent opening it is. But what really is the Old Testament? And what really was the beginning?

In one sense, one should look for 'the beginning' in the sun-baked reaches of southern Mesopotamia, the river lands between the Euphrates and the Tigris in what is now modern Iraq: the south-eastern end of the so-called Fertile Crescent which is generally regarded as the cradle of civilisation. It was at places like Uruk (Biblical Erech) in the ancient land of Sumer (Biblical Shinar) that everything began, long before the Bible was written or even conceived; because that was where *history* began, in the sense of written history. That was where man became a civilised social animal. That was where we meet, for the first time, the recorded mind of man.

So how does our growing recognition of how we began – man as a child of the universe – match the image presented in the Bible? In the last century, and particularly in the last decade, archaeology has done and is still doing a great deal to clarify and illuminate our understanding of the Bible as a document. From being our sole source about the origins and development of civilisation in the Middle East, the Bible can now be set in the much broader context of our growing knowledge about the human revolution that helped to shape our world.

Our purpose in this book is to explore the literary, historical, social, economic, theological and political perspectives throughout the Middle East that gave rise to the Bible. The

Bible does not exist in a vacuum. It was written long after the early events it purports to record, and only by understanding the cultural context in which it was written, and the society for which it was written, can we gain a clearer understanding of the work as a whole.

To this end, we must study the peoples and civilisations *around* ancient Israel and not just the story of the 'Holy Land' alone. Not only do they, directly and indirectly, tell us more about the history of Palestine than the Bible does; their idea of prehistory, their mythology, their legends, their world view, all informed and helped to mould the Biblical picture of the past.

For centuries, that picture was accepted as literal revealed truth, and inspired countless artists down the ages as well as leaving an ineradicable stamp on Western culture. Only 300 years ago, Archbishop James Ussher of Armagh, in Ireland, was able to use *Genesis* to 'prove' that the Creation took place in precisely 4004 BC; today, astronomers disagree on how the universe as we perceive it began, but the most conservative estimate of its age is 10,000 million years!

Similarly, Archbishop Ussher's world chronology was soon refined by Dr John Lightfoot, Vice-Chancellor of Cambridge University, who pinpointed the precise moment when Adam was created – 'on October 23, 4004 BC, at nine o'clock in the morning'. Today, we know that Dr Lightfoot was at least 35,000 years out in his reckoning, and that *Homo sapiens*, or Adam (the Hebrew word for 'man'), had been slowly evolving for hundreds of thousands of years even before that.

The emergence of *Homo sapiens* in the Middle East has been dramatically illustrated by archaeological excavations in the Valley of the Caves on the western flank of the Mount Carmel range of northern Israel. Here, a few miles south of Haifa and not far off the main coastal highway, the canyon-like cliffs are pocked with caves, four of which served as human dwellings in very ancient times. They were first excavated in the late twenties and early thirties by a joint British-American expedition led by Dr Dorothy Garrod and, later, T.D.McCown; work has been recently resumed under the direction of Dr Avram Ronen of Haifa University.

There was ample evidence that the caves had been used for tens of thousands of years by the ancestors of Man – nomadic hunters who used flint weapons and implements. Then, in the southernmost cave of the group (et-Tabun, 'the Oven'), Dr Garrod found a human skeleton lying on its back with its

Opposite above Jawa in north-eastern Jordan: to the right, remains of the earth-core dam built to trap flash-flood water from the Wadi Rajil.

Opposite below Uruk: north-eastern side of the ruined ziggurat

8

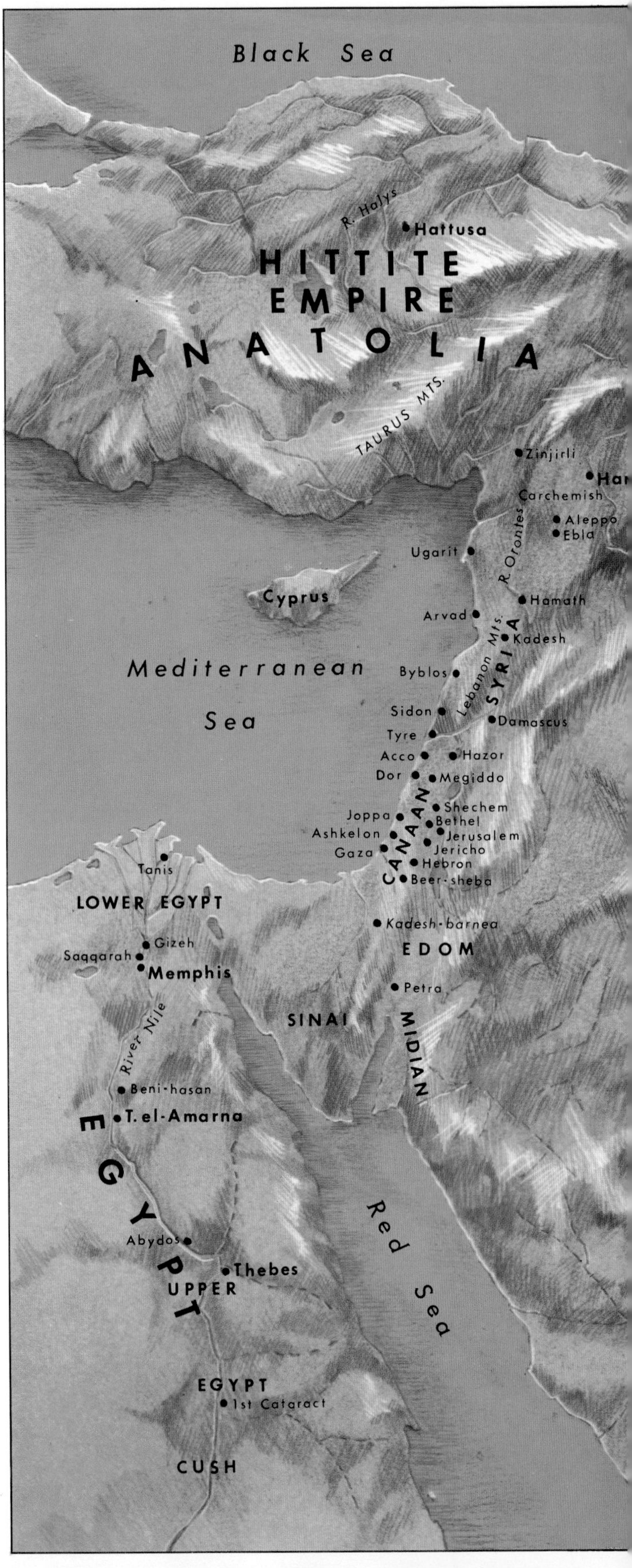

Black Sea

R. Holys

●Hattusa

HITTITE
EMPIRE
ANATOLIA

TAURUS MTS.

●Zinjirli

●Har

Carchemish

●Aleppo
●Ebla

Ugarit ●

R. Orontes

●Hamath

Arvad ●
●Kadesh

S
Y
R
I
A

Cyprus

Mediterranean

Byblos ●

Lebanon Mts.

Sea

Sidon ●
Tyre ●

●Damascus

Acco ● ●Hazor
Dor ● ●Megiddo

Joppa ● ●Shechem
Ashkelon ● ●Bethel
●Jerusalem
Gaza ● ●Jericho
●Hebron
●Beer-sheba

C
A
N
A
A
N

Tanis ●

LOWER EGYPT

●Kadesh-barnea

EDOM

●Gizeh
Saqqarah ●
●Memphis

●Petra

SINAI

M
I
D
I
A
N

River Nile

●Beni-hasan
●T. el-Amarna

Red

E
G
Y
P
T

Abydos ●
●Thebes

Sea

UPPER

EGYPT
●1st Cataract

CUSH

The Ancient Near East

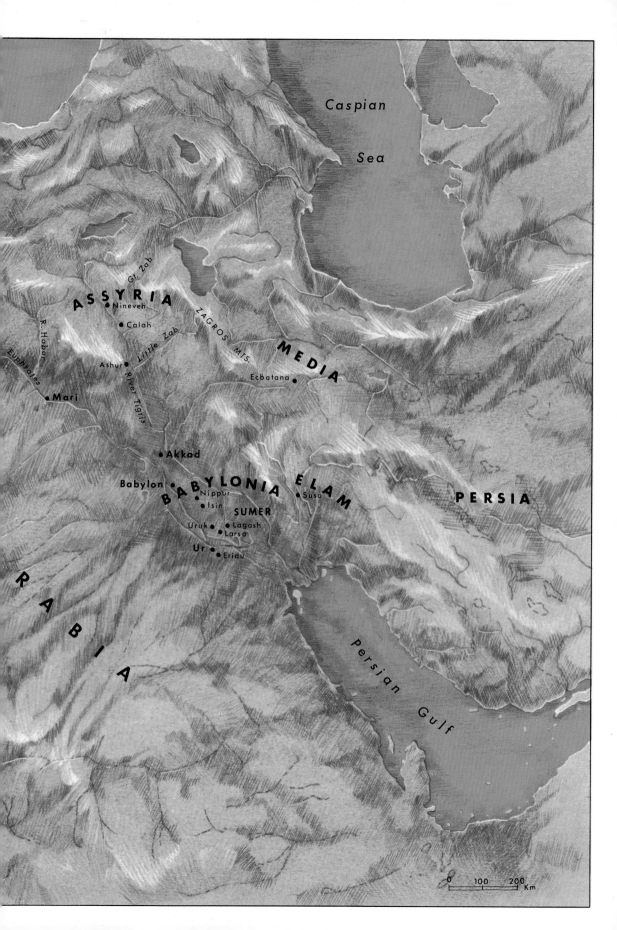

Caspian
Sea

ASSYRIA
Gt. Zab
•Nineveh
•Calah

ZAGROS MTS.

MEDIA

R. Habor
Little Zab
Ashur•
River Tigris
•Ecbatana

Euphrates

•Mari

•Akkad

Babylon•
BABYLONIA
ELAM
PERSIA
•Nippur
•Susa
•Isin
SUMER
Uruk• •Lagash
•Larsa
Ur• •Eridu

A
R
A
B
I
A

Persian
Gulf

0   100   200
Km

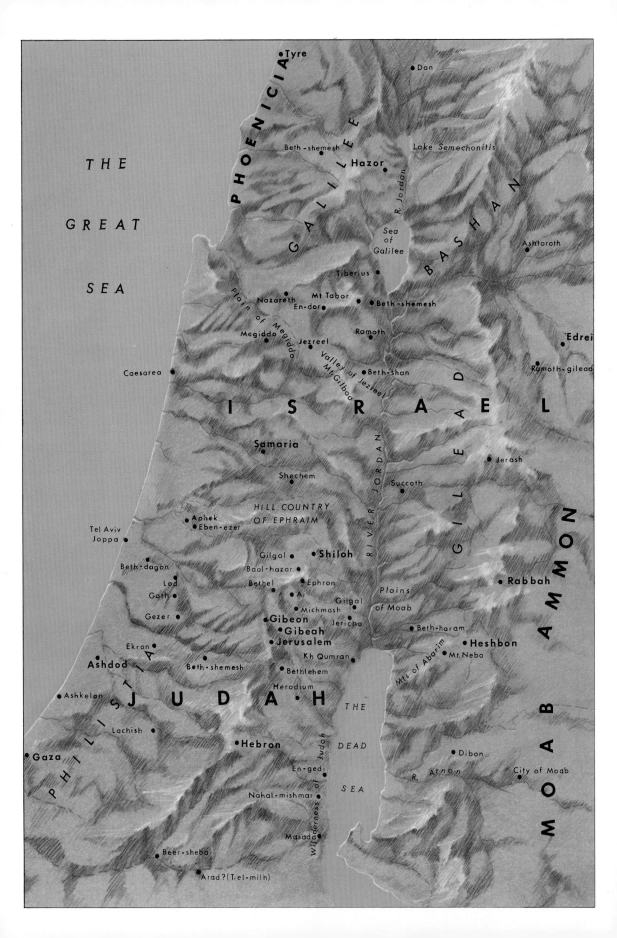

General view of the Valley of the Caves at Mount Carmel. To the right, et-Tabun (the Oven); to the left, es-Sukhul (the Kid).

Opposite
Palestine in Old Testament times.

legs flexed. This skeleton, which became celebrated as the Woman of Tabun, was that of a female of the Neanderthal form of man. The remains of Neanderthal Man (*Homo sapiens neanderthalensis*) have been found in many parts of the world, and he seems to have lived from c.150,000 BC to 40,000 BC, when he was gradually replaced by the modern form of man – *Homo sapiens sapiens*. The Woman of Tabun was dated c.40,000 BC; she was among the last of the Neanderthals.

In a neighbouring cave (es-Sukhul, 'the Kid') farther up the valley, the excavators came across a group of ten skeletons; it had evidently served as a burial ground in prehistoric times. These skeletons bore distinct characteristics of the modern form of *Homo sapiens*. Originally, the Tabun and Sukhul skeletons were thought to be contemporary with each other, and they were hailed as a hybrid form of Neanderthal and fully modern man – the missing link, as it were, to explain the final stage of the chain of man's evolution. Now, however, it is believed that the Sukhul skeletons should be dated 10,000 years later than the Woman of Tabun, around 30,000 BC, and that there is not necessarily any direct evolutionary relationship between the two.

The name of Mount Carmel is familiar to us from the Bible in connection with much later events (it was there that Elijah was said to have confounded the prophets of Baal, in the *First Book of Kings*). An even more celebrated Biblical place-name has afforded archaeologists a glimpse of the great leap forward from man as a nomadic hunter and cave-dweller

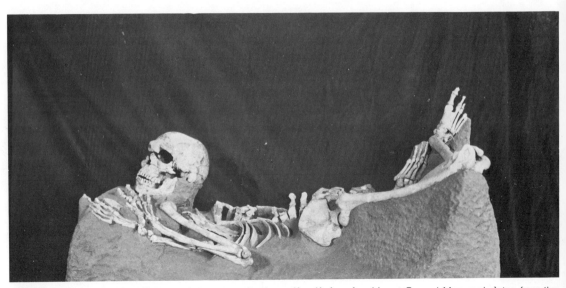

to man as a town-dweller, a peasant agriculturalist living in settled communities; that place is Jericho.

Jericho lies in the great rift of the Jordan Valley, a few kilometres north of the Dead Sea and 230 metres below sea-level. Most of the Jordan Valley is an arid wilderness, a white desert of baked stone and sand. Nothing can grow there. Yet it was in this barren valley that man made this significant step forward; and the key to it was water. One copious perennial spring created at Jericho a huge oasis of luxuriant green vegetation in the middle of the desert.

Water made the surrounding soil fertile. The tropical climate, winter and summer alike, encouraged not only growth, but planned growth. It inspired the deliberate cultivation of wheat and barley, instead of the haphazard collection of wild cereals. The 6000 gallons of water per hour that come bubbling out of the spring at Jericho made settlement possible – the first stage in the progress towards civilisation proper. It is what prehistorians call the Neolithic Revolution – Neolithic means New Stone Age – and it happened at Jericho around 10,000 BC. It was the crucial change from nomadic to settled life that is reflected in the Bible in the enmity between Abel, 'a keeper of sheep', and Cain, 'a tiller of the ground'.

The spring emerges at the foot of a great mound or *tell*, known as Tell es-Sultan, on the outskirts of modern Jericho. A *tell* is a man-made hill consisting of the ruins of settlements each built upon the debris of another. This was the ancient site of Jericho.

Jericho has been excavated on several occasions. But it

was not until the most recent dig, by Dame Kathleen Kenyon of the British School of Archaeology in Jerusalem in 1952-8, that the remarkable antiquity and significance of Jericho was revealed. Dame Kathleen showed that long before Jericho became a town, nomads had been coming to the oasis for rest and refuge, season after season, and had built a little sanctuary there – a small rectangular clay platform with a retaining stone wall. Some of the descendants of these early nomads then settled in Jericho, more or less permanently. Above bedrock, the excavators found an innumerable succession of tramped earthen floors and round house-walls.

Once fully sedentary occupation began, the community expanded very rapidly; and this explosive expansion can only have been associated with the development of new agricultural techniques. In turn, this can only be explained by the development of a complex irrigation system, to create larger areas of fertility. Such a development argues a considerable degree of social organisation, with a central authority based on the control and distribution of surplus agricultural supplies, capable of directing, and paying, an ample labour force for public works and enforcing standards of communal co-existence – a code of law, in effect.

The most astounding of these public works was the construction of massive fortifications consisting of a thick stone-built wall that still survived, when excavated, to a height of nearly seven metres in places. Outside it there was a broad ditch that had been gouged out of the bedrock. Even more spectacular was the discovery of a great stone tower, still

Neolithic house-fittings at Jericho: patterns imprinted on early floor levels by two overlapping circular rush-mats.

Neolithic Jericho: at the bottom levels, the earliest fortifications, underlying later walls.

standing to a height of ten metres, with a well-made interior staircase of stone giving access from inside the town to the top of the tower. Radiocarbon dates suggest that these prodigious fortifications were originally built around 8000 BC, but allowing for the known deviations that occur in radiocarbon dating in prehistoric times, this date should properly be corrected to nearly 10,000 BC. It makes Jericho the oldest walled city in the world that we yet know of.

It is a staggering thought, that man should have reached this remarkable level of communal organisation and architectural ability so early in time. To stand at the edge of the deep trench dug by Dame Kathleen, and to look down at this wonderfully preserved tower, never fails to awe the thousands of people who visit the site every year.

The Neolithic defence tower at Jericho: the grill at the top covers access to the internal stone staircase. At the bottom, the entrance to the tower itself.

The people who built the first city of Jericho and its fortifications made vessels of stone, not pottery, and so archaeologists call this period Pre-Pottery (or a-ceramic) Neolithic. But why were these huge walls built at all? Presumably for defence against a formidable enemy, not just marauding nomads who coveted its prosperity – a prosperity which must surely have been based on trade as well as local agriculture. The hypothesis seems proved by the fact that, after about a thousand years, Jericho was taken over by another Pre-Pottery people, who brought with them a new style of architecture. They also brought with them new forms of religion. The most striking evidence of this came from the discovery of ten human skulls which had been moulded with plaster into the likeness of human features;

13

the eye sockets were inlaid with shells, the ears, nose, eyebrows and mouth had been delicately modelled and tinted, giving the heads an extraordinarily lifelike appearance. They are masterpieces of artistic and technical skill, and must surely have been associated with a cult of ancestor worship.

The earliest inhabitants of Jericho did not know how to make pottery vessels. The development of pottery utensils – one of the many significant inventions of prehistoric man – can best be exemplified by the site of Çatal Hüyük, in what was once ancient Anatolia (now Turkey). Here, in the 1960s, the British archaeologist James Mellaart discovered the remains of one of the world's oldest towns, radiocarbon dated to 6000 BC (corrected date, c.7100 BC).

Çatal Hüyük, which lies about forty-five kilometres southeast of the town of Konya, is one of the largest Neolithic sites known in the Near and Middle East. It was a huge place, with a population of some 5-6000, at least four times larger than ancient Jericho. Its economy was based on advanced agriculture (with artificial irrigation) and trade, its urban life was sophisticated to a degree not yet encountered anywhere else in the world at this early date. In the earliest levels of habitation of the Çatal Hüyük site, Mellaart found a number of 'firsts' – the first textiles, the first mirrors, the first wooden vessels, the first paintings on plastered walls, and above all, the first pottery. It started with simple bowls of cream-burnished, straw-tempered clay, heavy and lumpy, but developed in refinement and technique until, by the end of the first period of occupation (c.6000 BC), the first attempts were being made to decorate the pottery with smears of paint.

The development of pottery was highly significant not only for civilisation itself, but for archaeology; because from now on, excavators could use pottery found in stratified levels as an aid to dating sites by comparing it with pottery found elsewhere. The Çatal Hüyük discoveries also made it clear that the development of civilisation was by no means limited to the Fertile Crescent itself, but could happen spontaneously elsewhere as well.

In the time-scale of man's early achievements, perhaps the most significant invention that followed pottery was the development of metallurgy. At Çatal Hüyük, Mellaart found evidence of experimentation with metals – lead and copper – to make trinkets and ornaments; but the Copper Age, or Chalcolithic Age as it is also called, meaning a period when both copper and stone were in use, is generally regarded as having started c.4000 BC.

One of the plastered skulls from Jericho.

Early pottery from Anatolia: boldly decorated vessel from Hacilar, which developed from the simple start at Çatal Hüyük.

The most superb hoard of copper objects ever found in the
Middle East was discovered in 1961 hidden in an almost
inaccessible cave in a canyon called Nahal Mishmar, overlooking the western shores of the Dead Sea, near the oasis of
En-gedi. The opening of the cave was near the top of a vertical
cliff nearly 300 metres high; the only access was by means of
a rope ladder from the top of the cliff. It was one of many caves
in the area explored by an Israeli expedition, after the discovery of the first Dead Sea Scrolls nearby (see Chapter 12).

The excavators, led by Pessah Bar-Adon of the Department of Antiquities in Jerusalem, found the cave had been used by Jewish refugees during the Roman occupation of Palestine. But underneath the debris and floors of beaten earth they had left behind there was evidence of an earlier occupation more than 3800 years before, dating to the Chalcolithic period, around 3500 BC.

On the eighth day of the excavation, a natural niche was found in the north wall of the cave, loosely covered by a sloping stone; inside the niche, there was an astonishing hoard of 429 handsome objects, carefully wrapped in a straw mat. All but thirteen of them were made of copper with a high arsenic content.

The objects were breathtaking not only in their quantity but in their quality. About 240 of them were interpreted as 'mace-heads' of various designs and shapes. There were also about eighty 'sceptres' or 'standards', some of them extremely elaborate and terminating in human faces or complex ibex heads. But perhaps the most remarkable of the objects were ten 'crowns'; they are decorated with striking ornamentation, a profusion of birds and human faces and gate-like projections. All the objects, which are on prominent display in the Israel Museum in Jerusalem, are evidence of a highly sophisticated skill in copper casting at a date much earlier than had previously been suspected.

But what had these objects been used for? And where had they come from? Israeli scholars are convinced that they were cultic objects from a temple that had been excavated at En-gedi, ten kilometres to the north, ten years earlier. There, on an escarpment high above the Dead Sea, an Israeli expedition led by Professor Benjamin Mazar of the Hebrew University of Jerusalem uncovered the remains of a substantial stone-built enclosure from the Chalcolithic period which was interpreted as a religious sanctuary. It contained several structures, including, right at the centre, a curious round platform that was assumed to have had some sort of cultic significance. Pottery finds enabled the enclosure to be dated to the period 3300-3200 BC, and the excavator has suggested that this was the central sanctuary of the villagers and shepherds of the Judean desert and its oases. The sanctuary was not destroyed, but was simply abandoned – and the suggestion is that all the cultic objects of copper were removed to a place of safety and hidden in the cave at Nahal Mishmar, but never retrieved.

No one is sure about the provenance of the objects. Israeli

Opposite above Tell Mardikh: general view of the excavation. In the foreground, part of the south-western gateway and its fortifications.

Opposite below Tell Mardikh: in the foreground, the repository in which the 15,000 tablets of the state archives of Ebla were found in 1975.

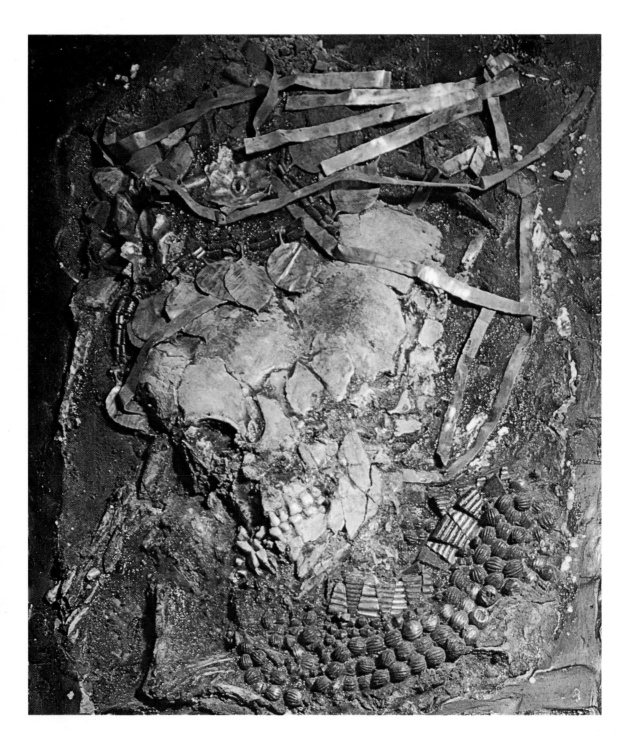

Opposite Skull and jewellery of a court lady from the Royal Cemetery at Ur. Above, a headband of 'beech leaves' made from thin gold foil. Round her neck she wore necklaces of gold, lapis lazuli and carnelian.

scholars would like to detect a native or local origin, but it is generally thought that they must be imports from far away to the north-east – Mesopotamia or Iran. But wherever the hoard came from originally, it is vivid evidence of man's great technological and artistic skill in the fourth millennium BC.

Man's capacity to cope with his environment in prehistoric times is being increasingly emphasised by recent archaeology. One of his most remarkable, and unlikely, achievements has just been revealed at a remote site in north-eastern Jordan, at a place called Jawa. It forms a large island of basalt rock in the middle of the desert, with no local water resources whatsoever; yet here, in the middle of the fourth millennium BC, settlers created a major town with a population of perhaps 5-6000, whose very existence depended entirely upon sophisticated hydro-engineering.

The site was excavated between 1973-5 by Dr Svend Helms, then of the Institute of Archaeology in London. From his preliminary reports, it is clear that Jawa was a fortified and well-planned town that flourished for about a century, long before urbanisation occurred elsewhere in Palestine. Yet there was no spring-water available, for the lava flows in the region are nearly a thousand metres thick; the only way the town could survive was by storing sufficient water from the rainy season to last throughout the dry season of five or six months.

Jawa was sited beside a *wadi*, or seasonal water-course, called Wadi Rajil. In order to trap and retain sufficient of the water that came flooding down the Wadi Rajil in the winter, the engineers of Jawa constructed an earth-core dam ninety metres long and thirty metres thick to create a huge reservoir with sufficient capacity to meet the needs of the townspeople and their livestock.

But how did the people survive while the great dam was being built? Which came first – the reservoir, or the town? It seems that the first settlers, who came to the site with previous experience of an urban culture, started by digging a series of rock-cut pools that were fed from the *wadi*. Then, as the town expanded, the dam proper was built – and built, apparently, in exactly the same way as a modern engineer would have built it.

Control of the water resources of a region has always been the key to development and prosperity in the Middle East, and it remains immensely important to this day. The massive new dam on the upper Euphrates at Tabqa, in northern

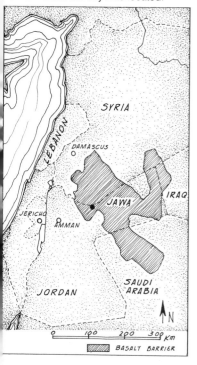

Jawa: map by the excavator, Svend Helms, showing the extensive basalt lava flow on which the city was located.

17

Syria, is a case in point: here, a vast lake has been created, eighty kilometres long and eight kilometres broad, to revitalise agriculture and industry in the region. Like the Aswan Dam in Egypt, this project inspired an international archaeological effort to excavate threatened sites before they were submerged. Sponsored by UNESCO and coordinated by the Directorate-General of Antiquities and Museums of Syria, no fewer than sixteen mission were sent to the area by ten countries – Belgium, France, Germany, Great Britain, Holland, Italy, Japan, Spain, the United States, and of course Syria itself – to salvage sites that spanned a range of 10,000 years, from Neolithic times to the Islamic period. The results of these heroic rescue digs were placed on display in Aleppo Museum.

Considering the overriding importance of water supplies, it is not surprising that Mesopotamia, the 'land between the rivers', should have provided the setting for the next major stage in man's progress towards civilisation, the means by which he stepped into history proper – the invention of writing.

Round about 3500 BC, it is believed, the Semitic population of southern Mesopotamia was infiltrated, or invaded, by a non-Semitic race who proceeded to found a number of city-states that came to be known, collectively, as Sumer. Remarkably enough, Sumer and the Sumerians only became known to historians a century ago, after having been 'lost' completely for 2000 years; it was only through the discovery of Assyrian inscriptions in the middle of the nineteenth century that the existence of Sumer was first hinted at, and then proved by archaeology.

The royal city-states of Sumer built their prosperity, as their predecessors at Jericho and Catal Hüyük had done, on complex irrigation systems, commerce, and now metallurgy as well. And by some special concatenation of circumstances, the conditions arose in which there evolved what can properly be called, for the first time, 'civilisation' – a civilisation that recorded its activities and thoughts in writing.

One of the earliest and most significant of these city-states of Sumer was Uruk (Biblical Erech, modern Warka), which has been extensively excavated by a number of German expeditions from 1912 onwards. It was a large city, covering an area of some 200 acres, and divided into three main quarters – official buildings, dwelling houses, and gardens and cemeteries. Today it is a dusty, arid place; but once it was, quite literally, a watershed for mankind, a bustling, beautiful city.

'In the beginning': excavated temple precincts at the Sumerian city of Uruk, looking south-west from the top of the ziggurat.

The site is still dominated by the ruined stump of a ziggurat, a rectangular staged mound that the Sumerians built as an artificial mountain of mud-brick to provide a sanctuary for the gods. Uruk was an important religious centre, for it was the home-city of the chief god of the Sumerians, the sky-god Anu, father of all the gods. He had a shrine on top of the ziggurat, and a fine temple on ground level decorated with patterned mosaics formed by terracotta cones with painted heads pressed into a bed of mud-plaster.

Temples like these were a reflection and a product of intensified economic growth. The temple was the administrative and social centre of the city; together, king and priest (and gods) formed a theocratic bureaucracy which ran the state. As the administration became more complex, it became necessary to develop a form of recording the daily transactions of the temple; and thus writing was born.

In one of the temples of Uruk, German archaeologists discovered early evidence of this: an archive of hundreds of small clay tablets inscribed with crude pictographic signs, dating from about 3100 BC. That was how writing began, using simplified pictures representing objects which gave rise to associated ideas. Later, this primitive system would be refined into a more stylised form called cuneiform, in which the symbols involved could be rapidly impressed on soft clay with a wedge-shaped stylus (cuneiform simply means 'wedge-shaped'), and the tablets would then be baked to harden and preserve them.

To start with, writing was used exclusively as a vehicle for administrative and commercial notation. But by about 2500 BC it had developed into a sophisticated *literary* form, capable of expressing complex mythological and historical concepts. And it is from these later documents that we learn about the gods of ancient Sumer.

The Sumerians had an extremely highly developed theology. They were also profoundly devout; innumerable figurines have been excavated showing people in attitudes of reverence, hands clasped, eyes wide with piety and awe, which had been deposited in temples as votive offerings to the gods. No doubt these votive figurines were meticulously recorded by scribes like the celebrated Dudu, amiable and podgy in his sheep's-fleece skirt, whose statuette proudly records in a pictographic inscription on his back the importance of his status. And it is scribes like Dudu that we have to thank for our knowledge of the Sumerian pantheon.

The supreme father of the gods was Anu, the source of all order and government. The god of wisdom was Enki (also called Ea), while Enlil was the storm-god. There was a sun-god (Shamash) and a moon-god (Sin). On the distaff side, the most potent of the goddesses was Ishtar (originally called Inanna in Sumer), who would become notorious in the Bible as Ashtoreth (Astarte), the mother of abominations. One of the earliest representations of her is to be seen on the magnificent Uruk Vase, a tall alabaster vessel dating to around 3000 BC, which shows her receiving offerings from a procession of naked priests.

Ishtar was a very complex deity. She was the goddess of fertility and sexual activity, the goddess of war, and in her astral manifestation, she was the Venus star in the sky. Kathleen Beatty, a young Canadian scholar at Birmingham University who is studying Mesopotamian religion, finds Ishtar (Inanna) the most intriguing of all the Sumerian divinities. She has detected hints that Ishtar was in some way

The scribe Dudu: temple votive offering from c.2500. The inscription on his back records the dedication of the statue, giving his name and profession, to one of the gods of Sumer.

Limestone plaque from a Sumerian temple at Ur: a naked priest accompanied by three female attendants pours a libation before a seated god.

responsible for the selection and sanctioning of the kings of the Sumerian city-states, who acted as stewards of the divine sovereigns. It was this, says Miss Beatty, which gave rise to the concept of sacred marriage, the 'temple prostitution' that the later Bible writers would find so abominable. The sacred marriage was a formal, highly stylised cultic institution, at one and the same time religious and political, enacted between the high priestess representing Ishtar, and the king in the role of high priest representing the city as the vicar of god; and through this act of sacred sexuality, the power of the divinity flowed down from heaven through the king to the people and the land.

One superb piece of jewellery, now in the Iraq Museum, symbolises the beauty and the love involved in this religious intimacy: a magnificent necklace of stone and carnelian beads bound by a silver string and framed in gold. An inscription on one of the parts states that Amar-Sin, king of Ur, presented the necklace to Abi-Simti, priestess of Uruk. Miss Beatty is in no doubt that Ishtar, patron goddess of Uruk, was thought of as being the divine embodiment of beauty; from the innumerable representations of her that were made down the ages, it is clear that she was the pin-up girl of ancient Mesopotamia.

However, it is the mythology of the Sumerians, rather than their theology, which is most germane to our exploration of the Bible saga. For the Sumerians recorded the oldest myths known to us – stories about the Creation that would be echoed many centuries later in the Creation myths in *Genesis*. But the most astonishing parallel between the Sumerian myths and the Biblical myths is the story of the Flood, when the gods decided to go back to the drawing-board and start the business of Creation all over again.

Several versions of the Sumerian Flood story have been found over the years, all of them pre-dating the Bible. The most sophisticated version forms part of an epic poem about one of the ancient semi-legendary kings of Uruk, a man called Gilgamesh. In one episode, he pays a visit to the only human survivor of the Great Flood, the Sumerian Noah, in effect, on whom the gods had bestowed immortality. The story he is told is so close in its details that the Biblical Flood story was obviously borrowed directly from the much earlier Sumerian original. The individual names may be different, but the specific parallels are unmistakable.

The Sumerian Flood story and its later versions form only a part of a general history of mankind and man's relationship

The Uruk Vase: an alabaster vessel, about a metre tall and dating from c.3000 BC, depicting a procession of naked priests bringing offerings to the goddess Ishtar.

with gods; so, too, does the Bible Flood story (*Genesis* 6-9). The Sumerian gods decided to destroy mankind by a Flood because the population of the earth had become so numerous and noisy; in *Genesis*, God repented of his decision to create mankind when men began to multiply on the face of the earth. The god Enki conspired to spare the life of one pious king (so that the practice of offering sacrifices to the gods might be continued); in the Bible, 'Noah found grace in the eyes of the Lord'. The pious king is instructed to build a huge cube-shaped vessel into which he should take 'the seed of all living things'; Noah is instructed to build a huge rectangular vessel of gopher wood, an Ark, into which he was to take two of every sort of every living thing of all flesh. The Sumerian Deluge lasted seven days; the Biblical Deluge lasted forty. The Sumerian Ark came to rest on 'Mount Nisir', presumed to be in the Kurdestan Mountains; Noah's Ark came to rest on Mount Ararat, in eastern Turkey. The Sumerian Noah sent out a dove, a swallow, and a raven; the Biblical Noah sent forth a raven and a dove (twice). The Sumerian Noah offered sacrifice to the gods, and 'the gods smelled the sweet savour'; the Biblical Noah built an altar and offered burnt offerings, 'and the Lord smelled a sweet savour'.

The story of the Great Flood has always haunted man's imagination, and tempted archaeologists and adventurers alike. When Sir Leonard Woolley was excavating the Sumerian city of Ur in the 1920s (see Chapter 2), he came across a two-metre layer of pure alluvial clay sandwiched between occupation levels, and sent an electrifying cable back to London: 'We have found the Flood.' Later archaeological discoveries showed that many sites had suffered destruction by flooding, but the dates varied widely, from 4000 to 2500 BC; they were the results of different local floods, not evidence of the Great Flood of Sumerian and Biblical tradition.

Similarly, the search for the remains of Noah's Ark has taken a number of optimistic expeditions and individuals to Mount Ararat, a towering mountain rising to a height of 17,000 feet on the borders of Turkey, Russia and Iran. A whole modern mythology has been built around the alleged 'evidence' provided by these expeditions – deathbed confessions that no one can check, hindsight identifications long after the event, aerial photographs showing anomalies that could be anything. One of the latest pieces of 'evidence' was a large piece of hand-worked timber pulled from a water-filled pocket deep in a crevasse on Ararat in 1955 by a French 'arkeologist', Fernand Navarra. The timber, partly fossilised,

Small terracotta plaque of a goddess, possibly Ishtar (Inanna). The head-dress indicates her divinity.

was dated by a Spanish laboratory to about 3000 BC (primarily on the basis of its colour and the extent of fossilisation). This was hailed in the newspapers as conclusive proof of the Flood story. Unfortunately, independent radiocarbon tests by British and American laboratories indicated a date around 450-750 AD, though this was less enthusiastically reported in the press.

The quest for Noah's Ark is self-evidently futile because the Flood story in the Bible is obviously a legend, and a borrowed and garbled one at that (in *Genesis* there are apparently two Flood stories which have been conflated into one). So what does this do to our understanding of the earlier chapters of *Genesis*? Does it discredit the 'authenticity' of the Bible as an epic document?

The distinguished American scholar Dr James B. Pritchard of the University Museum of Pennsylvania, editor of the authoritative anthology, *Ancient Near Eastern Texts*, certainly does not think so. He points out that although the first discovery of ancient Mesopotamian versions of the Creation and Flood stories profoundly altered the prevailing thinking about the uniqueness of the Hebrew view of cosmology, it established a new way of understanding the cultural milieu from which the Bible sprang. It proved that the Bible did not exist in a vacuum, that the Hebrew writers fully participated in the culture of their day, that they shared the current traditions about the creation of the world and mankind and adapted them as a means of presenting their own views about life and religion.

The fact that there was widespread knowledge of these ancient Mesopotamian traditions throughout the Middle East was attested in 1955 by the chance discovery of a cuneiform tablet containing forty lines of the Gilgamesh epic from the spoil-heap of an American excavation at Megiddo, in the heart of Palestine (see Chapter 8). Since the tablet was found on a rubbish dump by a shepherd, and had not been spotted by the original excavators in the stratified level from which it had come, it could only be dated from the style of the script. It certainly predates the Israelite presence in the Promised Land; but it shows that these traditions were common knowledge throughout the Fertile Crescent for a very long time. It is an indication of the spread of Sumerian culture.

This is not only evidenced by the way in which the art and use of writing was quickly adopted throughout Mesopotamia; it is also attested in one of the rescue digs of the Upper Euphrates project. At a site called Jebel 'Aruda on the west

Fragment of the Gilgamesh epic found at Megiddo in Palestine in 1955, dating from c.1400 BC.

bank of the northern reaches of the river, the Dutch excavator Dr H.J.Franken of Leiden University has uncovered the imposing remains of a large Sumerian temple of the fourth millennium, built on the Uruk model.

Jebel 'Aruda occupied an eminence some 180 metres above the surrounding plain and overlooking the Euphrates. It must have been an important commercial centre, strategically sited to dominate the trade route up and down the river. It has no traditional associations with any place-name mentioned in the Bible; and Dr Franken, for one, must be relieved, for he is the most astringent critic of so-called 'Biblical archaeology', of excavating with a Bible in one hand and a spade in the other. Expressed in its most simplified and extreme form, Dr Franken believes that to excavate a 'Biblical' site with preconceived ideas derived from possibly pseudo-historical statements in the Bible can only distort an archaeologists's interpretation of the objective evidence of the dig.

It is a view shared by many Syrian archaeologists, who tend to differentiate between 'real' archaeologists and 'Abraham-chasers'. Abraham is the first named character in the Bible that Biblical scholars nowadays are prepared to consider seriously as a possible historical figure, and he has been the subject of endless historical and theological debate.

Jebel 'Aruda: the Sumerian temple site is in the foreground. Behind is the valley of the Euphrates, now submerged under the lake created by the dam at Tabqa, in northern Syria.

2
The Abraham Years

When the Bible narrative gets past the more obviously mythological and derivative parts like the Creation and Noah's Ark, one powerful name forces its way out of the genealogical clutter of *Genesis*: the name of Abraham.

Abraham is presented in the Bible as the archetypal ancestor, the progenitor of the Children of Israel, the father of the people. With and through Abraham we enter the so-called 'Age of the Patriarchs'; and according to the received wisdom of Biblical scholarship until now, with Abraham we are supposed to enter the realm of actual history. The date tends to vary according to individual predilection, but it is frequently set at the start of the Middle Bronze Age – say 2000 BC, give or take a couple of centuries.

But now, all the thinking about the historicity of the Age of the Patriarchs is being radically re-examined. The somewhat facile assumptions of the past are under fierce scrutiny.

In addition, our picture of that whole period, especially in so far as it affects Syria and Palestine, is being totally revolutionised by a sensational excavation that is taking place at a site in Syria called Tell Mardikh, some forty kilometres south of Aleppo. Here a team of Italian archaeologists, working in cooperation with the Directorate-General of Antiquities and Museums of Syria, has recently discovered a huge palace archive – one of the oldest state archives in the world, containing no fewer than 15,000 inscribed clay documents. And they reveal the existence of a mighty Canaanite empire in Syria that also embraced Palestine around 2400 BC which no one had suspected before; its capital was at Tell Mardikh – an ancient, all-but-forgotten city called Ebla. Ebla, which scarcely rates a mention in even the most up-to-date textbooks, is going to become one of the outstanding names in the archaeology of the ancient Middle East; its discovery has given the history of Syria in particular, and of the Middle East in general, an entirely new dimension.

But what makes it doubly sensational for 'Biblical archaeology' is that the greatest of the kings of this mighty empire of Ebla had the same name as one of the legendary ancestors of Abraham, his great-great-great-great-grandfather: a king

Tell Mardikh: royal courtyard of the palace at Ebla. Left foreground, a dais for the king's throne. To the right, the base of the three-storeyed tower. The plaster on the walls is still visible.

called Ebrum, or Ebrium, which is the same as that of the Biblical Eber (*Genesis* 11), the eponymous ancestor of the Hebrews.

We also find in the tablets a number of personal names and place names with which the Bible would later make us all familiar: places like Sinai, Gaza, and Jerusalem, and people like Abraham, Ishmael, David, Saul, and most astonishingly of all, Israel.

Nothing was further from the minds of the Italian Archaeological Mission to Syria when they started digging at Tell Mardikh in 1964, directed by a brilliant young scholar from the University of Rome, Professor Paolo Matthiae. Tell Mardikh is one of the most imposing *tells* in northern Syria, rising sixteen metres above its surrounding plateau and covering an area of 140 acres. Dr Matthiae, who was only twenty-four at the time, wanted to obtain more information about the culture and history of Syria at the start of the Middle Bronze Age.

The ancient Middle East in this period was at a fascinating stage of its evolution. The non-Semitic city-states of Sumer had been overwhelmed by an aggressive new East Semitic dynasty headed by Sargon I of Akkad (Agade), thus creating the first true Mesopotamian empire, around 2350 BC. Later, the whole of Mesopotamia would be subjugated by a vigorous

West Semitic dynasty, the empire of Old Babylonia that is associated with its most dynamic ruler, King Hammurabi, around 1750 BC (see Chapter 11). Dr Matthiae wanted to find out what was happening in Syria at about this time, and he chose Tell Mardikh as the site on which to concentrate.

In the early seasons, Dr Matthiae found ample evidence that during the early part of the Middle Bronze period Tell Mardikh had been a large and prosperous city, one of the major commercial and cultural centres in Syria. He uncovered the ruins of a substantial royal palace which could be dated to c.1900 BC, and a large temple whose architectural pattern of vestibule, anteroom and sanctuary was strikingly similar to the tripartite structure of later Canaanite temples, and to Solomon's eventual temple in Jerusalem a thousand years later (see Chapter 8). The city was fortified by massive walls pierced by four gates; the ramparts were made of several strata of rubble and stamped earth, the so-called *glacis* fortification which archaeologists had previously associated with a rather later historical period in Palestine. The south-west gateway, as excavated, is still a magnificent structure: an outer gate leading to a small courtyard that gave access to the main gates – three pairs of monumental pylons delineated by huge blocks of dressed basalt, which housed a double pair of gates that swung open on clearly defined sockets.

The vigorous art of this period is exemplified by a monumental stone libation basin, with a line of four lions' heads emerging roaring from the base, below a frieze depicting the High King offering wine to a seated god, and a line of warriors carrying curved knives.

In 1968, the excavators came across a large fragment of a votive statue dedicated to the goddess Ishtar by a certain Ibit-Lim, king of the city of Ebla. At last the great mound had been positively identified: it was the ancient city of Ebla, until then only dimly known from casual inscriptions from Akkad and Babylon.

It was not until 1973, with the discovery of a wing of a royal palace lying buried under the western slopes of the city's acropolis, that the excavators realised that the Ebla of the Middle Bronze Age, which was destroyed c.1600 BC, had been built on top of an even earlier city. They found a three-storeyed building with a tower containing a staircase of four flights. This handsome building with its spacious paved rooms had been destroyed by fire c.2250 BC. In the ruins the excavators found a small cache of inscribed tablets in 1974; there were only forty-two of them, and all of them of

Professor Giovanni Pettinato, the epigraphist with the Tell Mardikh expedition, with some of the 15,000 clay tablets he is deciphering and cataloguing.

a commercial or administrative nature, but they were sufficient to allow the expedition's epigraphist, Professor Giovanni Pettinato of Rome University, to identify the language of the tablets as a previously unknown and very ancient form of north-western Semitic – a language he categorised as Early Canaanite.

In 1975, however, came the really sensational finds: two small rooms flanking the entrance to the palace proper, and adjoining some sort of open courtyard, turned out to be the repositories of the official state archives of Ebla between 2400 BC and 2250 BC. These inscribed clay tablets, of which 15,000 have so far come to light, had originally been stacked on wooden shelving that lined three of the walls – floor sockets for the supporting uprights can still be seen. During the great fire that destroyed the palace c.2250 BC, the shelves had been consumed and the tablets had fallen to the ground as they had been filed, stacked on edge like gramophone records for economy of space and ease of retrieval. The fierce heat had baked the clay tablets hard, and they are still in a marvellous state of preservation, the tiny cuneiform writing still perfectly legible.

The majority of the tablets dealt with the administration of trade and economics and international commerce, particularly in textiles, timber, copper and precious stones. They revealed that Ebla's commercial horizon was a vast one at this time, extending to all the known corners of the world. Other tablets contained royal edicts, state correspondence and diplomatic treaties with other cities, as well as lists of those cities subject to Ebla and the amounts of tribute exacted. There were a few literary texts containing stories with a mythological background. One text dealt with the Flood story, another with the Creation.

Above all, there were thirty-two bilingual dictionaries or vocabularies – the oldest such vocabularies in the world – in which about a thousand words from the non-Semitic Sumerian language were carefully translated into Early Canaanite. It is clear that the people of Ebla imported from Sumer the cuneiform system of writing in logograms (symbols that represent a whole word or context, in the way that the symbol '£' represents 'pound sterling'), and adapted it to their own language in which words were spelled out in syllables. And this Early Canaanite language of Ebla is the direct ancestor of Hebrew and other West Semitic languages.

From the texts, a vivid and startling new picture of Syria in the third millennium BC has emerged. Until now, because of the paucity of documentary and archaeological evidence, Syria and Palestine had been assumed to be a cultural backwater between the 'super-powers' of Mesopotamia and Egypt at this time, inhabited only by illiterate nomadic tribesmen. Now, as Dr Matthiae says, we must recognise that there was a third great commercial and political power at this time, whose capital was Ebla and which covered the whole of Syria and Palestine; this empire was specifically 'Canaanite', and in its heyday it was powerful enough to reduce Mesopotamia itself to vassalage.

Amongst the hundreds of place names in the commercial and diplomatic texts, of special interest to Biblical scholars are references to places and vassal cities in Palestine like Hazor, Gaza, Lachish, Megiddo, Akko, Sinai, and even Jerusalem itself (*Urusalima*).

But perhaps the most intriguing names are those personal names which also appear in the Bible: names from the 'Patriarchal Age' like Ab-ra-mu (Abraham), E-sa-um (Esau), Ish-ma-ilu (Ishmael), even Is-ra-ilu (Israel), and from later periods, names like Da-'u-dum (David) and Sa-'u-lum (Saul). The most tantalising adumbration is the name of Ebrum

(Biblical Eber), third and greatest of the six kings of the Ebla dynasty between 2400 and 2250 BC. He seems to have been placed on the throne of Ebla by Sargon the Great of Akkad after a punitive expedition in which Ebla was subjugated. But after Sargon died (c.2310 BC), Ebrum turned the tables on Akkad and reduced its cities to vassalage in turn. It was not until 2250 BC that Sargon's grandson, Narum-Sin of Akkad, was able to throw off the yoke of Ebla by conquering the city and putting it to the torch. Little wonder that he boasted of the exploit in his inscriptions! We now know that he had conquered one of the major powers of the ancient world.

It may well be pure coincidence that this powerful king of Ebla, King Ebrum, should have had the same name as Eber, from whom the Hebrews traced their descent. It may be pure coincidence that so many Biblical names like Abraham and Ishmael are attested in documents from the time of Ebrum. Dr Pettinato counsels us not to conclude from this that we have necessarily found the historical context of the Patriarchs themselves (even though, coincidentally, Arab historians have traditionally dated Abraham to c.2300 BC); but he thinks it not impossible that the Biblical traditions about Abraham do, in fact, enshrine legendary memories of the forgotten Canaanite empire of Ebla some 1500 years before the Bible began to take shape.

One other aspect of all this is bound to provoke endless argument in the future. All names like Ishmael, Michael and Israel are theophoric in form – that is to say, the suffix element (-ilu or -el) represents a divine name, in this case the paramount god El. But during the reign of Ebrum, Dr Pettinato noted a change in the theophoric element, from -el to -ya(w), so that Mi-ka-ilu became Mi-ka-ya(w), and so on. It is quite clear that both the endings are divine names, either names of gods or words simply meaning 'god'; so it looks as if Ebrum made some major alteration in the religion of Ebla at this time. Whether -ya(w) is related to the Biblical Yahweh, the One God of Israel whose name replaced the earlier form of El, is a matter for debate: but there will be many who will be tempted to see in this change an early version of the change from El to Yahweh in Hebrew theological tradition.

There is still an immense amount of work to be done at Tell Mardikh/Ebla, and a great deal of further study to be done on the decipherment and interpretation of the texts. But without doubt a new and significant chapter in the history of the Middle East has been opened, which is going to

The ziggurat of Ur, built by Ur-Nammu of the Third Dynasty c.2100 BC. It was originally four stages high; it has now been restored to the height of the first stage by the Iraqi authorities.

have a large and lasting impact on Biblical scholarship. Already, it has pushed back our concept of Canaan and Canaanite culture and language (see Chapter 5) by a full 1000 years; what it will eventually do to the argument about the historicity of the Patriarchal traditions in the Bible is still anyone's guess.

These traditions are encapsulated in the story of Abraham, which starts in *Genesis* 11:26: Abraham's father, Terah, was said to have lived in 'Ur of the Chaldees'. There, Abraham married Sarah, and at some unspecified time thereafter Terah moved with his family from Ur of the Chaldees to Haran, where Terah died and whence Abraham set out for the Promised Land of Canaan.

'Ur of the Chaldees' has always been one of the magic names in the Bible. Actually, it is a misnomer; Ur was originally one of the ancient city-states of Sumer, and did not become associated with the Chaldaeans until the first millennium BC, more than a thousand years after Abraham is thought to have been born there. So the name 'Ur of the Chaldees' in *Genesis* is clearly an anachronistic reference.

Ur is identified with Tell el-Muqayyar, the 'Mound of Pitch', in southern Iraq, about half-way between Baghdad and the head of the Persian Gulf. In olden times, the Euphrates flowed past it, but the river has changed course and is now nine kilometres away; where once there were fertile irrigated fields there is now a desert wasteland. Little remains of the once great city except for its ziggurat, which has recently been handsomely restored by the Iraqi authorities to the height of the first level.

31

Sir Leonard Woolley excavating at Ur.

Fifty years ago, 'Ur of the Chaldees' was the scene of the classical Biblical dig of its time. This was where Sir Leonard Woolley made his own name, and that of Ur, famous throughout the world. There, in thirteen spectacular seasons beginning in 1922, Woolley laid open before the astonished eyes of an avid public a record of royal wealth and power that no one had ever suspected to have existed so early in Mesopotamia.

The most remarkable finds came from a royal cemetery dating from the First Dynasty of Ur, as it is called, around 2500 BC. Here, kings and queens of Ur had been buried, surrounded by a retinue of attendants who had died by the score to accompany their dead master or mistress. The richness of the grave goods was breathtaking – a treasury of marvellous objects and ornaments fashioned from gold and precious stones. These magnificently furnished tombs with the gruesome evidence of wholesale human sacrifice excited public attention as much as the discovery of Tutankhamun's Tomb in Egypt had done five years before; yet these burials were 1500 years earlier in time.

Golden helmet and dagger with a lapis lazuli sheath: part of the rich treasure from the Royal Cemetery of Ur, c.2500 BC.

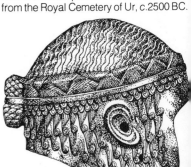

There was nothing directly relevant to the Bible in these finds, although the Biblically-minded Woolley fancied that the celebrated carving from one of the tombs of a goat on its hind-legs nibbling at a bush was an echo of the Biblical 'ram caught in a thicket' associated with Abraham's near-sacrifice of his son Isaac (*Genesis 22*), and he was later to convince himself that underneath the royal tombs he had found evidence of the Flood. But one thing at least was now certain: the city of 'Ur of the Chaldees', which previously had simply been an exotic name in the Bible, had actually existed; and for a lot of people everything was thereby proved. Ur of the Chaldees was real after all, so Abraham must have been 'real' as well.

And so, as Biblical archaeology burgeoned throughout the 1930s and later, scholars began to construct a compelling picture, an apparently historical context in which Abraham could have lived and moved. Ur succumbed to Sargon of Akkad c.2350 BC, like the other Sumerian city-states, then

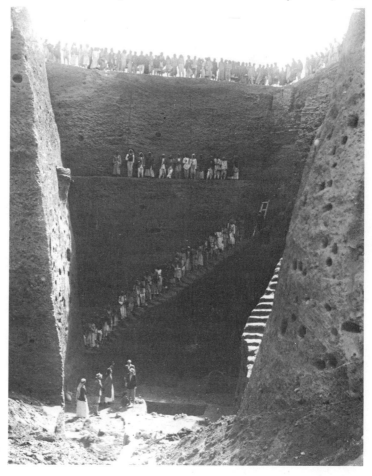

The great trench at Ur after Woolley's excavation of the Royal Cemetery. At the bottom, the start of the 'Flood' level.

enjoyed a short-lived resurgence of greatness under its Third
Dynasty, founded by Ur-Nammu c.2100 BC, until it was
overrun by Semitic nomads from the west c.2000 BC. Ur
managed to retain much of its prosperity, evidently, but the
period presents a picture of widespread and confused migration in Mesopotamia at this time. So what more natural, the
argument ran, than that Abraham's family should then have
left on their momentous journey as Ur's power waned?

But what sort of a place was it that they were leaving behind? A little to the east of the great ziggurat, and beyond the
royal cemeteries, Woolley excavated an area of the city that
made a profound impression on his thinking about the Bible.
It was one of the domestic quarters of the city – a warren of
narrow alleyways and open squares; and what astonished
him was the quality of the houses and shrines here, their walls
still standing to a height of three metres in places. They had

originally been luxurious: splendid two-storeyed private villas,
with ten or twelve or even fourteen rooms each, made of dur-
able baked brick with plastered and whitewashed walls.

The residential quarter of Ur excavated by Woolley, dating from c.2000 BC. It was here, according to Woolley, that Abraham and his family might have lived in 'Ur of the Chaldees'.

This, wrote Woolley, had been Abraham's Ur – a prosperous, elegant place with a high standard of private living based
on commerce. (Local guides even try to persuade the visitor
today that one of the houses was actually Abraham's house.)
So Woolley urged everyone to revise their view of Abraham
the Patriarch; he had not been a simple nomad in a tent, leading his little clan of shepherds in a quest for better things,
but a sophisticated city-dweller travelling the great caravan
routes of the Fertile Crescent as a merchant.

Out of all this archaeological speculation there arose a sort
of general presumption about the antiquity of the Biblical

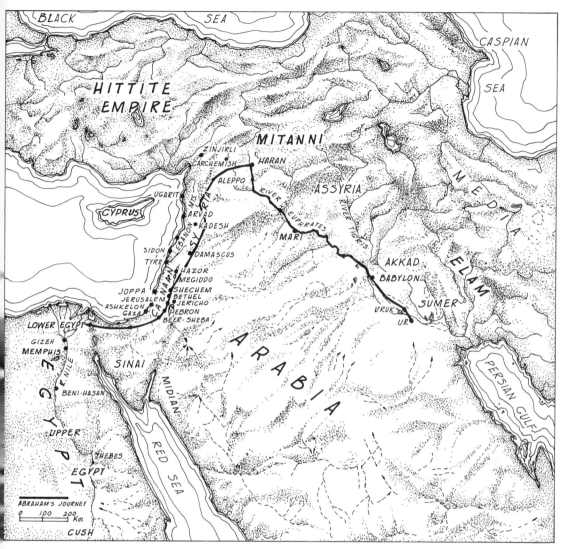

Abraham's presumed route from 'Ur of the Chaldees' to Shechem in Palestine, and his sojourn in Egypt.

traditions and the existence of Abraham as a historical personage. It ignored or dismissed the manifest contradictions of the Abraham traditions in the Bible itself, which portray him alternately as a nomad in the Bedouin mould and as landed gentry. Only ten years ago, anyone visiting Ur would have proclaimed, without much fear of contradiction, the words of the distinguished American scholar, the late W.F. Albright, to the effect that 'aside from a few diehards among older scholars, there is scarcely a single Biblical historian who has not been impressed by the rapid accumulation of data supporting the substantial historicity of patriarchal traditions'.

Today, however, as a result of the work of a new generation of more radically-minded scholars, no one can be quite so confident. But let us follow Albright and the Abraham

35

story in *Genesis* for a moment, and see where it takes us. It takes us to Haran via another of the great seminal sites of Biblical archaeology in Mesopotamia: the ancient city of Mari.

Mari lies on the west bank of the Euphrates just inside Syria, some twenty odd kilometres north of the Iraq frontier. Until 1933 it was simply an extensive *tell* known as Tell Hariri; but in 1933 a French archaeological expedition led by Professor André Parrot started to excavate it, and so impressive and significant were the finds there that Professor Parrot is still patiently excavating, season after season.

It turned out that Mari had been one of the most majestic cities in ancient Mesopotamia, the chief city of the middle Euphrates. It had two great periods of splendour; the first coincided with the rise of ancient Ebla in the third millennium BC, until it was subjugated by Sargon of Akkad, while the second and even more brilliant period was at the beginning of the second millennium BC until it was destroyed by Hammurabi of Babylon c.1750 BC.

This latter period is spectacularly represented by an enormous royal palace, the residence of the last king of Mari, Zimri-Lim. It contained more than 300 rooms and courtyards in a single vast block, richly furbished with statues and painted walls. The walls of these chambers are still standing to a great height, and it is impossible for the visitor not to be

Mari: one of the great halls of the vast palace of King Zimri-Lim, c.1750 BC. The palace contained more than 300 rooms.

Clay tablet from Mari: a letter from the king of Carchemish to King Zimri-Lim, suggesting punishment by burning for two men charged with an offence – or for their accuser, if the accusation is proved false.

overwhelmed by the sheer scale and grandeur of the place. Anyone travelling from Ur to Haran up the Euphrates, as Abraham and his family are assumed to have done in the Biblical account, would assuredly have passed by or through Mari on the way.

From the point of view of Biblical scholarship, the most striking discovery at Mari was the palace archive, which contained some 25,000 cuneiform tablets dating from c.2000-1750 BC. From them, scholars have been able to form a detailed picture of the international politics of the time and the social organisation of the kingdom of Mari. From the tablets, too, came Biblical-sounding names which caused a tremendous stir at the time. There were frequent references to a Semitic tribe of nomads called Bene-iamina, which Biblical scholars were quick to identify with the Benjaminites of Hebrew tradition. 'The Bene-iamina are sending fire-signals,' wrote one officer of the Mari desert police – and a reference to the 'fire-signals' of the Benjaminites is found in *Jeremiah* 6:1. The name 'David' was also detected in the form *davidum*, the leader of the Benjaminites, and interpreted as 'war-leader', which led scholars to wonder whether the Biblical David's name was really a title rather than a personal name. The reading *davidum* has now been abandoned by scholars, however.

Bene-iamina, on the other hand, simply means 'sons of the right hand', or 'sons of the south', and modern scholars tend to dismiss the apparent similarity in names as having any significance in the search for Biblical origins.

There is another name in the Mari tablets that seemed at the time to have direct Biblical importance: the name Habiru. They were a troublesome group, or tribe, or class, of robbers and plunderers who caused the Mari authorities endless difficulty, and many scholars at once connected them with the Hebrews.

The chain of argument seemed complete; the Mari documents portrayed a time of tribal movement, of Benjaminites and Hebrews, and social customs which would find an echo in many of the *mores* of the Children of Israel centuries later. This, surely, was the milieu of Abraham, the first of the Hebrew Patriarchs. At Mari, the Hebrews seemed to have entered the stage of Middle Eastern history as a well documented, properly authenticated people.

Today, however, the association of Habiru and Hebrews is no longer accepted so unquestioningly. The Habiru are also attested in Egyptian records, for instance, where they are clearly a particular class of people rather than an ethnic group; they are footloose bands who hire themselves as mercenaries, or even building labourers, or else make a living as raiders and brigands. Moreover, philologists are doubtful whether there is any real connection between the two words.

All in all, despite the magnificence of the site and its tremendous historical importance, Mari now feels rather dead from the Biblical point of view. The excitements and the certainties of the 1930s seem rather out of date now. The cast-iron historical context which Mari had seemed to provide for Abraham no longer inspires the same confidence that it did. In its time, however, it was the Mari archive that persuaded Professor Albright to place Abraham definitely at the start of the Middle Bronze Age, around 1900 BC, and send him on his momentous journey from Ur of the Chaldees, through Mari, and up the Euphrates to Turkey, to a place called Haran.

Haran was mentioned in the Mari texts as a religious centre for the West Semitic tribes, who worshipped at the temple of the moon-god, Sin. It also seems to have been a trading post of some importance, lying on an ancient caravan route from Mesopotamia to northern Syria and thence down to Palestine and Egypt. According to *Genesis*, Abraham lived in Haran until he was seventy-five years old, at which time the Lord sent him off to the Promised Land of Canaan.

Many scholars believe that Haran, and not Ur, was the real origin of the Patriarchal tradition. They consider the reference to 'Ur of the Chaldees' a later and anachronistic addition to the story, and point to the fact that in the Bible it was to the Haran area – 'my country' – that Abraham sent to find a wife for his son Isaac (*Genesis* 24). It was to this same area, Padan-Aram, the 'Plain of Aram', that Isaac later sent his son Jacob to find a wife amongst the family of his uncle, Laban (*Genesis* 28).

From Haran, Abraham is said to have travelled south to Shechem, in Canaan, some 1000 kilometres, with his family or clan. The Bible makes no mention of the places he would have passed on the way. Commentators who cast him in the role of a trader would take him down one of the major caravan routes, through Aleppo (where the vast covered bazaar, or *suk*, is still a magnet for visitors) and the Syrian capital, Damascus, which can claim to reflect the oldest urban traditions of any city in the Middle East, and from there down towards the Sea of Galilee and Israel. Those who see

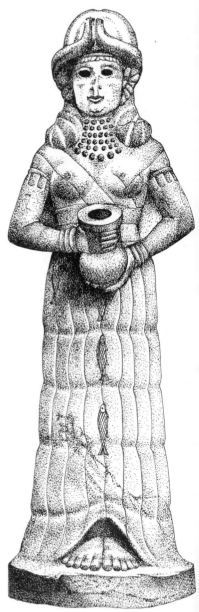

Life-size statue of a minor fertility goddess from Mari, dispensing 'living water' from a vase. Water could be made to flow from the vase and down her fish-decorated skirt by means of piping within the statue.

Abraham as a nomadic herdsman would move him in slower stages along the fringes of habitation until he came to Canaan. They picture Abraham's life-style as being not unlike that of the modern Bedouin in their tents, sharing many of the legal and social customs of the desert dwellers of today.

Both of these assumptions, however, beg the very question that is being asked with increasing insistence by younger scholars nowadays: was there a journey at all? Was Abraham a historical figure at all?

Two recent books have subjected the Abraham traditions to close examination: *The Historicity of the Patriarchal Narratives*, by Thomas L. Thomson of North Carolina, published in 1974, and *Abraham in History and Tradition* by John van Seters of University College, Toronto (1975). They both take a hard scholarly look at the traditional view that Abraham represents or sums up a nomadic tradition that is reflected in documents of the Middle Bronze Age – and they both, independently of one another, come to the conclusion that he does not.

Both find that the legal and social background reflected in the Patriarchal stories, which seems to be paralleled in these early documents, can be found just as easily in the first millennium BC as in the second. They point out the innumerable inconsistencies in the Biblical account, and argue strongly against the 'fundamentalist' view that the Biblical narratives can be used to reconstruct the history of the Middle East in a manner comparable to the archives of Mari or anywhere else, and vice versa.

The debate really centres on the questions of when the Biblical account was written, and why. There is a general and uncritical presumption that the Patriarchal stories were handed down orally, more or less unchanged, round the camp-fires of the nomadic Israelites until they came to be written down at the time of David and Solomon in the tenth century BC. This is contested by scholars who believe that the first books of the Bible were written considerably later, during the period of the Babylonian Exile in the sixth century BC (see Chapter 11). They reach this conclusion on grounds of textual and literary criticism chiefly, but also on social grounds: the trauma of the Exile created the need to construct and articulate a comprehensible historical past, a perspective of history which would give a meaningful context to the identity of the Hebrews and their special relationship, as they felt, with their god.

All this is still a matter of vigorous debate; there are many sides to the problem. But it is worth bearing in mind that the question is still a very open one.

Once Abraham is in Canaan, the Patriarchal traditions do little to inspire any greater confidence in their historicity. Folkloristic motifs abound. There are anachronisms, contradictions, inconsistencies. Many stories seem to be frankly aetiological – that is to say, they offer an explanation of origins of place names or particular situations, such as the naming of the twelve tribes, or to justify the reason for the political enmity between the Israelites and the Moabites and the Ammonites (they were said to be the offspring of incestuous unions between Lot and his daughters), and so on.

The story of Lot and his wife, and the destruction of Sodom and Gomorrah, is a case in point. It is one of the most memorable stories in *Genesis*, haunted by images of horror and catastrophe, resonant with echoes of universal themes of divine wrath and punishment. Down by the salt-encrusted shores of the Dead Sea, 1500 feet below sea level, where the cities of Sodom and Gomorrah were said to have stood, one can get a clear insight into how stories of this kind came about.

Everywhere in the world that you get weird natural shapes,

folklore tries to give them life: take the Witch of Wookey in England, for instance, or those curious lava formations in Iceland that folklore instantly transforms into dwarves and trolls who were caught by the rising sun and turned into stone. Down by the Dead Sea, it is easy to discern the origin of the fable about the wife of Lot, who 'looked back from behind him, and she became a pillar of salt'; because everything there is salt. The range of hills that border the sea is pure rock-salt. Even the Dead Sea itself is thirty-two per cent salt. Centuries of erosion have whittled and chiselled one particular outcrop of salt on top of the escarpment into a freestanding pillar which, from certain angles, might conceivably suggest the representation of a human female figure and face. People have always tried to see in the story of Sodom and Gomorrah and their destruction some kind of historical event – perhaps some volcanic catastrophe that overwhelmed them. But it seems more on a par with the legend of Atlantis, which may originally have had some kernel of historical memory, but whose violent destruction was interpreted as a punishment by the gods for the wickedness of its inhabitants.

At least in the case of Atlantis there are buried remains on the island of Santorini (ripped open by a volcanic eruption around 1450 BC) which might have occasioned the legend, or which the legend was created to explain. But despite strenuous efforts by archaeologists and romantics alike, no trace at all has ever been found of the Biblical cities of the Vale of Siddim, either in the ground or under the waters of the Dead Sea. Sodom and Gomorrah, and Lot's wife in her pillar of salt, remain forever petrified in the realm of legend.

People who have grown up in the religious and cultural traditions that derive from the Bible may find it unpalatable that the Old Testament text, 'Holy Writ' as it were, should be questioned at all. But to look objectively at its historicity is in no way to impugn its literary greatness or its theological profundity. Some theologians have rather unnecessarily backed themselves into a corner by insisting that since the Bible describes the purposeful intervention of God in the history of a particular people, then the account must either be historically authentic or else it is nothing. Yet it is surely possible to develop a view of the past which is not strict history in order to articulate a conviction about the past: a conviction that is inspired by factors which have nothing to do with historiography.

It is only human to want to find corroboration of such ideas, some physical evidence which can serve as a focus for reverence. It creates a sense of intimate contact, whether the evidence is authentic or not. In the Patriarchal context, the alleged burial place of Abraham in the city of Hebron, a site revered by Jews, Christians and Moslems alike, is an excellent example of this.

When the new religion of Islam was created by Mohammed early in the seventh century AD, he simply took over, wholesale, the major characters of both the Old Testament and the New. Thus, Moslems today revere both Moses and Jesus as major prophets. The ancestor of the Arabs is hailed as Ishmael, Abraham's outcast son by his Egyptian concubine, Hagar; so Abraham, too, was drawn into the fold of Islam. That is why a carp-pool near modern Haran in Turkey is held to be sacred to the memory of Abraham. Now, according to the Bible, Abraham was said to have bought from Ephron the Hittite the field and cave of Machpelah, at Hebron (*Genesis* 23). Pilgrims and tourists alike are today shown a cavern at the foot of the mosque in Hebron, and told that this was the very cave in which Abraham buried his wife Sarah. Eventually, the cave became the reputed burial site of the three major Patriarchal figures – Abraham, Isaac and Jacob; and in the seventh century AD the new Moslems built the mosque there to commemorate the joint founding fathers of both Judaism and Islam.

The only indisputable fact in all this is that the cave at Hebron cannot possibly be the Biblical Cave of Machpelah; it is in fact a man-made water-cistern, once carefully plastered to prevent the water seeping into the rock. But does that make the slightest difference to the religious convictions of those who believe in their god?

To return to our story: although the Patriarchs have now been laid to rest in the Cave of Machpelah, their story in the Bible is not yet done. Their destiny would lie for a time elsewhere, not in the Promised Land of Canaan but in a foreign place – Egypt.

3
Bondage in Egypt

The borderline between Africa and Asia is the line of the Suez Canal linking the Mediterranean and the Red Sea. It formed the approximate north-eastern boundary of Egypt. Egypt lay at one end of the Fertile Crescent, Mesopotamia at the other; and in between, the buffer lands of Palestine and Syria and the desert wastes of Sinai.

In days gone by, Asiatics from Palestine and beyond were continually crossing that Suez borderline to partake of the rich civilisation of the Nile, as traders, conquerors, captives, labourers, or just scroungers. According to the Bible, one such group of immigrants was a Semitic tribe, or clan, or group, who called themselves the Children of Israel.

According to the Biblical account, the Children of Israel spent precisely 430 years in Egypt, from the descent into Egypt in a time of famine in the wake of Joseph to the Exodus from Egypt under Moses for the trek to the Promised Land of Canaan (*Exodus* 12:40). On the face of it, such precision ought to make it easy to fit the Israelite presence in Egypt into an identifiable historical context; the history of Egypt is well documented, and the Biblical narratives are full of vivid detail.

Yet to this day there is no general agreement among scholars about the historical periods in which we can set the arrival of Joseph and his rise to power in the Egyptian court, or the time of the Bondage when the Children of Israel were conscripted to do forced labour for the Pharaoh, or the flight from Egypt and the miraculous crossing of the Red Sea. Indeed, there are scholars who tend to doubt whether the Egyptian interlude ever happened at all, at least in the way the Bible describes it.

Part of the problem is that, despite the mass of contemporary records that have been unearthed in Egypt, not one historical reference to the presence of the Israelites has yet been found there. Not a single mention of Joseph, the Pharaoh's 'Grand Vizier'. Not a word about Moses, or the spectacular flight from Egypt and the destruction of the pursuing Egyptian army.

And that silence in itself helps to put the powerful Biblical tradition into a much broader perspective.

Of course the descent into Egypt from Palestine was not the first Biblical encounter with Egypt. The Bible legends about the Patriarchs relate that Abraham himself once sojourned in Egypt for a while. The twelfth chapter of *Genesis* describes how Abraham went to Egypt because there was famine in Palestine; during his stay there, he pretended that his wife Sarah was actually his sister, for he was afraid that the Egyptians would kill him in order to enjoy her beauty for themselves, despite the fact that she was over seventy years old by then. The ruse apparently worked: Sarah was taken into the Pharaoh's harem and Abraham grew rich in consequence. Eventually the Lord visited Pharaoh and his household with plagues for the sin of adultery he had unwittingly committed, and Abraham and Sarah were expelled from Egypt.

The most celebrated piece of 'evidence' to illustrate Abraham's sojourn in Egypt is a wall-painting from the tomb of a high Egyptian official at Beni-Hasan, on the banks of the Nile some 300 kilometres south of Cairo. It represents a group of thirty-seven Semites with laden donkeys entering Egypt at a border post near Beni-Hasan and being escorted by frontier officials. The painting can be dated to around 1890 BC, and since this is assumed by many scholars to fit the Patriarchal Age, this tomb painting has been assiduously cited as being a representation of a nomadic or semi-nomadic Semitic family or clan 'like Abraham's', coming to Egypt for refuge in time of famine. The figures in the painting have been variously interpreted as a group of musicians, or travelling smiths, or Bedouin, or tinkers. In fact, the accompanying text makes it clear that they were traders bringing a cargo of lead sulphide (galena), which was used as an eye cosmetic and also for medicinal purposes; and in all probability they came not from Palestine but from the mountains along the Red Sea where lead sulphide was mined. Some commentators have seen in the garments of coloured striped material a foretaste of Joseph's 'coat of many colours' (*Genesis* 37:3); but recent textual studies have shown that this familiar phrase from the Authorised Version is a mistranslation, and that the phrase seems to mean 'a long, sleeved robe' (*New English Bible*).

The fact that the Beni-Hasan painting has no relevance for the Abraham story does not, of course, disprove the account of Abraham's sojourn in Egypt. It is quite clear from other Egyptian sources that Egypt, and especially the fertile East-

The Step Pyramid of Saqqara, the earliest monumental stone structure in Egypt, c.2750 BC. In the foreground, remains of the temple precincts, and an unfinished statue lying on its back.

ern Delta area, was prepared to offer refuge and succour through most periods of its history to starving tribes of desert nomads in times of famine; there are numerous official documents granting entry permits to foreigners and even specifying which grazings should be put at the disposal of their flocks. The real point is that this kind of migration happened throughout history, and there is no way of pinpointing the time of Abraham's alleged visit by appealing to this body of evidence.

However, on purely literary grounds, there is good reason for suspecting that the story may have no historical basis at all. It is noticeable that the ruse employed by Abraham, of concealing the fact that Sarah was his wife and passing her off as his sister in order to protect his own life and grow rich in the process, is featured three times in *Genesis*: Abraham does it again to Abimelech, king of Gerar (*Genesis* 20), and his son Isaac plays exactly the same trick on Abimelech (anachronistically called 'king of the Philistines') with his own wife Rebecca (*Genesis* 26). As John van Seters argues in his book on the Patriarchal tradition, we are dealing here with a folk-tale motif which was attached to the Patriarchs in variant forms and adapted in order to make certain moral and theological points.

Before we go any further, perhaps we ought to place Egypt more clearly in the wider historical context of the Near and Middle East. Egypt was already a very old country by the time that the Beni-Hasan tomb was painted around 1890 BC. For thousands of years there had been hunter-gatherers living off the fertile banks of the Nile. As elsewhere, they had been absorbed or replaced by settled agriculturalists who built villages and towns and learned to improve the fertility of the fields through controlled irrigation.

History proper – written history – began in Egypt at about the same time as, or slightly later than, in Sumer at the other end of the Fertile Crescent, with the unification of Upper and Lower Egypt around 3100 BC by a king called Menes, founder of the First Dynasty. The first period of Egyptian grandeur is known as the Old Kingdom, which started around 2700 BC with the Third Dynasty. This was when Egypt flowered into a major civilisation, the period of pyramid building, starting with the Step Pyramid at Saqqara and reaching its peak with the Great Pyramid at Gizeh around 2600 BC. The pyramids used to be called the oldest stone monuments in the world, but it is now clear that the megaliths of western Europe and the prehistoric temples of Malta were, in fact, considerably earlier; but the pyramids were certainly the most imposing structures the world had yet seen, and they reflected all the power and majesty of the Old Kingdom for the five centuries between 2700 and 2200 BC.

The Old Kingdom collapsed into anarchy at the end of the Sixth Dynasty, and it was not until around 2000 BC that Egypt was reunited by strong kings of the Eleventh and Twelfth Dynasties to create the Middle Kingdom period. Under kings like Sesostris III, who was the ruler of Egypt just after the time when the Beni-Hasan tomb painting was executed, Egypt enjoyed a brilliant new flowering of prosperity and culture, and extended her political, military and commercial influence over Palestine and much of Syria.

Throughout the eighteenth century BC, however, the imperial power and splendour of the Middle Kingdom declined. Once again, central government began to disintegrate.

The Great Pyramid at Gizeh; in the foreground, the Sphinx.

Lower (northern) Egypt was taken over by foreigners – Semitic immigrants or invaders whom Egyptian historians called the Hyksos ('rulers of foreign lands'). They seem to have infiltrated into the Delta area, where royal authority was weak, and to have established a rival kingdom there. According to the Egyptian historian Manetho of the third century BC, the Hyksos came to power through a fierce and bloody invasion from the east; but scholars now tend to discount the invasion theory in favour of a steady build-up of power from within, until the Hyksos set up their own dynasties around 1700 BC, while Upper (southern) Egypt continued to be ruled by princes of the old ruling house of Thebes.

The Hyksos kings established their capital in the Delta at a place called Avaris, where they installed a garrison of no fewer than 240,000 troops, according to Manetho. It was situated somewhere near the north-eastern frontier; but where, exactly? It is a question of more than academic interest to Biblical scholars, because long after the Hyksos were expelled from Egypt, Avaris would be rebuilt as a royal Delta residence by the powerful Pharaoh of the Nineteenth Dynasty, Ramesses II (Ramesses the Great). He named it Piramesse, the 'House of Ramesses', and it appears in the Bible as 'Raamses' (*New English Bible* 'Rameses'), one of the two royal store cities or treasure cities in the 'Land of Goshen' (the Eastern Delta area) which the Children of Israel were forced to build during the Bondage (*Exodus* 1:11).

Until recently, Avaris/Raamses has usually been identified with the ruins of the ancient Egyptian city of Tanis, near the modern fishing village of San el-Hagar, which was excavated in the 1920s and 1930s by Professor Pierre Montet of Strasbourg University. At Tanis he uncovered extensive temple ruins together with a great many statues, sphinxes, obelisks and stelae, many of them bearing the name of Ramesses II and his successors; there were also the remains of granaries and storehouses, as in all ancient Egyptian cities.

Today, however, Egyptologists have come round to the view that Avaris was not Tanis, but should be identified with a site thirty kilometres to the south, near the village of Khatana-Qantir. Here, Dr Labib Habachi, former Director of Fieldwork for the Egyptian Department of Antiquities, found evidence of the remains of royal palaces and temples, with pedestals for statues and obelisks, although there is nothing to be seen there now in the quiet pastoral landscape. He claimed that the missing statuary had been deliberately moved from the site and re-erected at Tanis on stone blocks

Opposite above The Beni-Hasan tomb-painting: in the upper register, to the right, two Egyptian frontier officials escort a group of Semites with a cargo of galena (lead sulphide).

Opposite below Corn in Egypt: the trio of pyramids at Gizeh dominate the fertile reaches of the Nile that attracted hosts of famished migrants from the desert down the centuries.

Sesostris III: granite statue of the warrior king of the Twelfth Dynasty, who conducted several military campaigns against the 'miserable Asiatics' of Palestine and Syria.

48

of a later period, thereby giving the impression that Ramesses II had actually built Tanis – whereas Tanis was not built until the eleventh century BC.

This thesis has now been brilliantly confirmed by Dr Manfred Bietak, head of the Austrian Archaeological Institute in Cairo, who is excavating a site called Tell el-Dab'a, some two kilometres south of Khatana-Qantir. Tell el-Dab'a is a mound which is situated beside what was once the easternmost branch of the Nile. Dr Bietak's excavations there have revealed a clear occupation sequence in which traces of the Hyksos period can be identified beyond question: on top of the Middle Kingdom Egyptian occupation is a layer which is culturally Semitic, associated with Palestine and Syria; and then, after a long hiatus, extensive rebuilding from the time of Ramesses II.

Dr Bietak has also succeeded in reconstructing in detail the ancient topography of the area. He has shown that Khatana-Qantir and Tell el-Dab'a were both part of a huge city complex which was served by an excellent harbour. But in the twelfth century BC, the branch of the Nile which was the arterial route for commerce began to silt up; strenuous efforts were made to dredge it, and build feeder canals, as is shown by the artificial dump-hills in the area. But eventually the attempt to save the city was abandoned, and at the same time the city of Tanis was founded further to the north, on a branch of the Nile that afforded easy access to the Mediterranean. It would explain why so much monumental material from Avaris/Raamses should have been found at Tanis; the Egyptian Pharaohs did not want to abandon all the valuable statuary, and so shipped it to the new capital when economic circumstances drove them from the original site. For most modern Egyptologists, the identification of Avaris with Khatana-Qantir/Tell el-Dab'a is now considered certain.

But to return to Avaris in the Hyksos period: it is clear that there was at this time a great influx of non-Egyptian, Semitic peoples, bringing new blood and new ideas, and it is into this period of intensive Semitic immigration from Palestine and beyond that Biblical scholars try to fit the story in *Genesis* of Joseph and his brothers.

The story of Joseph, youngest of the sons of the Patriarch Jacob, stands out sharply from the confused and rambling material of the earlier chapters of *Genesis*. It is a beautifully organised tale, tightly composed, polished and sophisticated; it is probably the best written short story in the whole of the Old Testament.

'And they drew and lifted up Joseph out of the pit, and sold Joseph to the Ishmaelites for twenty pieces of silver...And they took Joseph's coat, and killed a kid of the goats, and dipped the coat in the blood' (*Genesis* 37:28-31). Painting by Vernet.

In essence, the plot is simple and powerful. Jacob, the grandson of Abraham, had ten grown sons, and in his old age he begat an eleventh son, Joseph, whom he loved more than any other of his children, and gave him, amongst other favours, that celebrated long-sleeved 'coat of many colours'. The elder brothers grew jealous of this marked favouritism, and their feelings were further inflamed when the precocious child insisted on telling them his dreams, which suggested that one day not only his brothers, but his parents as well, would do obeisance to him. Enraged, the brothers seized him, stripped him of his coat of many colours, and sold him for twenty pieces of silver to a caravan of traders heading for Egypt.

In Egypt, Joseph was bought by an official called Potiphar, who quickly promoted him to be overseer of his household. Potiphar's wife then tried to seduce him, but when he refused her blandishments she accused him of trying to seduce her, and Joseph was flung into prison. In prison, he developed a reputation as an interpreter of dreams, and when the Pharaoh of Egypt had some disturbing dreams that no one could interpret, Joseph was summoned from his dungeon. Joseph told Pharaoh that his dreams meant that there would be seven years of abundance in Egypt, followed by seven years of famine, and that Pharaoh should appoint someone to hoard a portion of the abundance to tide the country over the lean years. Pharaoh was grateful, and appointed Joseph his chief minister, or Grand Vizier, to supervise the Seven Year Plan.

The famine affected Palestine as well, and Jacob sent his ten sons down to Egypt to buy corn. Joseph, unrecognised by his brothers, forced them to do obeisance to him, and humiliated them. Eventually he revealed his true identity, forgave them, and sent for his father, who also did obeisance to him. Then Joseph raised his family to high estate, and when his father died at a ripe old age he had his body mummified and taken for burial in the Cave of Machpelah at Hebron; and when Joseph himself died in the fullness of time, he himself was also mummified, according to Egyptian custom.

Such is the story of Joseph. In its present form in *Genesis*, it is frequently interrupted by digressions, but stripped of genealogical and theological accretions it stands apart as a beautifully wrought *novella*, with the dream motif used to provide the structure of the plot.

Fundamentalists who regard the Old Testament as literal truth try to slot the Joseph episode into the Hyksos period because it was the one time when an immigrant Semite might conceivably have risen to high office in Pharaonic Egypt; and they point to the apparent familiarity with the details of life in Egypt in ancient times.

However, Professor Donald Redford of Toronto University, who is now Director of the Akhenaten Temple Project in Egypt, disagrees. In a recent monograph, *A Study of the Biblical Story of Joseph*, he argues that the Egyptian elements in the story, and the plot motifs, reflect not the seventeenth century BC but the seventh century BC at the earliest; it has no independent historical validity. It is a late adaptation of a common folk-tale motif, or rather several motifs (boy-dreamer makes good, innocent man accused of seduction, wise man saves the king with sage advice, and so on), used in *Genesis* as a complete short story in itself to explain the cause of the descent into Egypt and the subsequent Bondage at a time in Hebrew history when another Bondage, the Babylonian Exile in the sixth century BC, was imminent.

51

Still, the theory of the Hyksos background for the Joseph episode remains an enticing one for many commentators, not least because it seems to provide an explanation for the Bondage that ensued (albeit three centuries later), when a Pharaoh came to the throne 'which knew not Joseph' (*Exodus* 1:8). Because round about 1550 BC, after ruling Lower Egypt for more than a century, the Hyksos were driven out of the country and the palmy days for Semitic immigrants came to an end.

During the period of Hyksos rule, Upper Egypt had been governed by a line of native Egyptian princes in the ancient capital of Thebes, the so-called Seventeenth Dynasty, as vassals of the Hyksos. It was from Thebes that the fight for freedom was launched. The first leader of the liberation movement seems to have been Seqenenre II, who apparently revolted against a provocative command from Avaris to 'silence the night-time roaring of the hippopotami in his pool' at Thebes; his mummified body, which was found in 1881, was twisted as if in agony, and there were five terrible wounds on the head and neck.

There is still doubt about the manner in which Seqenenre met his death, whether in battle or by treachery. But there is no doubt at all that his son and successor, Kamose, launched a full-scale attack on the Hyksos king, Apophis, and drove him back to the walls of his stronghold, Avaris. The account of his campaign was providentially discovered in 1954 by Dr Labib Habachi in the temple of Amon-Re at Karnak, where the limestone stela on which it was inscribed had been re-used in the foundation pedestal of the statue of a later king.  Kamose's mother, Queen Ahhotep, took an active part in rallying the people in the struggle, and was awarded military honours in the form of three golden flies. Kamose's younger brother and successor, Amosis I, who is regarded as the founder of the Eighteenth Dynasty, kept up the pressure; he laid siege to Avaris itself, which fell sometime around 1550 BC, and pursued the defeated Hyksos to Palestine.

The victory over the Hyksos heralded a long period of Egyptian strength and imperial expansion in the so-called New Kingdom (c. 1550-1080 BC), which would make Egypt for a time the greatest power in the world. Under a series of kings called Amenophis or Tuthmosis, Egyptian armies swept through Palestine and Syria time and again, laying waste cities and kingdoms all the way to the Euphrates. Their troops were now equipped with horse-drawn chariots and an improved composite bow (probably from the Hyksos), which gave them devastating mobility and firepower. Tuthmosis III, the most formidable of all the Pharaohs (c.1490-36 BC), campaigned repeatedly through Palestine and Syria. In the twenty-third year of his reign, c.1468, when he was still a young man in his twenties, he launched a historic invasion of Palestine against a confederation of local princes, chiefly descendants of the dispossessed Hyksos, whom he crushed in a decisive battle at Megiddo, a strongly fortified town overlooking the Plain of Esdraelon. The account of this crucial campaign, which brought Egypt to the zenith of her power, is recorded on the back of the Seventh Pylon which Tuthmosis erected in the Temple of Amon-Re at Karnak.

Some scholars like Dr Habachi, for instance, believe that Tuthmosis III was the Pharaoh 'which knew not Joseph', the Pharaoh of the Oppression who reduced the Children of Israel to servitude – or, as Dr Habachi prefers to describe it, recruited them along with the rest of the population of Egypt to take part in his major building projects. This theory can be corroborated by a selective use of the Biblical sources; for instance, according to the *First Book of Kings* (6:1), 480 years passed between the Deliverance from Egypt and the building of Solomon's Temple, which is usually dated c.960 BC – and this would give a date of c.1440 BC for the Deliverance, towards the end of the reign of Tuthmosis III. However, other scholars play their own version of the numbers game by assuming that the 480 years in the Bible represented twelve Biblical generations of forty years each, whereas a generation should more accurately be computed as merely twenty-five years. This would bring the date of the Deliverance forward to 1260 BC, and into the reign of another formidable Egyptian Pharaoh – Ramesses II, Ramesses the Great (c.1290-24 BC).

Ramesses II was the dominant monarch of the Nineteenth Dynasty, which was founded by his grandfather Ramesses I, c.1306. This Dynasty restored Egypt's fortunes after the empire had been all but lost through the internal weakness and confusion caused by the revolutionary religious policies of the celebrated 'heretic' Pharaoh, Akhenaten, in the middle of the fourteenth century. Ramesses II and his father before him (Seti I) energetically re-established Egyptian control of the garrison towns of Palestine. This aggressive policy reduced Palestine to vassalage again, but it also brought Ramesses II into conflict with the growing power of the Hittites in the north.

The Hittite New Kingdom, as it is called (c.1475-1200

The mummy of Seqenenre II: the five sword-wounds on the head and neck suggest he may have died in battle against the Hyksos.

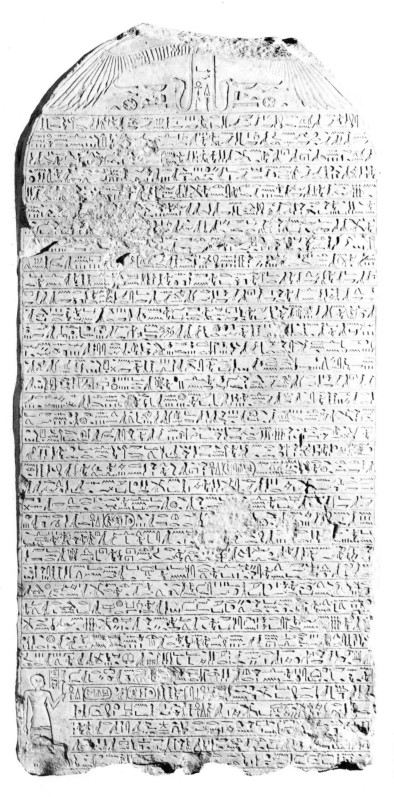

The Kamose stela: discovered in 1954 at Karnak by Dr Labib Habachi, it tells the story of Kamose's struggle against the Hyksos.

Ramesses II: relief carving from the temple at Abu Simbel. The upper register shows part of the Battle of Kadesh.

BC), had its power-base in the Anatolian plateau in modern Turkey. Hittite expansion was always aimed at Syria, in order to gain control of the important trade routes that passed through it, and during the period of Egypt's decline the greatest of the Hittite kings, Suppiluliama (c.1380-45), had taken firm hold of Syria. The resurgence of Egyptian military power under the Nineteenth Dynasty made a trial of strength between the super-powers over the control of Syria inevitable.

Soon after his accession to the throne c.1290 BC, Ramesses II led a huge army northward into Syria. About 150 kilometres north of Damascus, at a site now called Nebi Mend, near the city of Homs, the Egyptians were ambushed by the Hittites in an engagement known as the Battle of Kadesh. The extensive *tell* of Nebi Mend, scarcely touched by excavation as yet, dominates the broad valley of the Orontes River, just as the ancient city of Kadesh had done; today the valley is intensively farmed, and it was here that the Egyptian army,

The Battle of Kadesh: in the centre, a fortified town surrounded by a moat. On the left, the Egyptian army engages the Hittites; on the right, the Hittite king in his chariot. Relief from Abu Simbel.

marching in extended column, was almost annihilated by the fury and unexpectedness of the Hittite onslaught. Later, Ramesses was to boast in his inscriptions that his personal prowess had saved the day and turned near-defeat into a crushing victory; Hittite records, however, recently discovered at Boghazkoy, claim the outcome as a Hittite victory. Whatever the truth of it, Ramesses made a strategic withdrawal, and both sides apparently realised that they could not afford such expensive 'victories'; a few years later, the Egyptians and the Hittites concluded a peace treaty which gave Syria to the Hittites and Palestine to the Egyptians. Copies of the treaty, which was cemented by the marriage of a Hittite princess to Ramesses II around 1270 BC, have been found both in Egypt and at Boghazkoy in Anatolia.

Egyptian power and prestige had taken a severe drubbing as a result of the Kadesh adventure, and Ramesses II had to contend with a series of revolts in the cities of Palestine. In the Temple of Luxor at Thebes, Ramesses left a graphic illustration of the destruction he wrought in Palestine – buildings falling, trees being uprooted, gateways collapsing. The ferocity with which he quelled the uprisings seems to have left Palestine and its cities enfeebled for decades.

Ramesses II was perhaps the most vainglorious Pharaoh of all time. For the latter part of his reign he devoted himself to huge and grandiose building projects, largely designed to perpetuate his own name – the celebrated temples at Abu Simbel, for example. One of his major buildings was the Ramesseum, the mortuary temple on the west bank of the Nile at Thebes, now in ruins. It was this desolate site that inspired Shelley's poem *Ozymandias of Egypt*: 'My name is Ozymandias, king of kings: Look on my works, ye Mighty, and despair!'

How are the mighty fallen! That was the massive irony that informed Shelley's poem, and it is an irony that strikes the mind like a bludgeon when you stand at the head of the fallen remains of the largest statue in Egypt: the Colossus of Ramesses the Great. It was nearly twenty metres tall originally, one thousand tons of carved and polished granite now irretrievably ruined by some earthquake. His ears are over a metre long; his toes are nearly a metre and a half across; his shoulders are over seven metres broad. On his right upper arm are incised the well preserved hieroglyphics of one of his royal names, User-maat-re, which gave rise to the Greek version of 'Ozymandias'. But it is an even keener irony to reflect that it was not Ramesses the Great who was destined to change the way of the world, as he himself no doubt confidently expected. Instead, according to the way in which the majority of scholars tend to interpret the Biblical tradition of the Bondage, it was a small part of the most insignificant people of all those whom he reduced to servitude – the Children of Israel who had come into Egypt and grown rich there in the wake of Joseph and Jacob.

According to this view, it was the tyrant Ramesses (or perhaps his father Seti I) who grew alarmed at the way in which the Children of Israel had prospered and multiplied: 'Therefore they did set over them taskmasters to afflict them with their burdens. And they built for Pharaoh treasure cities, Pithom and Raamses...And the Egyptians made the Children of Israel to serve with rigour: and they made their lives bitter with hard bondage, in mortar, and in brick, and in all manner of service in the field...' (*Exodus* 1:11-14).

Contemporary Egyptian sources record the extensive use of forced labour for royal building projects during this period, and some of the state workers were recruited from among the 'Habiru'. Biblical commentators are fond of illustrating their thesis with the celebrated 'Bondage scenes' painted on the walls of the tomb of the vizier Rekhmire, which depict a group of workmen making bricks and building walls for the Temple of Amon-Re at Karnak. The fact that Rekhmire was the vizier of Tuthmosis III, two centuries before Ramesses II, and that the scenes do not refer to either Pithom or Raamses, is conveniently overlooked.

The Biblical scenario in *Exodus* continues with the birth of the man who was to save the Children of Israel from their ordeal and humiliation: a man with the uncompromisingly Egyptian name of Moses. 'Moses' is simply the suffix to be found in many Egyptian names, and means 'son of ', as in Ramesses ('son of Ra') or Tuthmosis ('son of Thoth'). According to the Bible, Moses was born at a time when Pharaoh, in an attempt to check the Israelite population explosion, ordered that every male child born to them should be killed; Moses's mother, to save him from this fate, hid him in a basket in the reeds of the river bank, where the infant was found by Pharaoh's daughter and brought up at the royal court.

The story is quite obviously a folk-tale, for it echoes almost word for word the birth legend of King Sargon the Great, who founded the dynasty of Akkad a thousand years earlier. The similarity is astonishing. The Bible says: 'And when she could no longer hide him, she took for him an ark of bulrushes (rush-basket, *New English Bible*), and daubed it with slime and with pitch (made it watertight with clay and tar, *New English Bible*), and put the child therein; and she laid it in the flags (reeds, *New English Bible*) by the river's brink' (*Exodus* 2:3). The Legend of Sargon, as translated in *Ancient Near Eastern Texts*, says 'Sargon, the mighty king, king of Agade [Akkad], am I. My mother was a changeling, my father I knew not...My changeling mother conceived me, in secret she bore me. She set me in a basket of rushes, with bitumen she sealed my lid. She cast me in the river which rose not over me...Akki, the drawer of water, took me as his son and reared me.'

The account of Moses's youth continues the folk-tale theme. Despite his Egyptianised upbringing, he still felt for his fellow Hebrews, and one day when he saw an Egyptian smiting a Hebrew he was so incensed that (after a quick look round to ensure that no one was watching) he killed the Egyptian and hid his body in the sand. Someone must have been watching after all, however, for it reached the ears of Pharaoh, and Moses was forced to flee to the land of Midian, to the copper-bearing mountains east of the Gulf of Aqaba, where he married the daughter of Jethro, the priest of Midian.

Eventually, according to the Bible, the king of Egypt died.

Ramesses II: all the power and majesty of the greatest Pharaoh of the Nineteenth Dynasty, at Thebes.

The Children of Israel still sighed under the yoke of servitude, and cried out to God. And God at last remembered his covenant with the Patriarchs 430 years earlier, when he had been known as El. He spoke to Moses from a burning bush, and revealed himself in the new name of Yahweh, and sent Moses back to Egypt to deliver his people from bondage.

The new Pharaoh, who would have been Merneptah, Ramesses II's successor, was reluctant to let his slave labour force emigrate, and added to their burdens by forcing them to make bricks without straw; whereupon the Lord, through Moses, concentrated Pharaoh's mind with a succession of plagues – bloodied water, frogs, lice, flies, cattle pestilence, boils, hailstorms, locusts and darkness. Finally, he produced the most terrible plague of all, that no amount of scientific rationalising can explain away: every first-born creature in the land of Egypt was struck dead at midnight, except in those Israelite houses which had a blood-mark on the door. This was the origin of the Feast of the Passover, when the Lord passed over the houses of the Israelites in Egypt when he struck the Egyptians.

Until the recent confirmation by Dr Bietak that the site of Avaris/Piramesse was to be found at Khatana-Qantir, scholars had assumed that the Biblical bond-city of Raamses was at Tanis. It certainly looks and feels the part. With its massively shattered ruins, its statues and obelisks lying in stricken disarray, it is a desolate scene which dramatically matches the thunderclap concept of the Passover. But despite the powerfully atmospheric impact of the ruins of Tanis, we have to remind ourselves that there is absolutely no objective proof, no contemporary evidence, that the Bondage or the Deliverance ever happened at all as particular, identifiable episodes in history, in any Delta city in the Biblical 'Land of Goshen'. And anyway, surely the circumstantial details of the birth of Moses and the flight from Raamses can be safely consigned to the realm of folklore? So how do modern scholars now look at it?

Dr Pritchard points out that the lack of evidence in the ancient Egyptian records of either the presence of the Hebrews or their deliverance need not necessarily surprise us. The Egyptian chroniclers were more interested in royal affairs than in social questions, and the activities of a small group of Semitic immigrants and their escape from the work-gangs would hardly engage their attention. On the other hand, it could also be that the undeniably powerful tradition of an Egyptian bondage might have arisen out of, or been emphas-

ised by, the cultic ritual of the celebration of the Passover – the ritual, in effect, helping to shape the tradition.

Dr Habachi, too, finds it unsurprising that there is no mention of Bondage or Exodus in the Egyptian records. The Hebrews were a minority people, and the Egyptians did not like to record anything that smacked of defeat or humiliation.

Interestingly enough, though, there *is* an Egyptian version of the story – or to be more accurate, a piece of counter-folklore from the Egyptian side – which was ascribed to the Egyptian historian Manetho in the third century BC, a thousand years after the assumed date of the Exodus. It is a highly scurrilous story, to the effect that the Hebrews had not escaped, but had been thrown out. It tells of a gang of Asiatic lepers and plague-bearers who had once been expelled from Egypt by force and driven back to Palestine where they founded Jerusalem and became the ancestors of the Jews.

Professor Donald Redford sees in this anti-Semitic story an Egyptian plot motif which might well hark back to the expulsion of the hated Hyksos, but which was reinforced by the waves of invasion which were to break over Egypt in the

60

first millennium BC. These invaders were always Asiatics, they always came from the north, they always wrought appalling destruction – the Assyrians, the Babylonians, the Persians. It is a timeless piece of patriotic xenophobia.

And what of Moses, the man who in the Biblical tradition plays so fundamental a part as the founder of Israel's faith? Outside the Bible, there is no evidence for his existence, although there is little doubt that his name goes back to a genuine Egyptian name-form. On the other hand, it is almost inconceivable that the powerful Biblical tradition about him does not rest on the memory of a charismatic personality of that name. As Israeli scholars say, 'Moses may not have existed, but he undoubtedly had a cousin called Moses!'

Whether the *Exodus* account gives a true picture of him is another question entirely. Professor Redford argues that the time when *Genesis* and *Exodus* crystallised in written form was in the seventh or sixth century BC, when the imminence or actuality of the Babylonian Exile provided the spur to rationalise and shape tradition into its present form: what the exiles needed to know, above all, was that there had been an earlier bondage, an earlier exile, from which their ancestors had been delivered. Looked at from this point of view, the story of the Bondage and the Deliverance is above all a statement of faith, rather than history.

4
Exodus

'Let my people go!' That was what Moses cried as he demanded the release of the Children of Israel from the bondage of
Pharaoh's slave labour gangs in Egypt. It is a cry that has
haunted the imagination of the oppressed and inspired the
dreams of liberators throughout history. It has also provided
a compelling picture for artists to impress on our folk culture
down the centuries: the deliverer Moses, eighty years old according to the Bible, confronting the all-powerful Pharaoh
of Egypt with that ringing challenge: 'Let my people go!'

Ultimately Pharaoh, stunned by the appalling consequen-
ces of the ten plagues which Moses called down upon Egypt,
agreed to let the Hebrews go. Indeed he was so glad to get rid
of these pestilential people that he allowed them to plunder
the Egyptians of as much silver and gold and raiment as they
could 'borrow' (*Exodus* 12:35-6). And the Children of Israel
set off on their Exodus from Egypt.

But where did they go? And what route did they take? The
Biblical account is bafflingly inconsistent, simultaneously
precise and vague, clear and confusing. Biblical scholars
have laboured without cease to establish a geography of the
Exodus; but their efforts are of necessity speculative, depend-
ing on different interpretations of the clues. As a result some
scholars would show us the Children of Israel wading knee-
deep through the shallows of the Mediterranean, while others
depict them fording the Red Sea itself, with numerous variations in between. A composite map of all the various routes
out of Egypt and through Sinai that have been suggested
over the years would look like the wanderings of a drunken
centipede.

There is also the problem of the scale of the Exodus.
According to Chapter 1 of the *Book of Numbers*, the Twelve
Tribes of Israel which took part in the Exodus could muster
no fewer than 603,550 males of military age; this implies that
the host of refugees must have numbered at least two million
– a figure that stretches even the most sympathetic credulity.
It is simply not believable that a host of this size could have
survived in the wilderness for forty years, as the Bible claims.

Besides, Egypt itself could not have afforded such a massive drain of its manpower; indeed, it is doubtful if the total population of Egypt in the New Kingdom period exceeded that figure. The Bible writers were perhaps aware of this objection when they portrayed Pharaoh coming to his senses after the catastrophic slaughter of the Passover, and repenting of his decision to 'let the people go'. He mustered a great army of chariots and set off in pursuit of the Children of Israel

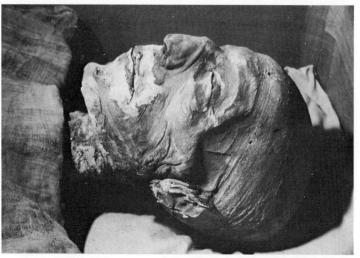

The mummy of Merneptah, the 'Pharaoh of the Exodus', who was once believed to have drowned in the Red Sea.

and overtook them 'encamping by the sea, beside Pihahiroth, before Baal-zephon' (*Exodus* 14:9). The sea in question, according to the traditional translation in the Authorised Version, was the Red Sea. And so the scene was set for the miracle of the Red Sea crossing, when Moses parted the waters to allow the Children of Israel to get over dryshod and then brought the seas crashing back to swamp and drown the pursuing Egyptian army, including the unfortunate Pharaoh.

On the assumption that the Pharaoh of the Bondage was Ramesses II, the Pharaoh of the Exodus was presumed to be Ramesses's successor, Merneptah. There was great excitement in 1881 when his mummified body was discovered in a tomb near Deir el-Bahri, on the west bank of the Nile at Thebes, though it was also a little disconcerting: if Merneptah had been drowned in the Red Sea, how could his body be buried in a tomb on dry land? Anxious fundamentalists were soothed by the information that the mummy bore substantial traces of salt on the skin: obviously, the Pharaoh's body must have been washed ashore after the mishap and buried in the normal Egyptian way. What was conveniently overlooked (or suppressed) at the time was the fact that *all* mummies show traces of salt on the skin, because mummification involved a period of treatment in natron, which contains salt.

63

Subsequent examination revealed that Merneptah's mummy had no more and no less salt on the skin than any other mummy.

On another level, Merneptah was a singularly bad candidate for the Pharaoh of the Exodus. He seems to have reigned from about 1224-11; and in the fifth year of his reign he campaigned in Palestine. On the stela with which he commemorated his exploits he listed the foes he had defeated: Canaan, Ashkelon, Gezer, and so on. It is a hymn of praise, a eulogy of victory, rather than a chronicle; and in it we find, strikingly, the only instance of the name 'Israel' in ancient Egyptian records: 'Israel is laid waste, his seed is not.' There is much debate on whether this refers to the state of Israel, or simply the people – the 'Children of Israel'. But either way, Merneptah could hardly have claimed victory over 'Israel' in Palestine if he had drowned in a vain attempt to stop them reaching Palestine in the first place.

Opposite Acacia trees in Sinai: despite the aridity, there is a surprising amount of vegetation in the desert. It was from acacia wood that the wandering Israelites were said to have constructed the Ark of the Covenant.

'Israel': detail from the Merneptah stela of *c.*1220 BC, with the only reference to Israel in ancient Egyptian records.

Those who like to be able to rationalise the Bible account of the Exodus, with its manifest contradictions, can point to the now recognised fact that the term 'Red Sea' is in itself a mistranslation. The Hebrew term is *yam suf*, which is now translated 'Sea of Reeds', not 'Red Sea', and this has opened the sluice-gates for a flood of suggestions of where this 'Reeds Sea' might have been. At least a dozen places have been proposed along the line of the Suez Canal and the Bitter Lakes; and since the topography of the Eastern Delta has changed so much since Biblical times, not least because of the construction of the Suez Canal, there is no way of verifying any of them. Any landscape which might have involved water and reeds could be pressed into service; it only needed a fortuitous drying wind to allow the Children of Israel to slip across while the chariots of the pursuing Egyptians were trapped in the mud and swamped when the wind changed and the waters returned.

There are now two distinct schools of thought on this subject: those who favour a northern route out of Egypt, and those who favour a southern route. Both factions rely on various permutations of the unidentifiable place names which

Opposite St Catherine's Monastery: in Christian tradition, it was built at the foot of Mount Sinai (Jebel Musa), where Moses received the tablets of law from the Lord

stud the Biblical narrative. And both of them choose to overlook the fact that elsewhere in the Bible, *yam suf* clearly does refer, geographically, to the Red Sea (Gulf of Aqaba), in the account of Solomon's naval and commercial activities at Ezion-geber (see Chapter 8).

There seems no way of resolving satisfactorily the many problems involved in this aspect of the Exodus. Dr Pritchard sums it up with his usual judiciousness: 'The route of the Exodus is one of the great problems in Biblical geography. There is a list of towns through which the Israelites passed – camping places, resting places, and so on – and this list can be read with no difficulty. The problem is that few of these places can be identified with any certainty. This is understandable because in the desert you do not have cities, and a camping place leaves no archaeological evidence. It is a vast area, and the area has not yet been combed, so it is quite understandable that this cannot be plotted on a present-day map. This does not say that the record in the Bible is not accurate; it says only that we have not found it yet.'

And thus, according to the Biblical narrative, the Children of Israel moved into the desert. 'Desert' is perhaps a misleading term. One tends to think of great stretches of sand dunes like the Sahara, but the Sinai is not like that at all. It is much more of a gravelly, dusty wilderness, and it supports a remarkable variety of life – not least several thousand Bedouin and their sheep, goats and camels. The leopard was hunted to extinction in the Sinai only quite recently; wolves, hyenas and lynxes are still found there, as well as the ibex, the mountain goats of the Bible. There is a surprising amount of vegetation, considering that the annual rainfall is only twenty-five millimetres: a mere two and a half centimetres a year. For herded livestock, there is a reasonably abundant supply of camel-thorn bushes, rather like the American tumbleweed so often featured blowing down deserted main streets of frontier towns in western movies; and as a last resort, of course, there is wormwood with its bitter taste.

For human travellers, migratory quails can sometimes be caught, especially in the northern reaches of the desert (*Exodus* 16:13, and *Numbers* 11:31-2). And there is that mysterious stuff called manna which helped to keep the Children of Israel alive (*Exodus* 16:15). Manna is in fact produced on various plants that flourish in the desert, particularly tamarisks; the Bible describes it as being like coriander seed, white like gum resin – and that is precisely what it is. It is a sap that exudes from the stalks of the bushes when they are pierced

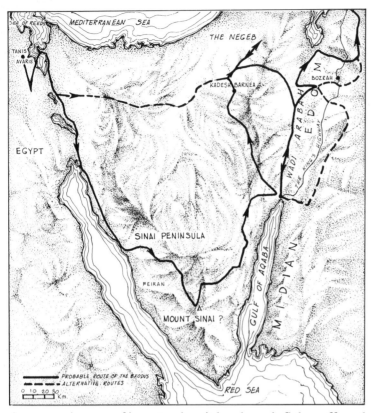

Probable route of the Exodus. But innumerable variations have been suggested over the years, and there is no general agreement among scholars.

by a certain type of insect; when it hardens, it flakes off, and its colour is white at first. There is really nothing miraculous about manna at all, except in the amount that the Bible suggests was available to sustain two million people for forty years. Today, anyone looking for sufficient manna to keep even one person alive in the desert would think it a miracle if he found it.

In the desert, survival is the major imperative. This is something that the Bedouin know better than anyone. Their social customs are largely based on the need to survive: the demands of sharing, the demands of hospitality to wayfarers, and the uncompromising punishments for breaking rules which might endanger the survival of the tribe. Scholars like Dr Clinton Bailey, lecturer in Bedouin culture at Tel Aviv University, point out that many of the customs and ethics of the desert Israelites can be mirrored in Bedouin society today; but this, of course, is not an argument for the age or historicity of the Biblical traditions about the wandering in the desert, for if these social customs are 'timeless', they can tell us nothing about the particular time that they were observed and incorporated into the Biblical tradition.

The climax and core of the desert experience for the Children of Israel took place at Mount Sinai (also called Mount Horeb), where Moses is said to have received the tablets of law from God. But where was it? Some would place it in the northern part of the Sinai peninsula. Others look for it on the east side of the Gulf of Aqaba, in the mountains of Midian where Moses spent most of his life, and where geological evidence of volcanic activity might have given rise to the Biblical description of a mountain peak wreathed in clouds and shot through with lightning (*Exodus* 19:16). There seems to be no way of making a conclusive identification.

The traditional site of Mount Sinai, for Christians at least, is the mountain of Jebel Musa (Mount Moses) near the southern end of the Sinai peninsula. As early as the fourth century AD, a devout lady traveller called Etheria noted that the Burning Bush was to be found at the foot of the mountain ('It is alive to this day and throws out shoots') and that it was tended by a group of hermits who had built a church nearby. In the sixth century AD the Emperor Justinian built a fortified monastery there for the protection of the holy men; it is still there, and still occupied by monks, and can claim to be the oldest continuously inhabited building in the world. Pilgrims and visitors can stay there overnight in somewhat spartan conditions if they want to climb the 2350 feet to the summit at dawn.

The monastery is dedicated to St Catherine, an Egyptian Christian said to have been martyred in Alexandria, after which her bones were carried to Jebel Musa by angels. The monastery itself is an enchanting place, redolent of history; its library has a marvellous collection of ancient manuscripts, and it was there that the magnificent *Codex Sinaiticus* was discovered in 1859. It was a Greek translation of the New Testament and parts of the Old dating from the fourth century AD, and was presented to the Tsar of Russia in exchange for a gift of 9000 roubles. After the Communist revolution in Russia, it was bought by the British Museum from the Soviet Government for £100,000.

The climb to the summit of Jebel Musa is both exhausting and invigorating. From the peak, where a small chapel has been built over the cave where Moses was supposed to have sheltered, there is a breathtaking panorama of the rugged desolation of the mountain ranges of the Sinai. Up there in the heart of an endless desert wilderness, there is nothing to contradict anything one might want to think, anything that a man might propose, or a god dispose. Up there, it is easy to think oneself into the presence of what many people consider one of the pivotal events in human history – the first personal encounter between man and god, in which details were hammered out of a covenant, a social contract, which said in effect: 'You look after me, and I'll look after you.'

Scholars are divided on the question of whether this spectacular episode actually was the birth of the concept of monotheism – the concept of a single creator god who could determine the day-to-day destinies of men and nations – or whether that was an interpretation which was imposed on the tradition by later prophets, with the benefit of hindsight. For the Biblical writers, it was seen as a transcendental occasion; God was no longer simply 'El' (plural 'Elohim'), but YHWH ('I am that I am'), which in the Authorised Version was transliterated as 'Jehovah' by combining the Hebrew consonants and the vowels of the Hebrew word for 'Lord' when excessive reverence had made later Jews reluctant to pronounce the divine name itself, nowadays called Yahweh. The covenant with Yahweh elevated the concept of worship from a hopeful appeasement of the wilful and haphazard forces of nature to a dynamic and determined arrangement with none other than the sole creator of the universe. This was no idle philosophical speculation about the nature of the Infinite, it was a specific deal that laid upon the Israelites (and through them the Western world) a terrible moral obligation of obedience in exchange for God's love.

Moses is depicted in the Bible as having had two of these meetings with Yahweh: the first to establish the broad lines of the contract – the Ten Commandments, which he duly transmitted to the assembled multitudes of Israelites down below – and the second a much longer session, lasting forty days, in which the details of the law code which would govern the social behaviour of his people were worked out. This law code, we are told, was inscribed by God on two stone tablets or 'tables'. For a long time, it was believed that this law code was literally the first such expression of social and ethical requirements; but archaeological discoveries in recent decades have shown that law codes of this kind were being recorded on stone stelae and clay tablets by rulers in Mesopotamia centuries earlier, such as the celebrated Law Code of King Hammurabi of Babylon in the eighteenth century BC, and that these early codes contained many of the concepts enshrined in the Mosaic code of the Bible.

Unfortunately, the stone tablets of Moses are not accessible to archaeology, because it seems that Moses smashed them in a rage when he got back to the Israelite encampment

The Wadi Arabah. In the foreground, the mountains of Edom; in the middle ground, the deep rift of the Wadi Arabah that runs north from the Gulf of Aqaba to the Dead Sea, in the far distance.

and discovered that all this lengthy negotiation with God had apparently been in vain: during his absence his brother, the priest Aaron, had turned the people to the making and worship not of Yahweh, but of a golden calf.

The golden calf episode, in which Aaron fashioned the image of a calf from the golden ear-rings of the Children of Israel (*Exodus* 32), is portrayed as backsliding, a reversion to the worship of Egyptian animal gods that was severely punished by Moses. But it would be repeated later in Israelite history, when the northern kingdom of Israel broke away from the official cult practices of Jerusalem (see Chapter 9), and should perhaps be interpreted as an allegory of the long struggle between the priests of monotheistic Judaism and the adherents of a more liberal pluralistic religion which apparently died hard. In *Exodus*, Moses diverted the image-making energies of his people to the making of the Ark of the Covenant and the Tabernacle, or curtained tent, which would serve as a mobile sanctuary to house it.

In the Bible, the description of the construction of the Ark from acacia wood, and the rich trappings of the Tabernacle, occupies six chapters (*Exodus* 35-40). This is more a measure of its cultic importance than a guarantee of its authenticity; attempted reconstructions of the Ark and the Tabernacle based on the Biblical account, such as the one by Tel Aviv

diamond merchant Moses Levine, on which he lavished fifteen years of his leisure time, become so elaborate and costly
that it is hard to think of them as part of the impedimenta of
a desert people – rather a back-projection of the ornate splendour of the Temple built by Solomon in Jerusalem in the
tenth century BC (see Chapter 8).

Be that as it may, the Biblical account continues in *Numbers*
to the effect that God made it clear that the Ark of the
Covenant was his symbolic residence by means of a pillar of
fire by night and a cloud by day that guided the Children of
Israel in their wanderings across the Sinai to their next significant staging post in the 'wilderness of Paran': a place called
Kadesh-Barnea.

Kadesh-Barnea was, and still is, an important oasis on the
north-eastern fringe of the Sinai. Historically, it became an
important fortress on the southern boundaries of the kingdom of Judah, and excavations in 1976 by Rudolf Cohen of
the Israel Department of Antiquities have revealed that
there was a pre-fortress settlement there from the tenth century BC (the period of Solomon) onwards. Before that, its
importance lay in its abundant spring water; for cross-coun-
try traders and nomads alike it provided a staging post with
ample water to supply all needs. Anyone coming out of the

'And Moses stretched forth his hand over
the sea...and the waters returned, and
covered the chariots, and the horsemen,
and all the host of Pharaoh that came into
the sea after them...' (*Exodus* 14:27-8).
Engraving by John Martin.

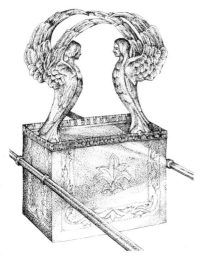

The Ark of the Covenant: detail from a miniature reconstruction based on the elaborate details given in *Exodus*, made by Tel Aviv diamond merchant Moses Levine.

desert would pause at Kadesh-Barnea; and Moses, apparently, was no exception. According to *Deuteronomy* (1:46), the Children of Israel spent a long time there, resting and watering their flocks – perhaps as long as a year.

At Kadesh-Barnea, they were right on the threshold of the Promised Land of Canaan. It is implied in the Bible that this was the point of entry into Canaan that Moses had originally planned; and being a prudent man, he sent a party of twelve scouts to spy out what lay ahead of them. One of them was a young man called Joshua, the son of Nun, who was to have an even larger part to play in the fullness of time.

The scouts returned after forty days (everything seems to happen in forties in the Bible), and reported that Canaan was indeed a land flowing with milk and honey; as proof of this they brought back with them a monster bunch of grapes so heavy that it had to be carried on a pole slung between the shoulders of two men – this is now, incidentally, the symbol of the Israeli Tourist Office. But they also reported that Canaan was densely populated, with walled and strongly fortified cities, and even a few giants thrown in for good measure; and against such opposition, it was feared, the Children of Israel would have little chance.

Frustrated by this bitterly disappointing news right on the threshold of the land they had been promised by their god, the Children of Israel 'murmured' against the Lord, and many of them were for turning round and heading straight back for the fleshpots of Egypt. But Moses, after due consultation with the Lord, decided instead to make a wide detour to the east, round the far side of the Dead Sea, in order to attack Canaan from across the River Jordan. But the Lord, to punish the Children of Israel for daring to call his promise into question, condemned them to take forty years of wandering in the wilderness (the same length of time in years as the scouting party had taken in days) before they reached their destination.

This eastern detour would take the Children of Israel through what is now the Hashemite Kingdom of Jordan. Once again, the various Biblical accounts of this stage of the journey are so inconsistent and even contradictory that no one has been able to create a coherent geographical picture from them. Biblical scholars tend, in consequence, to see them as a conflation of traditions about the wanderings of many groups, at different times, which accreted round the dominant figure of Moses.

Politically, Jordan was seen by the Bible writers as being

71

divided into three separate kingdoms: Edom in the south, reaching from the Gulf of Aqaba to the Dead Sea; then Moab, occupying most of the land to the east of the Dead Sea, centred on its capital at Heshbon; while north of Heshbon, the kingdom of Ammon occupied the land to the east of the River Jordan, with its capital in the region of the present capital of Jordan, the city of Amman. Through all these kingdoms ran one of the most important arterial trade routes in Palestine, the so-called 'King's Highway' from the Gulf of Aqaba straight to Damascus and Mesopotamia; the other major trunk road was the Via Maris, the 'Way of the Sea', that ran along the Mediterranean coast from Egypt to the Lebanon and Syria.

Ammonite king, dating from the late eighth century BC.

To get at Canaan from the east, across the River Jordan, Moses and his men would first have to get through or past the obstacles presented by Edom, Moab and Ammon. Edom was the most southerly, and had to be negotiated first. It was difficult and high hill country, guarded on its western flank by a formidable range of mountains and, according to the Bible (*Numbers* 20), by a formidable king. The most direct route was to travel up the King's Highway. Moses tried diplomacy; he sent messengers from Kadesh-Barnea to the King of Edom to seek permission to pass through the country along the Highway. He promised not to pass through any fields or vineyards, or take any water without paying for it. The King of Edom refused. 'And Edom came out against him with much people, and with a strong hand. Thus Edom refused to give Israel passage through his border; wherefore Israel turned away from him' (*Numbers* 20:20-1).

Other Biblical references imply that the capital of Edom was a city called Bozrah, in the north of the kingdom. Biblical Bozrah is identified with the present-day village of Buseirah, which lies just off the line of the King's Highway in the Wadi Arabah almost due east of Kadesh-Barnea. It is a reasonable assumption that any Israelite emissaries to the King of Edom would have gone to his capital at Bozrah. The name Bozrah originally meant 'fortress'; and the site of Buseirah has great natural advantages, with steep ravines guarding three sides. Clearly a fortified city there, commanding as it does the line of the King's Highway, would have been a place to be reckoned with; and obviously the Biblical account envisaged it as a well-garrisoned royal fastness with a powerful army, the 'strong hand' which denied the Children of Israel passage along the Highway.

72

The site of Buseirah (Biblical Bozrah): view from the King's Highway of the natural plateau in the middle distance on which the capital of Edom was situated. It was guarded by steep ravines on three sides.

That is the picture the Bible writers seem to have had in mind for Edom and Bozrah in the thirteenth century BC, if one assumes, as many scholars do, that the Exodus under Moses took place then. And it is a picture that archaeology once tended to reinforce by default, as it were. No Edomite site of the presumed Exodus period had ever been excavated until very recently; an archaeological survey of thirty years ago had turned up some stray bits of pottery from the surface of sites like Buseirah, and these potsherds were generally taken to belong to the thirteenth century BC, although nobody knew much about Edomite pottery then. It was rather a case of wishful thinking on the part of Biblical scholars who were subconsciously, perhaps, using the Bible to prove archaeological evidence, rather than the other way round.

That was the position in 1971 when Mrs Crystal Bennett, Director of the British School of Archaeology in Jerusalem, started excavating the site at Buseirah. Her intention, she admits, was to find evidence to confirm the Biblical account that there had been an Edomite royal city there in the thirteenth century BC: she was looking for Biblical Bozrah.

She found that the site was far more extensive than surface appearances had indicated. The city had been surrounded by formidable walls several feet thick. On the summit there was a walled citadel which included a temple or sanctuary area; and between the citadel and the outer walls she found a

73

Buseirah/Bozrah: general view of the acropolis during the 1974 season of excavation by Mrs Crystal Bennett.

great jumble of buildings superimposed one upon the other. There was also clear evidence of two separate destructions, when the city had been burned to the ground. But after four seasons of excavation, the conclusions she was forced to come to about the date of the city of Bozrah surprised herself no less than other archaeologists and Biblical scholars. She found that there had been no city there, no occupation of any kind, before the end of the eighth century BC – at least 500 years later than the presumed date of the Exodus. And if there had been no city there at the time of Moses, who were these kings of Edom that the Bible spoke about? The implications from Buseirah were unavoidable: the kings had simply been tribal sheiks, and their towns were tents. Mrs Bennett now has considerable doubts about whether there can be any historical validity in the Biblical traditions of the Exodus.

These doubts have been reinforced by another recent excavation in Jordan, at a site which is tentatively identified as the Moabite city of Heshbon. Heshbon was the setting for another encounter between the Children of Israel and the kings of Jordan, this time King Sihon, an Amorite king who had conquered Moab (*Numbers* 21:26).

According to the *Book of Numbers*, Moses had sent emissaries to Sihon, as he had done to the King of Edom, asking for safe passage through his territory. Sihon refused, and

fought a pitched battle with the Israelites, which he lost;
whereupon the Israelites took possession of all the land of
Moab and built (or rebuilt) Sihon's city of Heshbon.

Biblical Heshbon is identified with Tell Hesban, twenty-
six kilometres south of Amman on the main road. It is a
commanding *tell*, set on the edge of the rolling Plain of Moab,
rising 900 metres above sea level and surmounted by the
remains of a citadel. The present-day village of Hesban
covers the southern slopes of the *tell*.

Tell Hesban has recently been excavated for five seasons,
starting in 1968, by an American team sponsored by Andrews University of Berrien Springs, Michigan, and the
American Schools of Oriental Research. The excavation was
originally directed by the Dean of Andrews University, Dr
Siegfried Horn, who chose the site with the specific goal of
shedding more light on the Israelite incursion through
Jordan. His is a small Adventist university, and Dr Horn
(who retired in 1973) took a rather fundamentalist and literal
view of the Biblical account; he felt sure that Hesban would
yield irrefutable evidence of the presence of the Israelites
from around 1250-1200 BC onwards, and evidence of the
preceding Moabite city that the Israelites had destroyed after
defeating King Sihon.

In archaeological terms, the date 1200 BC is normally

75

regarded as the boundary between the late Bronze Age (c.1550-1200 BC) and the Iron Age (c.1200-c.580 BC) in Palestine. This shift is marked by a change in pottery styles that occurred in innumerable sites throughout Palestine; and because the Exodus and Conquest of Canaan are generally assumed to have taken place around this date, then the pottery of the first period of the Iron Age (Iron I) is assumed to be, and frequently is called, 'Israelite' pottery. Sometimes this casual nomenclature can lead to dangerously circular reasonings: the Bible is used to prove that Iron I pottery is 'Israelite', and 'Israelite' pottery is then used to prove the Bible!

Dr Horn's expectations were disappointed, however. As the excavators dug down through the layers of occupation, they found evidence that Heshbon had been a city of major proportions in the Iron II period (late eighth century BC onwards), but that in the Iron I period (1200-700 BC) there had only been very minor occupation – a village, at most. Practically nothing remained from this period, just a trace of some tattered house walls, some small pits, a possible cobblestone floor, and some fragments of pottery. Heshbon's urban development exactly matched that of Bozrah: there was no city there during the alleged period of Israelite occupation.

Not only that: as at Buseirah/Bozrah, the excavators found no traces at all of any Late Bronze occupation. At the time when the Bible suggests that Heshbon was the stronghold and capital of King Sihon, it was in fact totally deserted.

The final publication of these excavations is not yet available; but Dr James Sauer, the Director of the American Centre of Oriental Research in Amman, who took part in the dig and is a pottery expert, sums up the possible conclusions we can draw from the preliminary results. In the first place, we can conclude that the Biblical account is simply wrong, historically speaking; to explain this discrepancy, we would have to assume that the Bible writers projected backwards into time the kind of political rivalry that was happening in their own day, in order to explain that rivalry and perhaps justify the Israelite position over current border disputes. This interpretation implies that the writing of these early sections of the Bible happened much later than was formerly supposed – the seventh or sixth centuries BC, as many scholars, especially in Germany and the United States, are now beginning to believe. Thus, the validity of the Bible as a strictly historical source is undermined.

On the other hand, it is possible that Tell Hesban is not, after all, the Biblical city of Heshbon, and that archaeological

Tell Hesban: the earliest occupation level as evidenced by a small cistern and abutting wall, dating back to the start of the Iron Age (c.1200 BC).

investigation of some other site in the area – for instance, Tell Jalul – would reveal a totally different picture. And there is a third possibility – that the Israelite incursion certainly happened, but happened in a more complex way than the simplified picture presented in the Bible: by gradual infiltration rather than by military conquest, or by localised insurrections or social revolts triggered by relatively small groups of incomers.

So the picture of what was happening in Jordan in the thirteenth and twelfth centuries BC is unclear; certainly, it is much less clear than was previously assumed. The Jordanian archaeologist Dr Mouawiye Ibrahim has been unearthing Iron I ('Israelite') pottery at a site called Sahab, to the east of Amman, well beyond what was thought to have been the Israelite sphere of influence, which throws additional doubt on the automatic assumption that Iron I pottery is 'Israelite' – it might be an indigenous development rather than a pottery style brought in by immigrants.

The Bible narrative describes the Children of Israel gaining further victories and territory in the kingdom of Bashan, north of Amman as far as Mount Hermon, where the giant King Og was defeated. Archaeology can give us little illumination here as yet, but there is no reason to doubt that the pattern emerging from the excavation of Buseirah and Hesban would be confirmed further north; namely, that the role of the Bible as source material for the approach of the Israelites to the invasion of the Promised Land across the Jordan has to be critically and radically reassessed.

In Biblical terms, the Children of Israel took command of the East Bank of the Jordan, after forty years of wandering, and massed there for an assault on Canaan, with only the River Jordan between themselves and their objective. They had fought many battles – but one in particular, of a non-military nature, would be repeated practically throughout their future stay in Palestine; it was when 'the people began to commit whoredom with the daughters of Moab' (*Numbers* 25:1). The 'whoredom' complained of was not so much sexual, or not only sexual; it was basically religious. Although we do not know very much about Moabite religious practices, we can assume that what the Bible writers had in mind was the kind of polytheistic worship prevalent in Canaan (see Chapter 5); the carnage that Moses ordered in an attempt to purge the Israelites of their backsliding in *Numbers* symbolised the constant conflict between the sternly authoritarian monotheism of Yahwism and the more sophisticated and complex ritual cults of the Canaanites. It is becoming clear that such backsliding was much more common amongst the Israelites in Palestine than had previously been supposed – which perhaps explains the ferocity of the attempts by the priestly authorities to stamp it out.

Moses himself, according to the Bible, was not destined to set foot in the Promised Land: he was only allowed to glimpse it from the 'mountain of Nebo' right at the end of his life, when he was 120 years old (*Deuteronomy* 34). Mount Nebo is traditionally associated with the modern Jebel Neba (2650 ft), some thirty kilometres south-west of Amman. A little farther to the west is the broad and barren plateau of Ras Siyagha (2330 ft) which corresponds to Biblical Pisgah, the place from which the Lord is said to have allowed Moses his panoramic view of Canaan. In the distance to the west looms the dark mass of the Judean hills, and in the middle ground lies the sunken serpentine gorge of the Jordan flowing south to join the sullen sheen of the Dead Sea. Jericho stands out as a vivid splash of green; the towers of modern Jerusalem can just be glimpsed through binoculars. It is an impressive vantage point. Here Moses died, still hale and hearty, 'but no man knoweth of his sepulchre unto this day' (*Deuteronomy* 34:6).

However, by the fourth century AD, someone apparently did know of his sepulchre – a shepherd who was vouchsafed the information in a vision. A large Byzantine basilica was erected on the spot at Ras Siyagha, which has now been excavated by the Franciscan Biblical Institute of Jerusalem. There are remains of Roman masonry as well, but these monuments are all dated well over a thousand years after the supposed event. There is no archaeological evidence to substantiate the Biblical account, nothing to prove that this was where the colourful and dramatic career of Moses had its story-book ending, like some King Arthur of the ancient world.

So this is the image that the Bible leaves us with at this point: the Children of Israel poised on the threshold of the land they coveted, their charismatic leader dead, but with a successor already groomed to take them over the River Jordan: a brilliant young military strategist called Joshua.

5
A Land of Milk and Honey

The story of Joshua and the Israelite conquest of Canaan is firmly rooted in our folk culture: 'Joshua fit de battle of Jericho an' de walls cam' tumblin' down.' The actual crossing of the River Jordan into Canaan 'against Jericho', as the Bible puts it, on the eve of the invasion, was envisaged as taking place in the region of the old Allenby Bridge some eight kilometres upstream from the point where the river flows into the Dead Sea: it is also, incidentally, the traditional site of the baptism of Jesus, at Beth-Abarah.

The River Jordan is a natural geographical frontier, a natural barrier between territories on either side. It has never been fit for navigation, for its winding course from the Sea of Galilee to the Dead Sea is strewn with rocks. Indeed the Jordan, which most people imagine as a majestic broad river, is curiously disappointing at first sight: yellowy-brown in colour, and astonishingly narrow – only about ten metres wide. It looks relatively easy to ford; yet the crossing by the Israelites was apparently attended by a somewhat watered-down version of the miracle of the Red Sea crossing, so that the Israelites managed to ford the river dryshod (*Joshua* 3). Various earnest attempts have been made to show how such a phenomenon might have occurred naturally – damming as a result of an earthquake or a collapse of the river banks, and so on – but it always seems to me that such well-meaning apologias merely dilute the theological content of the Old Testament without reinforcing its historical value.

Be that as it may, when we come to examine the actual archaeological evidence from the territory of Canaan for this crucial period of the Bible version of early Israelite history we will find that there is considerable argument amongst scholars, not only about when or how the Conquest of Canaan took place, but also about whether it ever took place at all in the way that the Bible presents it.

The words 'Canaan' and 'Canaanite' require some definition. In the Bible they are used somewhat indiscriminately to cover those areas of Palestine which eventually became the kingdoms of Israel and Judah – that is to say, those areas that the Israelites mastered and then rationalised as having been

Opposite Dame Kathleen Kenyon filming on location at Jericho. Behind her, remains of the Middle Bronze Age fortifications of the city.

The Storm God: Baal, the god of thunder, brandishing a club in his right hand and a spear in his left (perhaps a stylised form of lightning). Limestone tablet from Ugarit.

Opposite Megiddo: the huge trench dug by the Chicago University expedition in the 1920s and 1930s, showing (centre) a fine Canaanite circular stone altar.

the 'Promised Land'. The Canaanites were thought of as the major, but by no means the only, element in the Semitic population dispossessed or absorbed by the Israelites. It is now clear, however, that 'Canaan' embraced a much larger area, from the borders of Egypt in the south to the north Syrian coast, including the Lebanon – the land-bridge, in effect, between Egypt and Mesopotamia.

This diverse area had no natural centralising or unifying feature, such as the River Nile, and it was seldom a coherent political entity. The recent discoveries at Tell Mardikh (see Chapter 2) suggest the existence of a great Canaanite empire in the second half of the third millennium BC. In the second millennium BC it was frequently under Egyptian influence or control, and in the New Kingdom period, from 1500-1200 BC, it was an Egyptian province. Politically and ethnically it was never a homogeneous area; settlement was concentrated round strongly fortified cities constantly seeking to exert their independence under feudal kings, and these cities tended to be richly cosmopolitan, particularly in the north. There the Canaanites absorbed and assimilated influences from all over the known world by virtue of their activities as mercantile middlemen – influences from Egypt, from Mesopotamia, from Arabia, from Anatolia, from Mycenae and the Aegean. From these influences they developed a sophisticated civilisation and culture whose wealth is steadily being revealed by archaeology.

One of the greatest of these cities was Ugarit on the north Syrian coast (modern Ras Shamra), just north of Latakia, which has been under excavation by French archaeological missions since 1929. Like so many great archaeological enterprises, it started as the result of an accidental find: in 1928 a Syrian peasant who was ploughing a field behind a tiny fishing haven called Minet el-Beida ('Whitehaven') disturbed a hewn stone which led into a large tomb. A team of archaeologists led by Claude Shaeffer hurried from Paris to investigate, and found themselves excavating a whole necropolis of tomb-vaults of a distinctly Mycenaean type. In the following spring, Dr Shaeffer turned his attention to a low *tell* about a mile inland known locally as Ras Shamra ('Fennel Head'), which seemed to have been the city to which the cemetery had belonged. Today, after forty seasons of excavation, Ugarit is one of the most impressive sites in the Middle East.

The main feature of the site is a huge royal palace dating from 1400-1200 BC, when Ugarit was at the peak of its great-

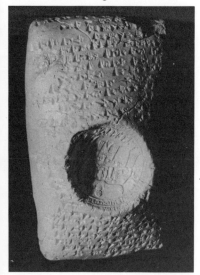

Ugarit (Ras Shamra): one of the many diplomatic texts found in the Ugarit archive with the seal of a king of the Hittites.

81

ness. It consisted of 120 rooms covering some 10,000 square metres, with interior courtyards and gardens and staircases. There is an extensive residential area, and two temples dedicated to gods whose names are familiar to us from the Bible – Baal and Dagon. The whole site is kept in magnificent condition for visitors by the Directorate-General of Antiquities and Museums of Syria.

But the most significant aspect of the discoveries at Ugarit was the palace library, in the form of a series of administrative, fiscal, economic, legal, commercial and diplomatic archives. In addition, there were two temple libraries consisting of religious and mythological texts.

The texts were written in a number of different languages and scripts, reflecting Ugarit's cosmopolitan role in world trade and politics at this time; but what really startled the world of Biblical scholarship was the discovery of a hitherto unknown cuneiform script (now called Ugaritic) which used for the first time an alphabet. The cuneiform scripts of Mesopotamia were syllabic, consisting of hundreds of signs representing syllables or words – a very complicated form of writing that could only be achieved by highly skilled experts. Ugaritic showed the evolution of an alphabet of thirty characters which made writing and reading infinitely easier and therefore more accessible to the common man. It is not, as is sometimes claimed, the oldest alphabet in the world; that distinction more properly belongs to the so-called 'Proto-Sinaitic' inscriptions dating from c.1500 BC that were found at the site of an Egyptian mining camp at Serabit el-Khadem in the western Sinai peninsula by Sir Flinders Petrie. This early Semitic script, which consisted of twenty-seven signs representing consonants, is the first known attempt to evolve a linear (not cuneiform) alphabet which could be written on a flat surface like pottery or papyrus. Nonetheless, the cuneiform alphabet of Ugarit represented a notable Canaanite contribution to human progress.

Gabriel Saade, writer and savant from the nearby city of Latakia, who has followed the excavations of Ugarit for more than forty years now, calls it 'one of the high places in the history of civilisation. Ugarit is, literally, a city that speaks.' Above all, he sees it as a quintessentially Canaanite city: its temples were dedicated to Canaanite gods, its mythological and religious poems were intimately related to the Canaanite pantheon, its West Semitic dialect was Canaanite.

Until the discoveries at Ugarit, we knew practically nothing about the Canaanites except for the imprecations of the

Ugarit: on a small clay tablet, the first cuneiform alphabet of thirty characters, reading left to right, starting 'a b g...'

Proto-Sinaitic inscription from a statue found by Petrie at Serabit el-Khadem, containing the phrase *lb'lt*, 'for Ba'alat'.

Ugarit: the great stone altar and pedestal from the temple of Baal.

Old Testament prophets who inveighed with such hostility against their religious 'abominations'. Now, thanks to the Ugarit texts, we have a clear idea of the theological organisation of the Canaanite pantheon and the functions and features of each of the many gods, expressed in mythological terms.

Paramount among the gods was El ('god'), the elderly father of the divine family and president of the divine assembly. He was known as the Creator God, the Kindly One, the Compassionate One. He expressed the concept of ordered government and social justice. It is noteworthy that the Bible never stigmatises the Canaanite worship of El, whose authority in social affairs was recognised by the Patriarchs. His consort was Asherah, the mother-goddess, represented in Canaanite sanctuaries by a natural or stylised tree (Hebrew *āshēra*).

Baal, one of the sons of El, was the executive god of the pantheon, the god of thunder and winter storms, the dynamic warrior god who champions the divine order against the menacing forces of chaos. He is also identified with vegetation and the seasonal fertility cycle. There is little evidence in the Ras Shamra texts of the sexual licence, the sympathetic magic aspects of the cult to secure the productivity of Nature, that the Bible writers found so abhorrent. On the contrary there is ample evidence that some of the aspects of Yahweh

83

reflected aspects of Baal as the Divine King, in the destruction of the sea-serpent Leviathan and the concept of everlasting kingly dominion; even some of the liturgical language is strikingly similar, like the wording of Psalm 68: 'To him that rideth upon the heavens of heavens', 'his strength is in the clouds', and so on.

Baal is sometimes called the 'son of Dagon'. Dagon was also a god of vegetation, specifically corn, which is what his his name means.

The chief fertility goddess was Astarte, the Canaanite equivalent of Ishtar, known in the Old Testament as Ashtoreth. She too incurred the opprobrium of the Bible writers, being associated with ritual temple prostitution. Scores of crude clay plaques of a nude female figure with emphatic feminine characteristics have been found, which are usually associated with the worship of Astarte; they seem to have been used as charms or magic amulets as an aid to fertility, and may perhaps have occasioned the stern prohibition in the Bible against the making of idols.

Apart from the temples of Baal and Dagon at Ugarit, several other Canaanite temples have been excavated in Palestine. A major feature of all these sanctuaries was the presence of standing stones, or stelae, called *massēbāh* (plural *massēbōt*) in the Old Testament. A superb miniature shrine which included an offering table was found at Hazor; it had a statuette of a seated god, and a row of stelae, on one of which

Hazor: the miniature stelae shrine. To the left, a seated deity which was originally found decapitated: in front, an offering table. On the central stela hands are raised in prayer towards the emblem of the moon-god.

was incised a pair of hands raised in prayer to a crescent emblem representing the moon-god. The most impressive open-air sanctuary is the great row of ten standing stones at the High Place of Gezer, dating from the middle of the second millennium BC. This custom of erecting standing stones to represent the gods seems to be reflected in the story of Jacob's Dream (*Genesis* 28:11-22), when he took the stone he had had for a pillow and set it up as a pillar and poured oil on top of it, and called the place Beth-el ('House of God').

As a result of our growing awareness of Canaanite civilisation and culture, it is now possible to take a much more sympathetic view of the Canaanites than the Bible writers did. Dr John Gray, Professor of Hebrew and Semitic Languages at Aberdeen University in Scotland, who is a leading authority on the Canaanites, recognises that their religion had a very real validity for them. He is a countryman himself, as well as being a Scottish theologian, and he sees in the great autumn festivals of the Canaanites (reflected in the festival of the Ingathering amongst the Israelites) a necessary and useful social safety-valve. As the summer drew to an end and the rains were due, the peasants would suffer a crisis of anxiety – would the rains come? By calling upon Baal, the rain god, and encouraging his intervention by rituals of imitative magic involving sexual union, their tensions were released and purged. Such rituals were subject to abuse, of course; and the prophets and reformers were anxious lest the simple Israelite peasants should be debauched by the abuses, and ignore the higher aims of Hebrew religion, the concept of obedience to the will of God rather than acts of worship or appeasement designed only to gain material agricultural benefit.

Dr James B.Pritchard of the University Museum of Pennsylvania shares Dr Gray's enthusiasm for the Canaanites, and feels that they have been greatly maligned. Having dug through many Canaanite levels in his excavations in Palestine, he thinks he would have found life among the ancient Canaanites very agreeable: 'They were a sophisticated people, they had a high material culture, and they had a religion which was in many ways similar to modern concepts in that they realised that there were multiple causes for certain phenomena in the world. For example they said that one god was responsible for such-and-such an area of human experience, another god was responsible for another, and so on. Now these explanations of human experience seem to fit into the modern scientific view in which certain determining factors

The Father of the Canaanite gods, El, seated on the right before a Canaanite king. From Ugarit.

Carved ivory plaque in Egyptian style from Megiddo: victory celebration with feasting, music and naked prisoners. Late Bronze Age.

are genes, others environmental, others economic – all sorts of forces that we do not control; and it seems to me the Canaanites had a glimpse of this idea which did not catch on, but which we are now able to recover from archaeological sources.'

Such, then, were the people whom the Children of Israel sought to dispossess in order to gain their Promised Land. According to the *Book of Joshua*, it was done by military conquest, a concerted effort by all Israel in three *blitzkrieg* campaigns after the initial destruction of Jericho: one through the centre of the lands to destroy the city of Ai (*Joshua* 7-8), one driving south-west to defeat a confederation of Canaanite kings at Gibeon (*Joshua* 10), and a third sweeping north to smash a coalition of northern kings and destroy their main centre at Hazor (*Joshua* 11).

Hazor (Tell el-Qedah), some fourteen kilometres north of the Sea of Galilee, was the scene of a spectacular excavation in the 1950s by the eminent Israeli archaeologist, Dr Yigael Yadin, Director of the Institute of Archaeology at the Hebrew University of Jerusalem. In the course of five seasons of digging, Dr Yadin (who was later to achieve even wider international fame as the excavator of Masada) found incontrovertible evidence of a violent destruction of the city around 1250-1225 BC which he unhesitatingly attributed to Joshua.

Hazor is a vast site, composed of two distinct parts: a wedge-shaped *tell* proper, pointing west, and a vast rectangular plateau, or enclosure, to the north, covering an area of 200 acres protected on three sides by huge earthen ramparts and on the fourth by the fortified city on the *tell*. Some trial soundings were made there in 1928 by Professor John Garstang of Liverpool University, then Director of Antiquities of the British Mandatory Administration in Palestine, who confirmed the identification of the site but who found nothing worth remarking from soundings he made in the enclosure area; as a result, he came to the conclusion that the

The goddess of love: terracotta plaque of Astarte, holding lotus blossoms in her upraised hands. Late Bronze Age, found in Palestine.

Hazor: in the vicinity of the miniature stelae temple, a potter's workshop, with small pottery mask for cultic purposes, and potter's wheel.

enclosure had been nothing more than a camp-site, or perhaps a parking lot for chariots.

Yadin's excavations, on the other hand, showed that the enclosure had been a huge city of 30-40,000 people, making Hazor by far the largest population centre in Canaan – the Lower City, as he called it – and that this city had been razed to the ground c.1225 and never rebuilt. At about the same time, the Upper City on the *tell* proper was also destroyed; the next occupation layer is represented only by silos, hearths, tent-bases and hut-footings, which suggest that it was abandoned to stray squatters using a simple style of pottery for a long period thereafter, and only rebuilt as a fortified city again in the tenth century BC, the time of Solomon.

At any site, it is the business of the excavator to try to establish a chronological sequence that will make sense of its history. At Hazor, Dr Yadin found lying on the floors of the last city before the final destruction the kind of Mycenaean pottery which was in common use throughout the thirteenth century, but which ceased to be imported into Palestine in the twelfth century. That gave him the date for the destruction; the appearance of the name 'Israel' on the Merneptah stela of c.1220 BC gave him a date for the presence of the Israelites in Canaan; the Bible did the rest.

Dr Yadin has written that he approaches a dig with a spade in one hand and a Bible in the other. The Bible account of the fate of Hazor in *Joshua* is plain and specific: after defeating the coalition of northern kings at the waters of Merom, 'Joshua at that time turned back, and took Hazor, and smote

87

the king thereof with the sword; for Hazor beforetime was the head of all those kingdoms. And they smote all the souls that were therein with the edge of the sword, utterly destroying them: there was not any left to breathe: and he burnt Hazor with fire...But as for the [others] that stood still in their strength [or 'on their mounds'], Israel burned none of them, save Hazor only; that did Joshua burn, (*Joshua* 11:10-13).

Dr Yadin argues that all the evidence at Hazor matched the Biblical account perfectly. The date matched the presumed date of the Israelite incursion into Canaan. The city was huge enough to have been 'the head of all those kingdoms'. It had been razed to the ground; and whereas the Lower City had never been occupied again, the Upper City had been given over to tent-dwellers and squatters – a sure sign that it had been reoccupied by a semi-nomadic people who were not yet used to living in cities. What is more, the various temples and sanctuaries excavated at Hazor showed signs of having been deliberately defaced, with the statuettes beheaded and standing stones felled – and had not the Children of Israel been enjoined to destroy all the cult-places of the Canaanites?

It is a strong case, and a plausible one, but not all scholars

Hazor during excavation: in the centre, the wedge-shaped *tell*, with a major excavation at its nearer (western) end. To the left, the start of the Lower City, with the huge earthen rampart in the foreground. The miniature stelae temple was found in the excavation area on the inside of the rampart, just left of centre.

are prepared to accept it uncritically. For one thing, the city could well have been burned by someone else, for this was a turbulent period when cities were always being burned, by rival neighbours or by Egyptian punitive expeditions. However tempting it is to seek to correlate the archaeological evidence with the historical tradition presented in the Bible, the theory cannot be considered proved beyond reasonable doubt. The only pottery evidence that distinguishes the Iron Age from the Bronze Age is the absence of Mycenaean imports; there is no distinctive artefact with which archaeologists can conclusively label a site as being Israelite.

Nor is the problem helped by the evidence, or lack of it, from other Biblical sites. Let us take the case of the city of Ai, near Bethel, which was said to be the target of Joshua's first lightning attack after the fall of Jericho. The Bible gives a clear and circumstantial account of its fate at Joshua's hands: 'And so it was, that all that fell that day, both of men and women, were twelve thousand, even all the men of Ai. For Joshua drew not his hand back, wherewith he stretched out the spear, until he had utterly destroyed all the inhabitants of Ai...And Joshua burnt Ai, and made it an heap for ever, even a desolation unto this day. And the king of Ai he hanged on a tree until eventide...' (*Joshua* 8:25-29). This merciless ferocity is justified in the Biblical account by the fact that the people of Ai had earlier inflicted a humiliating defeat on the Israelites.

The site of Ai (the name in Hebrew means 'ruin') is identified by most scholars with the mound of et-Tell, which has been exhaustively excavated, first in the 1930s by the Rothschild Expedition directed by Madame Judith Marquet-Krause and then by a major Joint Expedition from 1964-72 by a consortium of twenty institutions headed by the American Schools of Oriental Research, and directed by Dr Joseph A.Callaway of the Southern Baptist Theological Seminary of Louisville, Kentucky. The outcome of these excavations is simply stated: there was a major fortified city at Ai at the start of the Early Bronze Age (c.3000 BC) which, after several destructions and rebuildings, was violently destroyed by some unknown aggressor around 2400 BC and abandoned. Thereafter there was no further occupation of the site until the start of the Iron Age, around 1200 BC, when it gradually began to be settled by squatters and tent-dwellers who built an unwalled village there.

This means that unless the story has been transported from some other, differently-named site, Ai was in ruins when

Joshua is said to have arrived there, and had been in ruins for over a thousand years. The excavator, Dr Callaway, has since then made conscientious efforts to find some other nearby site that might have been Ai, but has come to the conclusion that the identification of Ai with et-Tell is correct.

Obviously, the archaeological evidence from Hazor and Ai cannot both tally with the Bible account. If Dr Yadin's interpretation of Hazor is correct, then the Bible must be wrong about Joshua at Ai; and if the Bible is wrong about

The site of Ai (et-Tell): excavations in the 1960s directed by Dr Joseph A.Callaway.

Joshua at Ai, what likelihood is there that it is correct about Joshua at Hazor? It looks very much as if the Ai story is one that was created by later generations to explain the presence of formidable ruins at a site, in terms of a remembered folk hero. Dr Yadin accepts that the Ai story is probably an aetiological one, but remains undismayed; he believes it to be an exception. Without wanting to take up an extreme position, he thinks that in some cases the Joshua stories may not be historical, but that others should be considered historical until it is proved that they are not.

But the real bone of contention is the first and most celebrated of all Joshua's conquests – the capture of Jericho. The story is told in *Joshua* in vivid and memorable detail. First he sent two spies into Jericho to gain up-to-date intelligence about the defences and the morale of the townspeople; they were given shelter in the house of Rahab the prostitute, whose family were assured of their lives for services rendered. Then came the miraculous crossing of the Jordan, led by priests carrying the Ark of the Covenant. Once safely across, the Israelites pitched camp at Gilgal, modern Khirbet el-Mefjir (see Chapter 7), and set up a row of twelve standing stones in thanksgiving and celebrated the Passover Festival.

Joshua now laid siege to Jericho in a rather unusual way, on the advice of an angel of the Lord. Day after day, for six days, his army marched round the walls in total silence. Then, on the seventh day, he struck: after six silent circuits of the walls, he suddenly gave the order for the trumpets to be sounded. His army raised a great war-cry, and the walls of Jericho promptly collapsed; the Israelites stormed in, killing every man, woman and child in the city, except for Rahab and her family, and burned it to the ground.

It is an incomparable story; and a story, surely, that should be more susceptible than most to the attentions of archaeological investigation. Surely archaeology should be able to confirm or disprove whether the walls of Jericho had collapsed in the middle of the thirteenth century BC, whether by human or by supernatural agency?

Jericho indeed has been a target for archaeologists for over a century now, ever since the Palestine Exploration Fund was founded to conduct Biblical excavations in 1865. Two years later, Captain Charles Warren was sent out to explore Jericho, but found nothing. There was an Austro-German expedition in 1907-9 which came across traces of two concentric rings of fortification consisting of thick walls of sun-dried clay bricks. These, it was suggested, were the famous

walls of Jericho; but since dating techniques had not been developed at the time, the excavators had no reliable method of identifying the period when they had been built. Argument raged for years, until a much larger expedition, directed by Professor John Garstang, was sent to Jericho in the 1930s in an attempt to shed new light on the problem. He studied the fortifications as carefully as he could, and identified four successive building stages, the last of which had been violently destroyed and burned, perhaps by a combination of earthquake and fire. This destruction he assigned to the period of the Israelite assault, which he dated to around 1400 BC, rather than the more generally accepted 1250-1225 BC. The problem seemed to have been solved: the walls of Jericho had indeed fallen down, catastrophically, probably during an earthquake, and the lurking Israelites under Joshua had seized the opportunity to ransack the stricken town. In the Bible, the natural phenomenon of an earthquake had been transposed into a blare of divinely inspired trumpets.

It was a tidy solution that suited fundamentalists and rationalists alike. But in the 1950s, Miss (now Dame) Kathleen Kenyon excavated Jericho again on behalf of the British

The site of ancient Jericho, from the north: centuries of erosion and decades of excavation make it look like a bomb-site. On the left side of the *tell*, just across the road, is the source of the spring that creates the oasis; on the far right, the edge of the crumbling refugee camp.

92

Jericho during Dame Kathleen Kenyon's excavations in the 1950s. Bottom left, work at the Neolithic level. The people on the top of the trench are standing at the level of Garstang's 'Joshua's Walls' – now proved to date back to 2300 BC, a thousand years earlier.

School of Archaeology in Jerusalem – and threw the problem right back into the melting-pot.

Her main concern was to illuminate the evolution of Neolithic Jericho (see Chapter 1); but in the course of reaching the earliest levels, she was able to elucidate afresh the question of the walls. She found that there had been a considerable Early Bronze Age city at Jericho throughout the third millennium BC, whose walls had fallen and been rebuilt no fewer than seventeen times between 3000 BC and 2300 BC, when the city suffered a catastrophic destruction. The last three stages of these fortifications had been built seven metres beyond the line of the original walls, farther down the slopes of the *tell*. These had been Garstang's celebrated walls that Joshua and the earthquake had apparently destroyed – except for the fact that they had been destroyed a thousand years before Joshua came on the scene.

For several centuries after the destruction of 2300 BC, Jericho was occupied only by squatter nomads. But then, around 1900 BC, a new city arose: the Jericho of the Middle Bronze Age. This was the period of Jericho's greatest prosperity. The fortifications were regularly improved; the final

93

Middle Bronze defences were great earthen banks with a facing of plaster that made them very hard to climb, the so-called *glacis* fortification, with a wall on top. This city flourished until the end of the Egyptian Hyksos period, when once again it came to a violent end, around 1550 BC; this destruction by fire was probably associated with the expulsion of the Hyksos from Egypt and the Egyptian pursuit.

Once again the site was abandoned, and the debris of all the ruined city began to be washed down the slopes of the *tell*. The site seems to have been reoccupied around 1400 BC on a much smaller scale. No new walls were built, but presumably the new inhabitants made do with what was left of the Middle Bronze walls. These second-hand walls, then, would have been the walls of Jericho that Joshua blew down. However, Dame Kathleen is adamant that the reoccupation of 1400 BC lasted for less than a century, before the town was wrecked or abandoned again no later than 1300 BC. Her conclusion is that Jericho, like Ai, must already have been a ruin by the time of the Israelite conquest, if that is correctly dated at 1250-1225 BC, right at the end of the Late Bronze Age and the start of the Iron Age.

Jericho: scanty evidence of Late Bronze Age occupation found by Dame Kathleen Kenyon and dated by her to c. 1350 BC. In the centre, a clay oven inside a house wall, with a juglet lying nearby.

94

Dr Yigael Yadin disputes her conclusions. He interprets the evidence differently, and believes that it proves that there *was* an occupation, albeit small, in the thirteenth century, although centuries of erosion have removed all evidence of what may have happened to the walls. (The speed with which mud-brick walls disintegrate when abandoned can be judged by the large refugee camps beside Jericho, which were built just after the War of Independence in 1948 and vacated after the 1967 war when Israel occupied the West Bank. After ten years they are crumbling fast.) It is a complex technical argument that involves a difference of interpretative method, and it shows how few certainties there can be in archaeology. Meanwhile, the lay visitor to the site can see remains of the great *glacis* fortification of the Middle Bronze Age, some stumps of Middle Bronze walls on the summit of the *tell*, and thin layers of ashes streaking the sides of the great trenches Dame Kathleen dug; and that is all.

Dame Kathleen does not find it surprising, or disappointing, that there should be no evidence of Joshua at Jericho. She believes that the Israelite occupation of Canaan was not achieved in one fell swoop, but was the result of a series of incursions by different groups at different times, some of whom may have come from Egypt, others who may have come from elsewhere, and who entered Canaan at different places. All these disparate events, in her opinion, were later combined by the Bible writers in an attempt to form a continuous story out of disjointed fragments of tradition. There seems to be some support for this theory in the Bible itself, for the first chapter of the *Book of Judges* gives a rather different picture of the conquest than *Joshua*, suggesting that the conquest of Palestine was a long process which was effected by the efforts of individual tribes, and only partially completed. This might explain a number of other sites, not associated with Joshua, which seem to have suffered destruction at the end of the late Bronze Age.

So far, archaeology has failed to provide conclusive proof for either of these alternatives – the short, sharp and bloody conquest by Joshua, or the more extended process by different groups. But there is a second theory, to the effect that the occupation was accomplished not by military means at all, but by peaceful infiltration. One of the main protagonists of this theory was the late Professor Yohanan Aharoni of Tel Aviv University, one of Israel's most distinguished archaeologists. Dr Yadin disagrees, however; he points out that there is no archaeological evidence for the settlement of infiltrators fifty or a hundred years before the downfall of the Late Bronze cities of Canaan, as there should be if the thesis were correct. He thinks that those who hold to this theory subconsciously cannot believe that migrant Israelite tribes could possibly have mustered sufficient strength or military skill to storm those heavily fortified Canaanite cities; whereas he himself thinks that the Late Bronze cities were already in decline, worn out by Egyptian attacks and economically enfeebled, and were ripe for the final assault by the tribes of Israel.

There is also a third thesis, advanced by Professor George E. Mendenhall of Michigan University. This postulates that there was neither a systematic conquest nor a large-scale infiltration, but a peasants' revolt against the domination of the great cities – a social and religious revolution within Canaan by underprivileged sections of the indigenous population, possibly associated with the arrival of a small number of immigrants from outside. Certainly, it is a theory which cannot be contradicted by the known archaeological facts at present.

Ultimately, the interpretation of the available evidence may all come down to the psychology of individual scholars. Professor Aharoni, who was born in Germany in 1919, came to Israel at the age of fourteen with his parents, who helped to found a kibbutz in which he lived for ten years; so he was perhaps predisposed in favour of the infiltration theory from his own experience of the development of the modern Israeli nation. Dr Yadin, on the other hand, was a distinguished soldier – Chief of Staff during the War of Independence in 1948 – and a protégé of David Ben-Gurion; by upbringing and training he is a dedicated Statist – so perhaps he is predisposed in favour of the military exploits of Joshua that would be repeated by the armies of the fledgling Israeli state under his command?

Archaeology may supply the definitive answers one day. Meanwhile, on a purely literary level, the *Book of Joshua* reads more like an adventure story than history. Wherever you find a really dramatic story of tactics and deception and ambush, or some gambit like the psychological warfare waged by Joshua against the people of Jericho to make their defences (if not their walls) crumble, there is no archaeological evidence to support it. Where you get a casual, almost offhand reference to a victory, such as Joshua's burning of Hazor, without elaboration, you are more likely to find archaeological evidence that might corroborate it. It is as if there were almost an inverse ratio between the vividness of the tale, and the

Opposite above Ashdod, ancient and modern: in the foreground, crumbling debris on the site of Philistine Ashdod. In the background, beyond the sand-dunes, the shimmering tower blocks of modern Ashdod.

Opposite below The Philistine coast at Ashkelon-on-Sea, now a popular holiday resort. Jutting out like gun-barrels, Roman pillars re-used by the Crusaders to strengthen the sea walls.

The late Professor Yohanan Aharoni of Tel Aviv University.

strength of the archaeological evidence.

Dr Yadin thinks that the controversy over Joshua is a little like the Shakespeare/Bacon controversy: if Shakespeare did not write the plays, then someone else called Shakespeare did. He believes that a man called Joshua existed, but that it is not necessary to take every detail of his history literally – in fact, the Bible does not explicitly claim that Joshua destroyed all the cities of Canaan. Dr Yadin answers his critics in this way: 'Suppose we were digging in a country like Israel, and there was no Bible to guide us, archaeologically speaking, what do we find? We find a phenomenon that at the end of the Late Bronze Age, let us say in the thirteenth century BC, several key cities are destroyed by fire; then there is a little gap, and on the ruins of these destroyed cities there grows a semi-nomadic settlement. The archaeological picture is quite clear – a disastrous upheaval, followed by occupation by newcomers. No one doubts that the Israelites became the sovereign people of Israel; so one time or another, one way or another, they conquered the country. That is the starting point, the fundamental fact. I agree that, as usual in science, it is nearly impossible to prove a thesis; it is always easier to disprove a thesis. I do not think we have managed to prove anything, but I believe that where the vital key cities are concerned no one has been able to disprove the conquest thesis.'

The argument over Joshua and the walls of Jericho will go on and on, no doubt, because Jericho, the oldest walled city in the world that we know of, has a very special hold on people's imaginations – as the Bible story demonstrates. But at about the same time as the Israelites were conquering Canaan, or infiltrating into Canaan, or emerging in Canaan, another people were making their presence felt elsewhere in Palestine and the Mediterranean coast. These were the Philistines; and they would not give the Israelites much time to enjoy the fruits of victory.

6
The Philistines

The Philistines have always been given a bad press; and perhaps as a result, I have always had a certain sympathy for them.

In the Bible they are consistently portrayed as depraved heathens worshipping crude gods and brute strength, and much addicted to hard drinking bouts: all brawn and no brain. Goliath, for instance, their giant champion, was laid low by a mere stripling of a shepherd lad, the boy David. They were devious, too: they used a treacherous lover like Delilah to ensnare the mighty folk hero Samson. In Western tradition, their name has become a synonym for coarse and uncultured materialism – a usage much encouraged by Matthew Arnold through his essay on *Culture and Anarchy* in 1869; and all because they committed the unforgivable sin: they dared to lay sacrilegious hands on the Ark of the Covenant and destroy the Israelite cultic sanctuary at Shiloh. (It is one of the ironies of history that the enemy whom the Israelites hated most, the Philistines, should eventually have given their name to the whole Biblical area, for the name 'Palestine' is derived from them.)

Yet this 'Philistine' image as applied to the Philistines has recently been shown to be neither fair nor accurate. Thanks to archaeology and other branches of Biblical research, we now have a much clearer picture of the Philistines than the one the writers of the Bible painted: who they were, where they came from, how they lived, and what they were really like.

One thing at least is quite certain: there can be few peoples who made quite such a dramatic entry on to the stage of world history as the Philistines did.

Round about 1190 BC, Ramesses III, Pharaoh of Egypt, met and checked, both on land and at sea, a massive invasion by a confederation of allies known in the history books as 'the Sea Peoples'. Among them were the Philistines, or Peleset as the Egyptian records called them – tall, slim warriors who wore tasselled kilts and distinctive ribbed caps or helmets.

The story of the onslaught by the Sea Peoples is recorded

Medinet Habu: the funerary temple of Ramesses III, viewed from the back. The reliefs of the Battles with the Sea Peoples are carved on the outside of the left-hand walls of the temple.

in words and pictures in the triumphal relief carvings which decorate the walls of the funerary temple that Ramesses III built for himself at Medinet Habu ('Town of Habu') on the west bank of the Nile at Thebes.

This great temple is a whole library carved in stone, a massive historical document now blurred and worn by wind and weather. The main battle scene is carved on the outside of the north wall of the temple, and is best looked at very early in the morning, in the oblique light of the rising sun. It is one of our major sources of information, albeit one-sided and no doubt simplified, about the turbulence that convulsed the eastern Mediterranean at the end of the thirteenth century BC, the start of the Iron Age.

The main cause of the upheavals seems to have been famine. There was severe famine in Anatolia, for instance, about 1220 BC, which was only relieved by a fleet of grain ships from Egypt, according to the records of the reigning Pharaoh, Merneptah. Three years later came the first assault by the Sea Peoples, when starving Libyans reinforced by seafaring northern tribes reached the western fringes of the Delta before being stopped.

The famine continued, and so did the raids of the Sea Peoples. Documents dating from the last days of Ugarit mention severe famine in Anatolia at the end of the century, and report attacks from the sea. Cyprus was engulfed by invaders. Round about 1200 BC, the Hittite New Kingdom in Anatolia collapsed. Ugarit fell. The whole Middle East was in turmoil.

The inscriptions on the temple at Medinet Habu describe the situation as seen through Egyptian eyes:

Detail of prisoners from the battles with the Sea Peoples at Medinet Habu: the man in the middle is a Philistine, distinguished by his characteristic ribbed cap and tasselled kilt.

In the eighth year of the reign of Ramesses III...the foreign countries made a conspiracy in their islands [*or* the lands of the north were agitated]. All at once the lands were dislodged and scattered in the fray. No country could withstand their arms, from Hatti [the land of the Hittites], Kode [northern Syria], Carchemish [on the Euphrates], Arzawa [Cilicia in southern Anatolia], and Alashiya [Cyprus] onwards...A camp was set up in one place in Amor [Amurru, in the northern plain of Syria]. They desolated its people, and its land was as if it had never existed. They advanced towards Egypt, while the flame was prepared before them...They laid hands upon every land to the farthest ends of the earth, their hearts confident and trusting: 'Our plans will succeed!' (Adapted from *Ancient Near Eastern Texts*).

The great battle relief at Medinet Habu shows glimpses of this irresistible tide of armed migrants, marching in a human avalanche down the coast of Syria and Palestine, destroying and burning everything that stood in their way. With them came their families, long-haired women and children, riding in large ox-carts with solid wheels pulled by double teams of humped Anatolian oxen. These were whole nations driven by famine, trekking in search of new lands and new larders, supported by menacing fleets that foraged the coasts alongside them.

Ramesses III mobilised all his forces, according to the inscription on the right-hand tower of the Second Pylon at Medinet Habu:

But the heart of this god, the Lord of the Gods, was prepared and ready to ensnare them like birds...I organised my frontier in Djahi [Palestine/Syria?] and prepared my armies before them: princes, garrison commanders and warriors. I turned the river-mouths of the Delta into a strong wall, with warships, galleys and skiffs, fully equipped and manned both fore and aft with valiant warriors under arms. The infantry were the pick of all Egypt, like lions roaring on the mountain tops. The chariot squadrons had the swiftest runners and every first-class charioteer available. Their horses quivered in every sinew, ready to crush the foreign countries beneath their hooves. I was the valiant Montu, god of war, standing fast at their head, so that they might gaze upon the capturing of my hands...As for those who reached my boundary, their seed is not. Their hearts and their souls are finished unto all eternity.

The sixth scene on the north wall of Medinet Habu shows the king in his chariot shooting arrows against the Philistines, identified by their distinctive ribbed caps. The seventh scene shows the Egyptian army on the march, while Pharaoh indulges in a little lion-hunting en route to deal with the enemy fleet that threatened the Delta. But the main theme of the great relief is the naval battle that followed the Egyptian victory on land.

Those who came forward together on the sea, the full flame was in front of them at the river-mouths, while a stockade of lances surrounded them on the shore. They were dragged in, enclosed, and prostrated on the beach, killed, and made into heaps from tail to head. Their ships and their equipment were as if swallowed up in the water. I have made the lands turn back from even mentioning Egypt; for when they pronounce my name in their land, then they are burned up...

In one superb, crowded scene (the eighth), the artist has contrived to telescope the various phases of the engagement. On the right, the giant figure of Pharaoh stands on the prostrate bodies of captives, firing arrows from the shore. Egyptian vessels, denoted by lion-headed prows and banks of oarsmen, are seen laying down a murderous barrage of arrows. The enemy ships are distinguished by ducks' heads at stern and prow, and castles fore and aft; but they have no oarsmen, only sails, and these sails are reefed. Clearly it was a windless day, and the ships of the Sea Peoples were hopelessly out-manoeuvred. After the barrage from the archers, they are seen being grappled, or rammed and capsized. The sea is full of drowning men. The Egyptian ships turn for the shore, laden with pinioned captives. The victory is complete.

In the ninth scene, the dead are being counted on the beach by hacking off their hands and piling them up in heaps. The

captives are herded into a camp, interrogated by Egyptian scribes, and branded as prisoners of war. Prominent among them are the Philistines.

Medinet Habu: the naval battle with the Sea Peoples. The duck-headed ships of the invaders are shown being rammed and capsized, with bodies falling into the water.

The Philistines were only one of several tribes who made up the confederation of the Sea Peoples, and there has been lively argument among scholars about the identity and origins of the various peoples. Earlier authorities tended to seek romantic associations far and wide throughout the Aegean: the Denyen, for instance, were thought to be none other than the Danaoi of Homer's *Iliad*; the Akawasha were the Achaeans of Mycenaean Greece, the Teresh were the Tyrsenoi, ancestors of the Etruscans, the Shekelesh were the Siculi of Sicily, the Sherden were Sardinians, and so on. However, recent advances in our knowledge of Anatolian sources suggest less fanciful equations: the Teresh and Denyen seem rather to represent two Cilician cities on the south coast of Anatolia mentioned in Hittite sources, Tarsa and Adaniya; the Akawasha should be equated with the Ahhiyawa of

south-western Anatolia; the Sherden are much more likely to be associated with Cyprus than Sardinia.

All this has considerable bearing on the origin of the Philistines, because although everyone is agreed that the Peleset of the Egyptian texts *are* the Philistines, there is no clue as to their precise provenance. According to the much later Biblical traditions, the Philistines came from the island of Caphtor, which is frequently identified with Crete: 'Have not I brought up Israel out of the land of Egypt, and the Philistines from Caphtor?' (*Amos* 9:7). But the tendency of modern authorities on ancient Anatolia, like James Mellaart, is to equate *all* the Sea Peoples with peoples from the south coast of Turkey and its associated islands, seafarers familiar with the eastern Mediterranean who were caught up in the famines at the end of the thirteenth century BC. Mellaart associates the Peleset, along with the Shekelesh and the Tjekker, with Lukka (Lycian) people from the Pamphylian area: less exotic, perhaps, than seeing them as Cretan throwbacks to the great Minoan civilisation that had collapsed two centuries earlier.

There is no conclusive evidence at present; but the odds seem to be shifting in favour of an Anatolian origin for the Philistines.

Although there is still doubt as to where the Philistines came from, there is no doubt what happened to them after the defeat of the Sea Peoples by Ramesses III. The magnificent Harris Papyrus No.1, now in the British Museum, which may originally have come from the state archives of the temple at Medinet Habu, presents a summary of the wars fought by Ramesses III and their outcome:

> I extended all the frontiers of Egypt and overthrew those who had attacked them from their lands. I slew the Denyen in their islands, while the Tjekker and the Peleset were made ashes. The Sherden and the Weshesh of the Sea were made non-existent, captured all together and brought in captivity to Egypt like the sands of the shore. I settled them in strongholds, bound in my name. Their military classes were as numerous as hundred-thousands. I assigned portions for them all with clothing and provisions from the treasuries and granaries every year.

In other words, the Philistines had not been annihilated, only defeated; Ramesses now used them to garrison the Egyptian fortresses that commanded strategic points on the major trade routes through Egyptian provinces, especially

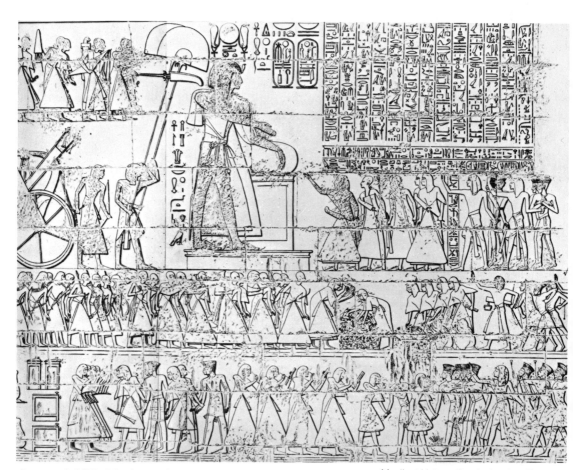

the crucial Via Maris up the coastal plain of Palestine. Thus, despite their apparently overwhelming defeat, early in the twelfth century BC we find the Philistines settled comfortably in towns along the Palestine shore from the Negev desert to Joppa (modern Tel Aviv), with the Tjekker installed farther north at harbours like Dor. The great victory, as it turned out, had been a Pyrrhic one; the battles on land and sea had exhausted Egypt, and given the Philistines a new lease of life! While the Egyptian kingdom rapidly disintegrated after the death of Ramesses III (c.1170 BC) the Philistines became masters of the area they had settled under Egyptian sufferance.

Excavations have been carried out at a dozen Philistine sites – that is to say, sites which have yielded clear evidence of Philistine occupation from about 1200 to 1000 BC, when the Philistine culture began to grow less distinct. Not all of these sites, however, can be definitely equated with towns and cities mentioned in the historical texts.

The best known Philistine cities were the five major

Medinet Habu: after the battles. The massive figure of Ramesses III is depicted receiving prisoners. In the bottom register, files of Philistine prisoners are shown being interrogated and listed by scribes. In the middle register, clerks count the piles of hands severed from the corpses of the enemy – the normal Egyptian method of counting casualties.

centres known from the Bible as the Philistine Pentapolis, a league of five cities each controlled by a *seren*, or 'chief'. These were Ashkelon, Ashdod, Gaza, Ekron and Gath – all names that reverberate through the pages of the Old Testament.

The first three – Ashkelon, Ashdod, and Gaza – were all situated on or beside the sea-coast, straddling the line of the Via Maris. There is no doubt about their identification with modern communities with similar names. The other two, Ekron and Gath, were inland cities situated on the plain somewhere to the east of the three coastal cities; but attempts by scholars and archaeologists to pin down their precise location have not yet found general agreement.

Ashkelon-on-Sea is a tidy new community established in 1953. Two kilometres to the south lies ancient Ashkelon, which was established about 4000 years ago. The 160-acre site is like a great semicircular bowl, open to the sea, rimmed by the impressive remains of a ruined Crusader wall. It is now attractively laid out as a National Park, and at week-ends the old Philistine shore teems with sun-bathing Israelis.

The core of the ancient city was an artificial mound which has been picked at cursorily by several excavators. Rich Roman remains have been found, which are on display in the Park itself. The Philistine level was excavated sufficiently to reveal a destruction level at the start of the Iron Age, which presumably relates to the arrival of the Sea Peoples around 1200 BC, and a subsequent rebuilding by the Philistines themselves. But systematic excavation would undoubtedly reveal a great deal more.

Throughout the second millennium BC (Middle and Late Bronze Age), Ashkelon was a key city, for it had the only harbour in southern Philistia; this harbour has been washed away now by the action of the sea, but on the beach one can still see reused Roman pillars jutting out of the rampart walls like the barrels of artillery guns – all that is left of later attempts to reinforce the sea-walls. Ashkelon's relations with Egypt throughout the second millennium seem to have been ambivalent; as Egyptian imperial power waned, Ashkelon would rise in rebellion, and there is a carved relief showing the reconquest of Ashkelon by Ramesses II (Ramesses the Great) around 1280 BC on a wall of the Great Hypostyle Hall at Karnak. Here the city is shown as a fortified tower on a hilltop, its defenders surrendering abjectly: 'The wretched town which his majesty took when it was wicked Ashkelon.'

Wicked Ashkelon was how the Israelites thought of it, too. Long after the Philistines had ceased to be a threat to the Israelites, or even to have a separate identity, the Old Testament prophets fulminated against Ashkelon and the other Philistine cities: 'For Gaza shall be forsaken, and Ashkelon a desolation...Woe unto the inhabitants of the sea coast...' cried the Hebrew prophet Zephaniah, with the undoubted benefit of historical hindsight (*Zephaniah* 2:4 1-5).

But Ashkelon survived, to reach a new peak of prosperity under Herod the Great who, according to one tradition at least, was a native of Ashkelon and embellished his birthplace with palaces and temples that effectively obliterated the Philistine streets. Ashkelon was finally destroyed by the Mameluke Sultan Beibars in AD 1270, never to rise again.

A few kilometres farther up the coast from Ashkelon, and four kilometres inland, stood the chief religious centre of the Philistines, Ashdod. It lay just behind the broad band of sand-dunes that border the coast. Today it is a large, low mound covering some ninety acres, scarred here and there by recent archaeological excavations. From the summit of the mound one can see, five kilometres away to the north-west across the sand-dunes, the gleaming high-rise tower blocks of modern Ashdod shimmering on the horizon like some science-fiction city. Ancient Ashdod had utilised a small river estuary seven kilometres away as a haven for its maritime trade; modern industrial Ashdod, which was only founded in 1957, has improved on this by constructing right on its own doorstep a new deep-water harbour, the largest in the southern part of Israel.

Seven seasons of excavations at Ashdod were carried out in the 1960s and early 1970s by a joint Israeli-American expedition headed by Dr Moshe Dothan of the Israel Department of Antiquities and Museums. They demonstrated that the ancient city had consisted of an acropolis covering some twenty acres, which later, during the Philistine period, spread into a much larger lower city surrounded by a fortified wall. The excavations also confirmed contemporary written sources from Ugarit that Ashdod had been an important trading city in the second half of the second millennium BC: 'traders from Ashdod' are specifically mentioned.

Late in the thirteenth century BC, the city was destroyed; the archaeological remains dating from this period were covered by a thick layer of burnt debris, and it is assumed that this destruction should be attributed to the Sea Peoples as they surged south towards Egypt. A brief hiatus seems to have followed; shortly afterwards, the Philistines rebuilt the city on top of the ruins of the Canaanite city they had so recently destroyed, and this is seen as clear corroboration of the historical pattern suggested in the Egyptian records, of a deliberate policy of Philistine resettlement at key points under the aegis of Egypt as buffers to protect Egypt's borders to the north.

What makes archaeologists so sure that they can identify a particular stratum, or layer, of their excavation as being specifically 'Philistine' is the distinctive style of the decorative motifs on their pottery.

Locally-produced Philistine pottery occurs all over the territory which the Biblical traditions say was occupied by the Philistines – and only there, as far as is known at present. It is based on a style which is called, in technical terms, Late Helladic IIIc, which was developed in the Aegean in the late thirteenth century BC. It extended to Cyprus, and to the expert eye is quite unmistakable. 'Philistine' pottery is basically Late Helladic IIIc, but it also combines elements of native Cypriot pottery, Egyptian pottery, and local Palestinian or Canaanite pottery. This cultural mix reflects the fortunes of a people who came from somewhere in the eastern Mediterranean (southern Anatolia, with Cypriot associations), and were then subjected to Egyptian and Palestinian influences which they blended in a style peculiar to themselves.

A great deal of Philistine pottery has been found and very handsome it is – bowls, stirrup-vases, three-handled jars, kraters. Of the motifs, which include looped spirals, Maltese crosses, lattice patterns and checkerboards, the most striking is a highly stylised bird like a swan with upraised wings pluming itself. As time goes on, it becomes more and more abstract and geometric, until it becomes almost unrecognisable as a bird at all.

According to the Biblical traditions, Ashdod at one time or another housed the central shrine to the principal Philistine god, Dagon. The Bible also mentions two other Philistine deities and their temples: Baal-Zebub, who was said to have had an oracle at Ekron, and the principal goddess, Astarte (Ashtoreth), who had a temple at Beth-shan. Dagon was depicted as a powerful warrior god associated with rain and agricultural fertility; Baal-Zebub was one of the many aspects of Baal, 'Lord'; and Astarte was the chief fertility goddess, the Sumerian Ishtar. All these were common (sometimes under other names) to the various Semitic cultures and civilisations of the ancient Near East. It cannot

Philistine pottery, showing the distinctive and elegantly stylised bird motif.

107

be said that any recognisable representations of these deities have been found in early Philistine levels. At Ashdod, a small clay statuette of a goddess schematically portrayed as a seated figure, with her body forming part of a throne, was found in the twelfth-century level, and has beeen affectionately nicknamed 'Ashdoda' by the excavators. Various other small figurines have been found, but nothing on the scale of the huge statues described in the Bible. It rather looks as if the Biblical stories about the Philistines are too generalised and stereotyped to have much independent value as source material for Philistine religion or culture. Even the accepted idea of the political organisation of the Philistines as given in the Bible – a league of five city-states – whose capital apparently changed on a rota basis from city to city – should be treated with caution, in the absence of any corroboratory evidence; for alas, no Philistine written archives have yet been found. The Philistines seem to have adopted the local Semitic language fairly quickly, along with other Canaanite influences, and any specifically Philistine script that may have existed was soon replaced by the alphabetic Phoenician/ Hebrew script (see Chapter 8).

It is clear from the archaeological record at Ashdod and elsewhere that the incoming Philistines, once they had settled and refortified the old Canaanite cities of Philistia, did not take long to establish themselves as a power in the land. As Egyptian influence waned, so Philistine strength waxed. In the middle of the eleventh century BC, around 1050, say, the city of Ashdod spread outside the central acropolis. A section of the excavations has been roofed over to protect the imposing remains of a towered gate and strong walls of sun-dried bricks reinforced with stone.

It was this period of unmistakable expansion of Philistine power and prosperity that is reflected in the Biblical folktales about the legendary guerrilla leader, Samson: 'And the children of Israel did evil again in the sight of the Lord; and the Lord delivered them into the hand of the Philistines forty years. And there was a certain man of Zorah, of the family of the Danites, whose name was Manoah; and his wife was barren, and bare not. And the angel of the Lord appeared unto the woman, and said unto her, Behold now, thou art barren, and bearest not: but thou shalt conceive, and bear a son. Now therefore beware, I pray thee, and drink not wine nor strong drink, and eat not any unclean thing: For, lo, thou shalt conceive, and bear a son; and no razor shall come on his head: for the child shall be a Nazarite unto

Clay statuette of 'Ashdoda', found in the Philistine levels of Ashdod, dating from the twelfth century BC.

God from the womb: and he shall begin to deliver Israel out of the hand of the Philistines' (*Judges* 13:1-5).

And thus, suitably embellished with theological exhortations, Samson enters the Bible story.

Samson is an archetypal saga figure. He was thirteenth of the so-called 'Judges', charismatic leaders who emerged as symbols of Israelite resistance to the Philistines. But what makes the stories about them more than merely a collection of legends and folk-tales is the didactic gloss they have been given: they seek to explain Israelite weakness in the face of Philistine military might entirely in terms of the people's religious backsliding. Hence the emphasis on Samson as a Nazarite – a strict Yahwist sect whose adherents never cut their hair; Samson's story is presented as a parable of obedience to the tenets of religious law.

Samson was born, it is said, in the Valley of Sorek, in the foothills of the mountains of Judah, near Beth-shemesh. This was frontier country between the Philistines on the plain and the Israelites up in the hill country, so it was an apt setting for the kind of border incidents exemplified in Samson's story. Despite the patently folkloristic nature of his exploits as recorded, he was clearly a man for the times; and recently archaeology has uncovered some highly suggestive evidence that might give a clue about how the story of his most celebrated exploit – the destruction of the temple at Gaza – may have been born.

Samson's early career had all the conventional feats of the budding rebel hero. He tore a young lion limb from limb with his bare hands. In a fit of pique after his marriage ended, he entered the Philistine stronghold of Ashkelon and killed thirty men single-handed. He ruined a Philistine harvest by releasing into the grain-fields 300 jackals with flaming torches tied to their tails. He even contrived to slay a thousand Philistines with the jaw-bone of an ass. Samson was clearly becoming an unmitigated nuisance to the Philistines; and so they bribed a Philistine harlot to ensnare him: a woman whose name has become a byword for female treachery – Delilah. The Philistine lords each promised her eleven hundred pieces of silver if she could persuade Samson to tell her the secret of his great strength.

For a long time Samson treated her questions as a teasing love-game. But in the end he told her the secret: no razor had ever touched his head because he was a Nazarite, consecrated to God from the day of his birth – if his head were shaved he would become as weak as any normal man. So while Samson slept, Delilah had his locks cut off, and this time when the Philistines came he was helpless. They gouged out his eyes and brought him down to Gaza. There they bound him with fetters of bronze, and he was set to grinding corn in the prison.

Today, Gaza is an Arab city, associated in most people's minds with the 'Gaza Strip' and the problem of Palestinian refugees. In ancient times it was the southernmost of the Philistine cities, a site of great strategic importance as the last city in Philistia before entering the Negev desert. Every power in the Middle East down the centuries has sought to control it.

All that is left of ancient Gaza is a *tell* in the north-eastern quarter of the city. Archaeologically speaking, almost nothing has been found of the Philistine city where Samson was blinded and bound with fetters of bronze – Gaza has been a battle-field too long for much that is ancient to have survived. What has survived, however, is the tragedy of Samson, which gave rise to Milton's celebrated lines about him –

Eyeless in Gaza at the Mill with slaves,
Himself in bonds under Philistian Yoke.

All the time, Samson's hair was growing again, and his strength was returning, until the terrible climax in the Temple of Dagon in Gaza which Samson was said to have pulled down upon 3000 of his enemies, and himself, in a last gesture of defiance and revenge. Not a trace of that remains, if it ever existed. But quite recently, Israeli archaeologists have found and excavated a Philistine temple, the first and only one so far, at a settlement mound called Tell Qasile, on the northern outskirts of Tel Aviv.

Tell Qasile is a relatively small mound, only four acres in area, situated on the north bank of the Yarkon River about two kilometres from its mouth. It first came to notice in the 1940s with the chance discovery of two inscribed potsherds lying on the surface; one of them said, 'Gold of Ophir to Beth Horon...thirty shekels'.

Admittedly, the script on the sherd (or ostracon, to give it its proper name) was post-Philistine – ninth or eighth century BC. But Professor Benjamin Mazar, who interpreted 'Beth Horon' as being not a city of that name, but the more literal rendering 'House of [the Canaanite god] Horon', reckoned that it was a pointer to the presence of a temple somewhere on the *tell*. So in the summer of 1949 he started digging Tell Qasile – which, incidentally, was the first official archaeological excavation undertaken by the new State of Israel after the Declaration of Independence in 1948.

In the course of four seasons (1949-51, and 1959), he uncovered part of a Philistine town that had been built in the twelfth century on virgin soil. It had obviously been built there in order to utilise the Yarkon River as a harbour for maritime trade with Phoenicia on the coast of Lebanon (indeed, the Yarkon River used to flow even closer to Tell Qasile than it does now). It was a well-planned city with straight, parallel streets, and regular housing schemes containing private dwellings and shops and workshops; each house, measuring about ten metres by eight metres, was about the same size as the apartments in the modern tower blocks of Tel Aviv nearby. The houses were of the classical Iron Age pattern, with three living-rooms and a store-room with an open courtyard, that seems to have been common to Philistines, Canaanites, and Israelites alike.

But one thing that Professor Mazor did *not* find was the temple of Horon that he was sure was somewhere in the vicinity.

And Samson took hold of the two middle pillars upon which the house stood...And Samson said, Let me die with the Philistines. And he bowed himself with all his might; and the house fell upon the lords, and upon all the people that were therein' (*Judges* 16:29-30). Engraving by Gustave Dore.

111

Then, in 1971, the municipality of Tel Aviv decided to turn Tell Qasile into an archaeological and educational park, and the excavations were resumed, this time by Professor Benjamin Mazar's nephew, Dr Amihay Mazar of the Hebrew University of Jerusalem. Dr Mazar started on the other side of the *tell*, working on exactly the same contour as that on which his uncle had laid bare a section of the city – and almost at once he came across the elusive temple.

In four seasons of excavation, from 1971-4, he uncovered an extensive sacred area, of which the core was a Philistine temple: not just one, in fact, but three temples superimposed on one another, the last dating from the eleventh century BC (the presumed period of the Judges). This third and upper-most temple, along with the rest of the city, had been violently destroyed by fire early in the tenth century, presumably by the Israelites; the city and the temple had then been rebuilt, not by the conquerors, apparently, but by the surviving Philistine population.

The temple was built with walls over a metre thick, made of sun-dried mud bricks on a stone foundation. It was enter-ed through a wide doorway into an antechamber lined with stepped plastered benches, for offerings. One then turned right (west) into the main hall; at the far end was a raised platform (*bāmāh*), about a metre high, made of mud bricks and plastered over, the focal point of the building. Beyond the far wall was a small storage room, which was found cram-med with hundreds of pottery cultic vessels.

But the most striking feature of the main hall was that the roof had originally been supported by two wooden pillars which had been set on round, well-made stone bases. There were traces of timber still adhering to these bases, and on analysis it was proved that the pillars that had held up the roof were made of cedar of Lebanon. And instantly, of course, the story of Samson in the temple of Gaza springs to mind: 'And Samson called unto the Lord, and said, O Lord God, remember me, I pray thee, and strengthen me, I pray thee, only this once, O God, that I may be at once avenged of the Philistines for my two eyes. And Samson took hold of the two middle pillars upon which the house stood, and on which it was borne up, of the one with his right hand, and of the other with his left. And Samson said, Let me die with the Philistines. And he bowed himself with all his might; and the house fell upon the lords, and upon all the people that were therein' (*Judges* 16:28-30).

Now, if one were built like a gorilla, it would be possible

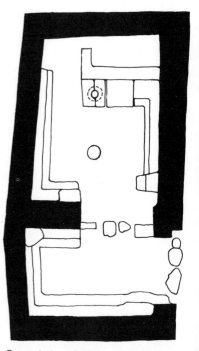

Ground plan of the temple at Tell Qasile: the entrance was bottom right. The bases of the two pillars are in the centre of the main hall. At the top, behind the altar plat-form, the storage room for cultic vessels.

112

Pottery incense stand from Tell Qasile: in the upper tier, the figure of a man with his arms spread as if braced against the pillars on either side – but actually part of a procession of four going round the vessel.

to reach both pillars in the Tell Qasile temple with one's outstretched arms: not to get a grip round them, perhaps, but at least to get purchase against them.

And then, in the Biblical phrase, one would bow oneself with all one's might and pull down the temple, killing all the Philistines who had gathered in and on it.

The only snag with this rather attractive scenario is the size of the temple itself. It is unexpectedly small. The main hall measures only 7.5 metres by 5.5 metres – not much larger than a good-sized living-room. By no stretch of the imagination could one pack 3000 festive Philistines either inside or on top of the temple; and although this is the only Philistine temple that has yet been discovered, there is no reason to suppose that any others will turn out to be larger. Only in Egypt does one find the kind of monumental stone temples that the Samson story obviously envisaged – and even in Egypt the public was never allowed into the temple itself; that was a privilege strictly reserved for the priests. Temples were not churches or synagogues, built to house a congregation. So in this one spectacular particular, the Samson story is quite simply wrong.

So how did the story come about? Obviously one can dismiss it out of hand as the kind of far-fetched legend that accretes around any strong-arm folk hero. But there is one rather intriguing hint to be gleaned from one of the pottery cult vessels that was found inside the ruins of the Tell Qasile temple – lying right up against the base of one of the pillars, in fact.

It is a cylindrical incense stand with two tiers; each tier has a series of 'windows' separating pillars. Between the pillars of the upper tier, in each of the four windows there stands the figure of a man with his arms extended sideways against the pillars. The whole is no doubt designed to represent a procession; but individually, the stance of the figures is temptingly suggestive.

By no stretch of the imagination can it be called a 'representation' of the Samson legend. But it is not too fanciful, perhaps, to see in a cultic vessel like this the germ of a folk-tale. As the conquering Israelites swept through cities and temples like Tell Qasile, they came across these odd cultic vessels, and by the quirks of association to which folk-tales are subject, memories of great Egyptian temples merged with stories of a legendary guerrilla leader and were fed by the thought of figures apparently pushing down the pillars of a temple. And thus an imperishable legend was born.

But there was nothing legendary or far-fetched about the historical plight in which the Israelites found themselves around the middle of the eleventh century. The haphazard and unsystematic emergence of 'charismatic' leaders like Deborah and Gideon to cope with crises as and when they arose failed them ('charismatic' is a technical term used to describe God's grace in such situations). The Philistines were growing stronger all the time. They had a flourishing economy, based on maritime commerce and control of the overland coastal trade route, the Via Maris. They had a formidable war machine based on a warrior-aristocracy, and the army consisted of archers, cavalry, and chariots, and was divided into hundreds and thousands. Compared with the Israelites in the hill country, they were an advanced commercial and industrial society. According to Biblical traditions, the Philistines had a monopoly of iron-working which they carefully kept from the Israelites. It was a technology that presumably they had learned in Anatolia before they moved south to Philistia: 'Now there was no smith found throughout all the land of Israel: for the Philistines said, Lest the Hebrews make them swords or spears: But all the Israelites went down to the Philistines, to sharpen every man his share, and his coulter, and his axe, and his mattock' (*I Samuel* 13:19-20).

The crisis came around the year 1050 BC, as nearly as can be deduced, when the Israelites met the Philistines in pitched battle for the first recorded time – a tribal rabble armed with farm implements against a disciplined army equipped with iron weapons: 'Now Israel went out against the Philistines to battle, and pitched beside Eben-ezer: and the Philistines pitched in Aphek' (*I Samuel* 4:1).

Tell Aphek lies about thirteen kilometres east of Tel Aviv. It is situated in a highly strategic position beside the abundant sources of the River Yarkon, dominating the eastern branch of the Via Maris. It is one of the most handsome sites in Palestine, looking for all the world like some ancient British castle (Caernarvon, for instance) set in well-kept rolling parkland. The *tell* itself is large, with an area of some thirty acres, crowned by the imposing ruined walls of a Turkish fort that was built there in 1571. Aphek was the north-eastern outpost of Philistine territory; and it was no doubt in an attempt to stop any further Philistine encroachment into the hill country that the Israelites were drawn into battle there around 1050.

Systematic excavation has been going on at Tell Aphek

Tell Aphek: in the centre, the ruins of the Turkish fort. The main excavated area within it (centre left) revealed traces of a Canaanite palace burned and robbed by the Philistines. Top left, the sources of the Yarkon River. Foreground, excavated area from the Roman period when Aphek was rebuilt by Herod the Great.

every season since 1972, led by Dr Moshe Kochavi, head of the Institute of Archaeology at Tel Aviv University; the work is being carried out in conjunction with the neighbouring municipality of Petah Tiqva, which is developing the whole site as a National Park. These excavations have already confirmed that Aphek was one of the oldest walled cities in Palestine, the earliest remains dating from c.3000 BC, the start of the Early Bronze Age. In the intervening 5000 years it has never lost its importance. Herod the Great rebuilt it extensively and named it Antipatris, after his father Antipater; the Crusaders built a little citadel on it, the Turks refortified it, the British used it as a camp in the 1930s, and during the 1948 War of Independence it was used by the Iraqis as an artillery post.

Inside the Turkish citadel itself a large section has now been excavated which seems to confirm its capture and

occupation by the Philistines. A large Canaanite palace in what had been the acropolis of the city had been destroyed by fire around 1200 BC. No Philistine buildings have been uncovered as yet in the acropolis – but all the available evidence points to the Philistines as being the cause of the destruction; because there are tell-tale signs of robber trenches that had been dug down through the debris to get at the stone foundations of the Canaanite palace walls for reuse, and these robber trenches are filled with sherds of Philistine pottery. What Philistine remains there may have been in this quarter were obliterated by the later building activities of the Turks.

Tell Aphek: part of the stairway leading to the tower of the Canaanite palace within the walls of the Turkish fort, dated to the thirteenth century BC.

It was from this formidable fortress that the Philistine army marched out to meet the tribal levies of Israelites at the place called Eben-ezer. They had gathered somewhere to the east of Aphek, to deny the Philistines access to the hill country of their homelands. But where *was* Eben-ezer?

Dr Kochavi reasoned that it must be at the nearest Israelite site to Tell Aphek; and the nearest potential site that he could see was the high ground of Izbet Sarta, three kilometres east of Tell Aphek, which had been pinpointed during an earlier archaeological survey. From Izbet Sarta, Tell Aphek

116

is just visible to the naked eye, clothed in trees, beside the Yarkon springs. This, Dr Kochavi reasoned, was as close as the Israelite settlers would have dared to come.

He made a trial dig there in 1975, and at once uncovered a stone house which could be interpreted as an Israelite structure of the eleventh century BC. The small settlement there had apparently been abandoned by its inhabitants in the middle of the century. For Dr Kochavi, the archaeological evidence suggested strongly that Izbet Sarta could be Eben-ezer, and that the fateful battle had been fought on the plain between it and Tell Aphek.

And fateful it was, from the Israelite point of view. At the first encounter the Israelite army was broken, and according to the Bible, 4000 were killed. In this dire emergency, the elders of Israel decided to play their trump card: they sent messengers to Shiloh to fetch the Ark of the Covenant of the Lord, the sacred talisman of the tribal league, to stiffen the morale of the troops. Shiloh seems to have been the major cult centre of the early days of the tribal league in Canaan. There the Ark of the Covenant, the portable throne of the invisible Yahweh, had been deposited in a tent-shrine, or Tabernacle.

Unfortunately, not even the presence on the battlefield of the Ark of the Covenant with all its potent associations could turn the tide. At the next encounter the Israelites were annihilated. They were slaughtered in their thousands. And worse still, the Ark itself was captured by the Philistines.

The Biblical town of Shiloh lay about twenty-seven kilometres north of Jerusalem. Today it is just another *tell*, about twelve acres in area, identified with Khirbet Seilun – a jumble of stone-walled terraces on which local farmers grow patches of barley amongst the ancient ruins. And no trace has ever been found of the site of the sacred shrine which was the sanctuary of the tribal cult before it was formalised with the building of the Temple in Jerusalem.

To this place, a messenger came running from the battlefield at Eben-ezer to bring the dire news. The chief priest, Eli, who was in charge of the Ark, was an old man of ninety-eight by then, and blind; and he was sitting on a seat by the wayside waiting to hear what had happened. The messenger went to him and told him that the army had been routed. No response. Then he told him that his two sons, who had been the guardians of the Ark, had been killed. No response. Then he told him that the Ark of the Covenant had fallen into the hands of the Philistines – and only with that third piece of news did the old man respond; he fell backwards off his seat, and broke his neck, and died (*I Samuel* 4:12-18).

The Philistine victory was complete. They occupied all the hill country, putting garrisons at all strategic points. And it looks as if the Philistine army also marched on Shiloh itself, to destroy the sanctuary; the Bible does not say so directly, but it would be the logical thing to do, and what archaeological evidence there is seems to support such an assumption. When Shiloh was excavated in the early 1920s by a Danish team led by Hans Kjaer they found an Iron Age house which seemed to have been destroyed by fire around 1050 BC.

The Bible chroniclers were quick to point out that capturing the Ark did the Philistines no good at all. When they carried it off in triumph to the temple of Dagon at Ashdod it caused a plague of tumours and rats, and the people of Ashdod passed it like a hot potato to Gath. Gath promptly suffered a similar plague of tumours and rats, and passed the Ark on to Ekron, which fared no better. Eventually, after seven months of this treatment, the Philistines sent the Ark back to the Israelites with their compliments and a wry gift of five tumours and five rats modelled in gold!

Nevertheless, the Hebrew tribal league was in utter disarray, with their hill country occupied and their sanctuary destroyed. It was a moment of desperate crisis. But then, as so often happens both in fact and in fiction, the moment produced the man – a man called Saul; and a boy called David.

7
The House of David

The story of King Saul and his tragic relationship with his former favourite, David, is an intensely human story, a passionate interplay of powerful personalities and flawed characters, a story of love and treachery and jealousy and ambition – and all apparently justified by the theological and political imperatives that are the hallmarks of the Biblical narratives.

In Biblical terms, Saul represented the first ruler whom the Children of Israel were prepared to accept as a 'king' after the sporadic and unstable charismatic leadership of the Judges. It was his ultimately tragic reign that paved the way for the rise of the United Monarchy under David, and the creation of Jerusalem as the City of David, round about the year 1000 BC.

In any account of Biblical history, Jerusalem is a focal point – for Moslems and for Christians as well, but most especially for the Jews; because Jerusalem was hailed by them as a Holy City centuries before the two other major world religions laid claim to a share of it. The story of how, and why, Jerusalem became the Jewish Holy City, the City of David, is central to this, yet seems at first sight a curiously inconsequential tale: for it came about simply because David, having learned from Saul's mistakes, wanted a royal city that he could call his own.

The story of Saul's kingship starts round about 1025 BC when the fortunes of the Children of Israel were at their lowest ebb. The hated Philistines had captured the Ark of the Covenant, they had destroyed their ancient cultic centre at Shiloh, and occupied their land. But at a place called Gilgal, about two kilometres from Jericho, at the very spot where Joshua was said to have pitched his camp at the start of his campaign to conquer the Promised Land and hallowed his invasion by setting up twelve standing stones, the tide began to turn for the Israelites because of Saul, the son of Kish.

The site of Gilgal is commonly identified as Khirbet-el-Mefjir, where archaeological soundings twenty years ago produced quantities of pottery sherds indicating settlement there dating from the early Iron Age (1200 BC), which matches the Biblical account. Today, Khirbet-el-Mefjir attracts more attention for the imposing ruins of the palace of Hisham, one of the Caliphs of the early Moslem era; inscriptions show that it was begun in AD 724 and finished in AD 743, only to be destroyed by earthquake four years later.

It was at Gilgal, according to one of three somewhat contradictory Biblical versions, that Saul was acclaimed the first king in Israel after leading an Israelite army on a successful foray to relieve the beleaguered city of Jabesh-gilead, east of the Jordan. In this account, Saul is depicted as behaving in a characteristically charismatic way (*I Samuel* 11): when he heard of the plight of Jabesh-gilead, the spirit of God suddenly seized him, and he chopped up a pair of oxen and sent portions to all the tribes, partly to raise the fiery cross and partly as a threat to those who hesitated to follow him into battle.

The other versions feature the prophet Samuel, who reluctantly anointed Saul in response to a popular demand for a king. Samuel is said to have felt that the Israelites already had a king, namely God, and that this clamour for a secular king like other contemporary states was a matter of backsliding. Samuel's reluctant compliance soon turned to active opposition, however, when Saul showed too many signs of acting independently of the prophet-priests – among them Samuel himself. The Bible represents both Samuel and God repenting that they had bestowed kingship on Saul – indeed, God went so far as actually to withdraw the charisma, the divine grace, with which Saul had originally been endowed. Professor Abraham Malamat, a Biblical historian at the Hebrew University of Jerusalem, sees Saul as a hybrid figure – the last of the Deliverer Judges, and the first of the institutionalised kings. The Saul/Samuel story represents the conflict between the idea of a secular monarchy and the idea of divinely-inspired tribal leadership through elders and prophets.

It has to be remembered that the Biblical accounts of Saul are profoundly biased against him; the whole Saul and David relationship is written up as propaganda in David's favour, so the stories about Saul's increasing moodiness, his pathological jealousy of David, and his mental instability should be taken with a pinch of salt. Folk-stories about prowess in war, and dramas of human relationship, have been manipulated for the specific purpose of glorifying David and vilifying Saul. We are dealing with saga, not history.

Yet Saul started well enough. As a charismatic guerrilla

David and Jonathan by Cima. 'Therefore David ran, and stood upon the Philistine, and took his sword...and cut off his head therewith...And it came to pass...that the soul of Jonathan was knit with the soul of David' (*I Samuel* 17-18).

leader, he skirmished successfully against the occupying Philistine forces; and he achieved a resounding victory at the pass of Michmash, north of Jerusalem, where the Philistines were routed after Saul's son, Jonathan, had infiltrated their camp in a daring commando raid (*I Samuel* 14). Today there is an Arab village at the site of the encounter; and during the First World War, a British army officer used the tactics described in the Bible to infiltrate the Turkish positions through the same narrow pass where there were two sharp columns of rock, called Bozez and Seneh (*I Samuel* 14:4).

The victory effectively cleared the occupying forces from the Judean hills, giving Saul much greater freedom to move in his new 'kingdom'. The tribes rallied round him gratefully – all except Samuel, who feared that Saul was usurping his priestly functions, and publicly revoked Saul's designation as king. Saul, however, was able to consolidate his position as war-leader by taking over the Philistine fortress at his home town, Gibeah of Saul, some five kilometres north of Jerusalem.

Gibeah is the modern Tell-el-Ful, a commanding mound beside the main road from Jerusalem to Nablus (Shechem). In the mid-1960s, King Hussein of Jordan started to build a palace on the summit, for this area was then under Jordanian rule. The Six-Day War in June 1967 put an abrupt end to the

121

scheme when the West Bank came under Israeli military administration. The royal palace remains an unfinished folly, a monument to war and a kind of peace, a symbol of the eddyings of military fortune, as it was in Saul's day.

Archaeologists have excavated this site, the first time in the 1920s under the direction of W.F.Albright when it was positively identified, and then again in 1964 in a six-week rescue dig directed by Paul W.Lapp before the building of the palace began. Lapp deduced that an Iron Age town had been founded there in the twelfth century BC, and that it had been fortified as a citadel in the eleventh century, presumably by the Philistines as part of the chain of garrisons they set up throughout the Judean hill country after their sweeping victory at Eben-ezer.

But late in the eleventh century BC, the place was apparently refortified and its walls strengthened with improved masonry and workmanship. The excavators presumed that this phase corresponded with the period of Saul, who recaptured his native town and turned it into his own royal citadel. It was rather a small fortress, to be sure (52 metres by 35, with a reinforcing tower at each corner), much smaller than King Hussein's palace complex was planned to be; but according to the Biblical accounts, it would have been in that ancient stronghold that King Saul first met the young shepherd who was destined to play such a decisive part in the history of the Children of Israel – the boy David.

Once again, the Bible gives three conflicting and irreconcilable versions of how David rose to a position of influence in Saul's court. In one (*I Samuel* 16:14-23), David, the youngest son of Jesse of Bethlehem, is summoned to court as a skilled harpist to soothe Saul's troubled spirits whenever an evil spirit from the Lord troubled him. In another (*I Samuel* 16:1-13), David was secretly anointed by Samuel as king-to-be as part of his (and God's) rejection of Saul. The third version is the most celebrated one (*I Samuel* 17): David the shepherd boy emerges as a folk hero by volunteering to take on the giant Philistine champion, Goliath, in single combat and killing him with a well-aimed sling-stone. This encounter, which is said to have taken place in the Valley of Elah some thirty kilometres west of Jerusalem, saved the Israelite army from annihilation, kindled the love of Saul's son Jonathan for David, and sowed the first seeds of Saul's jealousy. But it is a typical saga situation, folk-tale exalted into history; and it is worth noting that elsewhere in the Bible (*II Samuel* 21:19), the credit for killing Goliath is attributed to a certain Elhanan, the son of Jair of Bethlehem.

Be that as it may, David now became one of Saul's army commanders and his son-in-law, having won the hand of Saul's daughter Michal for his exploit against Goliath. But his growing success, according to the *First Book of Samuel*, only increased Saul's jealousy, until David was forced to flee the court and become an outlaw. He took refuge in the wilds of his native Judah, living as an outlaw in the rugged and mountainous wilderness on the shores of the Dead Sea, in the region around En-gedi, the site of the great copper hoard (see Chapter 1). He gathered about him a band of fugitives whom he forged into a tough fighting force, 'and dwelt in strongholds at En-gedi'.

En-gedi is a spectacular region: a facade of high, rearing mountains gashed by deep ravines that wind down through rocky slopes towards the Dead Sea. There is a welcome oasis at the bottom, watered by a beautiful spring whose name commemorates David's exile in the mountains above – 'David's Fountain'. It was in one of the caves high above the spring that David is alleged to have spared Saul's life, cutting off the hem of his robe as he slept to show that he could have killed him had he wanted (*I Samuel* 24:4). Apart from tradition and legend, however, there is as yet no archaeological evidence for David's sojourn at En-gedi. One of the 'strongholds at En-gedi' was excavated in 1949 and again in the 1960s by Israeli archaeologists led by Dr Benjamin Mazar; it was the settlement of Tell el-Jurn, perched on an elongated narrow hillock rising high above the valley of the north-western part of the oasis. From these investigations it was clear that the settlement was not founded until late in the seventh century BC – almost four centuries after the period of David's exile. It is difficult to avoid the conclusion that some, at least, of the traditions about David were furbished with anachronistic environmental details that date from the period of the writing up of the story of the Kings, several centuries after the alleged events.

Even in the impregnable mountains of En-gedi, David soon found his position untenable, apparently, and he took the only course open to him to escape Saul's relentless pursuit – he defected to the enemy: taking his band of hardened partisans, he offered his services to Achish, the Philistine king of Gath (*I Samuel* 27:2). The Philistines welcomed him with open arms, and gave him a town in the Negev as a feudal holding. The Biblical account, which is heavily slanted in David's favour, tries to make out that David was all the time

The Suicide of Saul by Breughel. 'Then said Saul unto his armourbearer, Draw thy sword, and thrust me through therewith...But his armourbearer would not; for he was sore afraid. Therefore Saul took a sword, and fell upon it' (*I Samuel* 31:4).

acting as a double agent, pretending to help the Philistines against Israel but meanwhile helping the Israelite settlements in southern Judah and building up support for himself amongst them; but there can be no escaping the implication that David threw in his lot with the Philistines against Saul, and became a Philistine vassal. When the Philistines next mustered an army for a final military showdown with Saul, David marched with them.

Once again, just as before the battle of Eben-ezer, the Philistines marshalled their forces at Aphek. Here the other Philistine war-lords looked askance at David, doubtless concerned about the loyalty of a mercenary who had already turned his coat once, and he was sent back – thus being spared the final treachery of taking the field against his own people. From Aphek the Philistines marched north; they did not want to engage Saul in the hill country, so instead they moved northwards across the coastal plain to the Plain of Jezreel (Esdraelon), the largest valley in Israel, between the mountains of Galilee to the north and the mountains of Samaria to the south. Here was good fighting terrain for their chariots; and here they encamped, and waited for Saul to come and challenge them.

And Saul came. Inexplicably, he allowed himself to be lured down from the hill country he knew best, and positioned his army at the foot of Mount Gilboa (*I Samuel* 31:1).

The result of the battle was practically a foregone conclusion; the Israelites were cut to pieces. Three of Saul's sons, including Jonathan, fell. And Saul himself, severely wounded by Philistine arrows, took his own life. The victorious Philistines found his body and marched off with it to the nearest garrison town of Beth-shan.

Today the ancient site of Beth-shan (Tell el Husn) is an imposing *tell* just to the north of the modern town. It rises stark and steep, and its bleakness is emphasised by a solitary withered tree that stands on the edge of the summit like a gibbet. Up on the *tell*, it is not hard to visualise the scene described in the Bible after Saul's suicide (*I Samuel* 31). The Philistines celebrated their victory by putting Saul's body on triumphal display. The headless corpse they impaled 'on the wall of Beth-shan'. The head itself they placed in the temple of their chief god, Dagon (*I Chronicles* 10:10), while his armour was set up as a trophy of war in the temple of their fertility goddess, Astarte (Ashtoreth).

When Beth-shan was excavated by a large American team from the University of Pennsylvania some fifty years ago, they uncovered many levels of intensive occupation over many centuries, slicing several metres off the top of the *tell* like a layer-cake. When they got down to the period of Saul in the late eleventh century BC, they uncovered the foundation walls of two large public buildings, which they interpreted as temples. But they were specifically Philistine temples – the temples, perhaps, of Dagon and Astarte? Indeed, was Beth-shan ever a Philistine city, as such, at all? From the archaeological evidence alone (which was gathered, remember, fifty years ago, when techniques were less refined than they are now) it is impossible to tell whether the city at this time was Philistine, or Canaanite, or even Israelite. But what is quite clear is that not long beforehand it had been an *Egyptian* base, superintending an important junction of the arterial Via Maris – and that it may well have been garrisoned then by Philistine mercenaries after the defeat of the Sea Peoples around 1190 BC according to the Egyptian records (see Chapter 6).

From the ruins came a statue of Ramesses III, the Pharaoh who had repelled the Sea Peoples in the great battles depicted on the walls of the temple at Medinet Habu in Egypt. But there had been an Egyptian presence in Beth-shan before that, especially in the period of Egyptian dominance in Canaan during the New Kingdom. A victory stela of Seti I (1308-1304) was found and a miniature stela dedicated by an

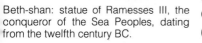

Beth-shan: statue of Ramesses III, the conqueror of the Sea Peoples, dating from the twelfth century BC.

Egyptian in memory of his father depicting them both worshipping Mekal, the patron god of Beth-shan – 'Mekal, the great god, the lord of Beth-shan', as the inscription has it. No incontrovertibly Philistine pottery sherds were found, however, which is puzzling if the Biblical account is true of Beth-shan as a Philistine stronghold on whose walls Saul's body was impaled.

However, some very intriguing evidence was found in the extensive cemetery that cut into the cliff-face of the river just opposite the mound. From this cemetery came a number of anthropoid clay coffins – that is to say, coffins with removable lids with representations of human faces on them, both naturalistic and caricatured. Some of these faces were surmounted by the characteristic ribbed head-dress of the Philistines already familiar from the reliefs at Medinet Habu. This remarkable correspondence has encouraged scholars to call them 'Philistine coffins'. The trouble is that these coffins are known to have originated in Egypt, where they have been found in burials in the Nile Delta. To explain this point, the argument runs that the Philistines adopted this particular burial custom from the Egyptians while they were acting as garrison troops in Egyptian towns in Canaan.

Even so, the 'Philistine coffins' at Beth-shan are thought by some scholars, in particular Professor Yigael Yadin, to be *earlier* than the time of Saul – twelfth century BC, or at the latest, perhaps, early eleventh century, whereas Saul is dated to the end of the eleventh century BC. Professor Yadin explains this difficulty by arguing that by Saul's time the Philistines had become so culturally assimilated in Canaan that they had stopped producing the typical Philistine pottery of earlier times; so that there is neither proof nor disproof of the Bible account of Saul's death from the archaeological point of view.

The leading Israeli authority on the material culture of the Philistines, Dr Trude Dothan, remains convinced, however, that the Beth-shan coffins are distinctively Philistine and can without question be dated to the period of Saul. In 1972 she excavated three anthropoid coffins from a cemetery beneath the sand-dunes thirteen kilometres south of Gaza, at Deir el-Balah. The burials were undisturbed for the most part, and yielded a great wealth of jewellery and other grave-goods. She dates these particular coffins to the fourteenth-thirteenth centuries BC, and certainly they are very Egyptianised; but it was burials like these in Philistia that the Philistines later took over and made their own.

Victory stela of Seti I, found at Beth-shan: the text gives an account of the king's success in overthrowing a coalition of Asiatic princes.

After studying the Philistines for many years now, Dr Dothan has the highest respect for the standard of culture which they brought with them to Canaan – a highly sophisticated culture which was superior to that of the Israelites and the Canaanites, and which is expressed particularly in their handsome pottery, their buildings, and their social organisation. It is hardly surprising that for a long time the Israelites found them such a formidable foe and wrote bitterly about them afterwards.

With the crushing defeat at Mount Gilboa, and the humiliation of Saul's body at Beth-shan, the Israelites were once again at the Philistines' mercy. It is quite clear that the Bible chroniclers saw this period as Israel's darkest hour – if only to set the scene for the dawn that was to come; for a saviour was at hand in the person of the hated rival whom Saul had outlawed and hounded for so long: David.

David emerged from his exile amongst the Philistines. After mourning Saul and Jonathan: 'Tell it not in Gath, publish it not in the streets of Ashkelon...' (*II Samuel* 1:20), he was acclaimed and anointed King of Judah at the ancient shrine of Hebron, no doubt with Philistine approval. But Saul's military commander, Abner, threw his support behind one of Saul's sons, Eshbaal, who formed a kind of government in exile across the Jordan River, laying claim to the northern kingdom of Israel. For the first time, the concept of 'Judah' and 'Israel' as separate integral entities now begins to emerge.

There was considerable diplomatic rivalry between the two opposing camps; and this rivalry is vividly illustrated in the Biblical tradition in a bizarre encounter that took place by 'the pool of Gibeon' (*II Samuel* 2). It was a meeting between Eshbaal's army commander, Abner, and David's army commander, Joab, presumably to discuss terms for a treaty between the two kings, because relations between them had been somewhat strained. But it went disastrously wrong. Each army commander had with him a contingent of young men; and they sat, according to the Bible, on opposite sides of the 'pool of Gibeon'. Then, after the talks, some sort of ritual or military ceremonial must have been planned, perhaps to seal the terms of the treaty, because twelve young men of each side 'arose to play before them', as the Bible puts it. But it turned out to be a very rough game indeed. Each man suddenly seized his opposite number by the head and thrust his sword into his side, so that all twenty-four of them dropped dead on the spot.

Philistine anthropoid coffin: the distinctive ribbed cap is exactly the same as in the depiction of the Philistines at Medinet Habu.

The Pool of Gibeon: a great water-shaft sunk into the bed-rock to reach the water-table. It meant excavating 3000 tons of limestone.

But where, or what, was this pool of Gibeon? The name of Gibeon will always be associated with the place where the sun stood still at Joshua's command; it was when Joshua was said to have rushed to the aid of the beleaguered city of Gibeon, and in order to give himself more time to complete the slaughter of the routed enemy he cried out, 'Sun, stand thou still upon Gibeon; and thou, Moon, in the valley of Ajalon' (*Joshua* 10:12). Whereupon the sun obligingly stayed its course, and 'hasted not to go down about a whole day'. Gibeon also achieved fame of a less heroic kind through Joshua, when the Gibeonites disguised themselves in old clothes, carrying worn-out patched wine-bottles, and persuaded Joshua that they were poor vagrants from a distant country instead of prosperous merchants from the rich wine-producing town of Gibeon, and thus obtained a covenant of peace with him. When Joshua discovered the ruse he did not repudiate the covenant, but condemned the Gibeonites to be 'hewers of wood and drawers of water' (*Joshua* 9:27).

The site of Biblical Gibeon has traditionally been associated with the Arab village of el-Jib, some twelve kilometres north

Opposite Phoenician ivory found at Nimrud, inlaid with gold, lapis lazuli and carnelian, showing a lioness attacking a young Negro. Dated to the eighth century BC.

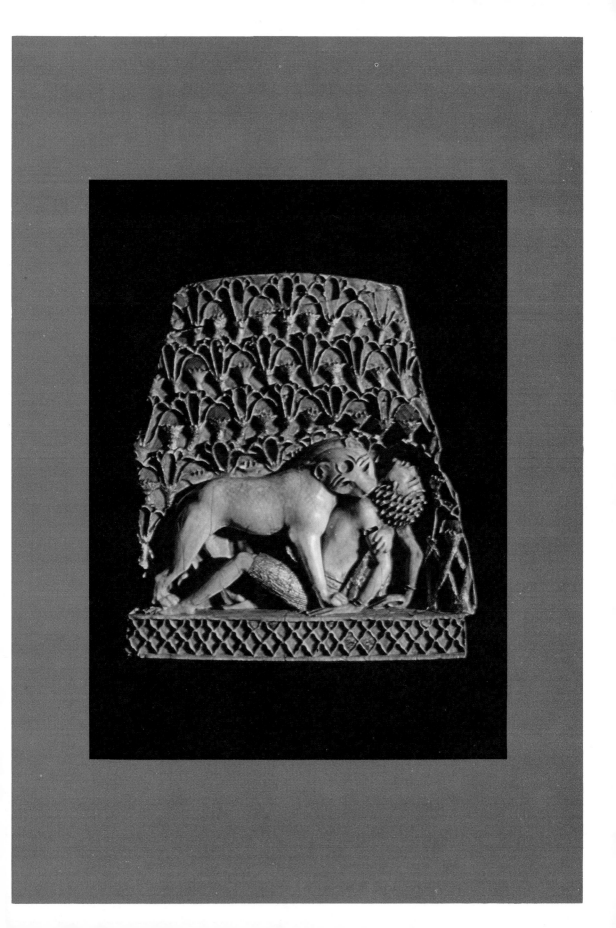

of Jerusalem, in what was in David's day a kind of no-man's-land between the two factions. But there were some puzzling aspects to the identification. Why had Joshua cursed the Gibeonites to be 'drawers of water' in particular? And what about the reference to the 'pool of Gibeon' in that gruesome incident that occurred in David's early days as King of Judah?

The problems of Gibeon were solved in the 1950s, when the site at el-Jib was excavated by Dr James B.Pritchard. He came upon the pool right away in his first season in 1956; actually it was not a pool, but a water system, a means of supplying water from a deep source within the city boundaries. Some civic ruler had dug 3000 tons of rock from the solid limestone of the hill, twelve metres in diameter and eleven metres in depth, with a spiral stairway winding down the edge of the shaft. From the bottom of this huge shaft, a spiral tunnel continued for another fifteen metres down to the reservoir of water that lay twenty-seven metres below the ground surface.

When Dr Pritchard discovered the pool, it was filled to the brim with debris. It took two years of work to clear it. In the debris, he came across a jar handle on which the word 'Gibeon' had been scratched in archaic script of the seventh century BC. For an archaeologist to find the name of an ancient site on the site itself is almost too good to be true, and at first Dr Pritchard suspected a hoax; but ultimately no fewer than fifty-six of these inscribed jar handles turned up, all marked 'Gibeon' or 'vineyard of Gibeon', sometimes followed by a personal name. There could be little doubt that the 'pool of Gibeon' had been found.

The only way of dating it was by the jar handles, and they were all of the seventh century BC. It is impossible to tell for how long before that the pool had been in use; but this was

One of the inscribed jar-handles found by Dr Pritchard in the Pool of Gibeon. The letters read *gb'n gdr* –'vineyard of Gibeon'.

surely the setting that the later Bible chroniclers had in mind when they penned the story of the encounter at the pool-side.

The abundance of jar handles in the pool was soon explained. In 1959, Dr Pritchard's team from the University of Pennsylvania came across a number of curious cellar-like cuttings down into the bedrock of the ground surface; they had a small circular opening at the top which opened out into a jug-shaped tank some six feet deep. In one of them, they found a large storage jar with a capacity of nearly ten gallons. With that, everything fell into place: the rock-cuttings had been storage cellars for wine-jars. It turned out that the temperature of these cellars, even during the hottest summer months, stays at a constant 65 degrees Fahrenheit – exactly the same temperature at which wine in the nearby winery at Latroun monastery is stored today. In addition to sixty-three of these cellars, which had a total storage capacity in excess of 25,000 gallons of wine, the excavators found wine-presses in the area as well, so it is clear that in the seventh century BC, at least, Gibeon was the Bordeaux of Palestine. And with all these findings, the story about the Gibeonites

Gibeon: excavating the wine-cellars gouged out of the bed-rock.

concealing their prosperity as wine-makers, and being condemned to be 'drawers of water', was given a new and vivid context.

David's star was now in the ascendant. Both Abner, Eshbaal's commander, and Eshbaal himself were murdered, and David apparently managed to avoid any suspicion of complicity in these highly convenient events. With their deaths, the dynastic claim of the House of Saul to the throne came to an abrupt end; and so at the ancient town of Hebron with all its powerful religious traditions, where Abraham and the other Patriarchs were reputed to be buried, and where David himself had already been elected king of the southern state of Judah, the elders of the northern state of Israel now came to David and offered him the kingship of Israel as well (*II Samuel* 5:1-5).

This amalgamation of Judah and Israel under their vassal, David, was something the Philistines could not overlook, and they mobilised an expedition against him – they 'came up to seek David' (*II Samuel* 5:17). But already it was too late. As a Philistine mercenary, David had had ample opportunity of learning all about Philistine military tactics; and now, with his own army of veteran professionals he met the Philistines twice in battle, and beat them. These victories were apparently so decisive that the Philistines simply ceased to be a major power in the land. From now on they would be limited to their original territories in the coastal plain of Philistia, and David was free to develop his own political power-base from which to build up an empire. After reigning from Hebron for seven and a half years, he decided it was time that he founded a capital of his own.

It so happened that such a place was ready to hand: the Jebusite city of Jerusalem, which lay between Judah and Israel, and which cut off direct communications between the two states. Jerusalem would make an effective half-way house between them, and also provide David with a royal city of his own, if he could capture it with his own troops. And that is precisely what he now set out to do, according to the Biblical accounts (*II Samuel* 5:6-8, and *I Chronicles* 11:4-6). The year was around 1000 BC.

Down in the Kidron Valley, in the south-eastern quarter of Jerusalem, and just opposite the Arab enclave of Silwan, there is a rock-cut passage that leads down to a wire grill. Behind it there is a fresh-water spring which is known as the spring of Gihon, which was the main source of water for the Jebusite city of Jerusalem higher up the slopes. Later tradi-

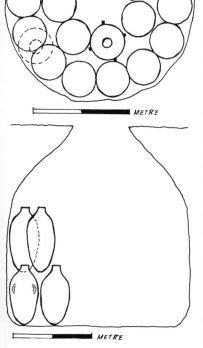

Gibeon: plan of the floor of one of the wine storage cellars. Below, section of a wine-cellar, showing how the storage jars were stacked at a constant temperature.

METRE

METRE

tions would dub this the 'Virgin's Spring', because of the legend that the Virgin Mary washed the swaddling clothes of the infant Jesus in it. But that was much later. In David's time, if we are to believe the Biblical accounts, there was a secret method of entry into Jerusalem through a water-shaft or 'gutter' that the Jebusites had dug from inside their city down to the spring outside their walls, and David apparently knew of this. The Biblical texts are badly garbled at this point, but the burden of the story seems to be that David

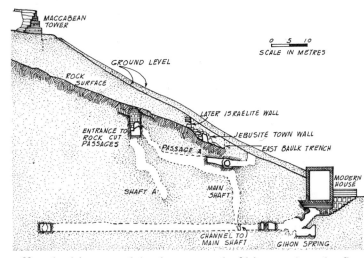

'Warren's Shaft' at the Gihon spring. Shaft A was abortive, so the Jebusites dug Passage A until they reached an easier place to bore a shaft (Main Shaft) down to the waters of the spring, outside the Jebusite town wall.

offered a big reward (and command of his army) to the first man who would climb up this 'gutter' or water-shaft and lead an attack on the Jebusite defenders from behind; and this, it seems, was how the city was taken.

Just over a hundred years ago, in 1867, a British engineer, Captain Charles Warren, who was making a survey in Jerusalem, went to visit the 'Virgin's Spring' as a tourist, and he noticed that in the roof of the cavern above the spring there was a crevice. He came back next day armed with mountaineering tackle and wormed his way into the crevice and up a shaft which brought him out, to his great surprise, into broad daylight half-way up the hill behind the spring. From then on, this shaft was assumed to be the 'gutter' that David's commandos had used to capture the city.

There was, however, a serious snag to this theory, because in those days the walls of early Jerusalem were assumed to have been right up on the crest of the hill – and yet the shaft came out only half-way up the hill; so why had the Jebusites dug at great labour a shaft to their water supply which did not start inside their walls? And what was the point of David's men climbing it?

Dame Kathleen Kenyon's excavation of the eastern slope of the Ophel Hill: right of centre, the great trench running downhill from the 'Tower of David' on the crest of the hill. Background, top, sections of the medieval walls of Jerusalem.

It was with this discrepancy in mind that Dame Kathleen Kenyon started digging for the remains of the earliest Jerusalem on that hillside in 1961.

The first thing she discovered was that the structure that previous excavators had called the 'Tower of David' on the crest of the hill (the Ophel Hill, as it is called) had actually been built on ruins that could be dated some 400 years *later* than David's time, and therefore could not be considered part of the original Jebusite walls. So Dame Kathleen dug a great trench straight down the side of the steep hill. It was an extremely difficult operation, and it had to be shored and terraced all the way down. She had to dig through a mass of ruined debris from later centuries, but eventually she came across what she had been looking for: a thick city wall that could be dated well before the time of David. She had found the line of the eastern wall of the Jebusite city – and as she expected, it was well *below* the entrance to the Warren Shaft, but *above* the Gihon spring. The short stretch of wall which she uncovered turned obliquely up the slope at the point where she came across it; so from this tiny portion she was able to deduce the general outline of the city limits of Jebus-

133

ite Jerusalem, and therefore David's Jerusalem. It was one of the most spectacular and satisfying finds in the history of archaeology in Palestine.

The City of David: in the centre, the short stretch of the original Jebusite wall found by Dame Kathleen Kenyon at the point where it turned uphill. On the right, a later Israelite wall. In the background, the stone revetment walls built by the excavators to shore up the trench.

David's Royal City turned out to have been rather small, covering an area of only some eleven or twelve acres across the ridge of the Ophel Hill. But it was enough. David quickly consolidated his position by making Jerusalem the religious as well as the political capital of the united kingdoms. With great ceremony, he fetched the Ark of the Covenant that had lain for many years discredited after its ignominious capture and return by the Philistines. Saul had completely ignored this potent sacral symbol; but now David brought it to Jerusalem and installed it in a tented shrine he had prepared for it, dancing and capering with such abandon that his wife was ashamed of him for exposing his genitals to the crowd.

Professor Abraham Malamat thinks that this was the masterstroke of David's political genius – to create a fusion, a merger, of what he calls the 'earth-bound' Jerusalem and the 'sky-bound' or celestial Jerusalem. With this one move, David established both the Ark and its priesthood in a new official national shrine. From now on, David's place in the

134

hagiography of Israel was assured, whatever wrongs he might commit.

And wrongs there certainly were. Even the eulogistic accounts of David penned by later redactors made no attempt to conceal the discreditable episode of his seduction of Bathsheba, wife of one of his army officers, Uriah the Hittite; David had Uriah sent to the front line, to his certain death, so that he could continue to enjoy the favours of the delectable Bathsheba (*II Samuel* 11-12).

Nonetheless, David is represented in the Bible as *the* king par excellence. Some scholars think that the accounts of his exploits are exaggerated, particularly where the extent of his empire is concerned. But Professor Malamat has no doubt that David's achievements were not only faithfully recorded, but make sense in the historical perspective of the times. There was a power vacuum in the Middle East in the tenth century BC, which David exploited with great political skill to create an empire for Israel at a time when the superpowers in Egypt and Mesopotamia were quiescent. Dr Malamat summarises David's career in schematic form, involving five concentric rings:

First was his playing off of the Philistines when he was their vassal – the Philistines were interested in a divide-and-rule policy for Judah and Israel, and were happy to let him take over Judah as their vassal.

Second was his careful diplomatic wooing of the northern state of Israel, to overcome the traditional animosity between the two states. Thereby he combined all the tribes of Israel.

Third was his decisive defeat of the Philistines, whereby he broke their claim to Canaan and became himself a 'successor-state' to the former Egyptian hegemony over Canaan.

Fourth was his annexation of the nations of Jordan – Edom, Moab, and Ammon – which gave him control of the major trade artery, the King's Highway, from the Red Sea to Mesopotamia.

And fifth was his inevitable clash with Syria, where the Aramaeans were trying to carve out an empire for themselves, and could not stand by while David annexed their buffer states like Ammon. By defeating the Aramaeans three times, David extended his empire all the way from the borders of Egypt to the Euphrates.

It is a splendidly logical structure, justifying the Biblical account in terms of its own inner logic. But it begs the question of the accuracy, the historicity, of the Biblical account itself – when it was written in its present form, why it was

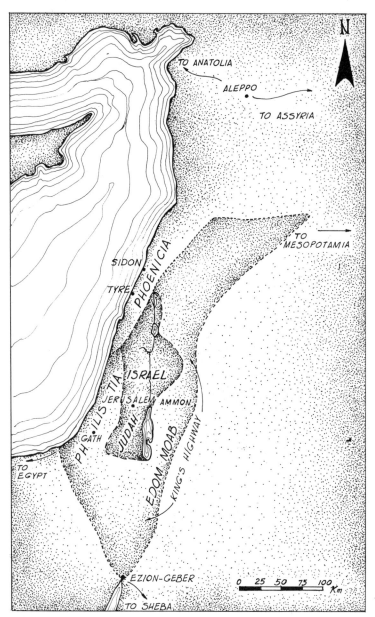

David's conquests: a reconstruction of the possible limits of David's empire by Dame Kathleen Kenyon.

written, and for whom it was written. In terms of saga, as opposed to history, it also has a compelling narrative logic: for now *hubris* overtakes the ageing king.

David's last years as king were clouded by a series of palace intrigues of Byzantine complexity, and profound personal sorrow when his favourite son, Absalom, rebelled against him and was done to death (*II Samuel* 13-19). The Biblical accounts seem to be concerned mainly with explaining how it was that all of David's sons were disqualified from inheriting the kingdom, one by one, except for Solomon, his son by

Bathsheba; on his deathbed the old king was importuned by Bathsheba to have Solomon acclaimed and anointed as the next king, on the very same day as yet another of his sons, Adonijah, was declaring himself king (*I Kings* 1).

The picture of David that we are offered is that of a man who had fulfilled his primary purpose in establishing a united Hebrew monarchy for the first time, but whose sins had been so great that he was not considered worthy to carry out the ultimate function that Jerusalem was to have in the eyes of later commentators, namely to be the religious and political capital of the Jews through the building of a Temple. But David prepared the ground and made all things possible for his illustrious successor, Solomon. One of the most significant things he did in the view of the later Bible writers was to purchase, by charter, a piece of land just outside the City of David: a threshing-floor, as the Bible calls it, on a high place outside the walls, for which he paid fifty shekels of silver and on which he set up an altar unto the Lord (*II Samuel* 24). And it was on that high place, just beyond the original City of David, that his son Solomon would consummate the Biblical narrative by building the First Temple.

8
Jerusalem the Golden

In all the long history of religions and their holy places, the Temple Mount in Jerusalem has had a busier and more chequered story than most over the past 3-4000 years; because there the legends and traditions of three major world religions come together.

In chronological order, it was the place associated with Abraham's ordeal of faith on one of the mountains in the Land of Moriah where he was said to have been prepared to sacrifice his son Isaac (*Genesis* 22). It was where King David was said to have bought a threshing-floor on Mount Moriah on which he set up an altar to the Lord (*II Chronicles* 3:1). This was where Solomon built a great Temple and Herod another; and this was where Jesus was said to have cleansed that Temple of its money-changers. It was from the Temple Mount that the prophet Mohammed was supposed to have ascended to Heaven and where the Moslems built, in AD 691, one of the most beautiful mosques in the Islamic world, the Dome of the Rock. Today, the Temple Mount (or the Haram es-Sherif, as the Moslems call the sacred area) is venerated by adherents of three religions – so much so, indeed, in the case of strictly orthodox Jews, that they will not set foot in its precincts lest they inadvertently desecrate the place by treading on the unknown site of the Holy of Holies of Solomon's Temple.

The building of the First Temple in Jerusalem was the first major enterprise of Solomon's reign and, in the eyes of the later Bible writers, much the most significant. Solomon succeeded his father David as king of the United Kingdom of Israel and Judah around 965 BC, though some scholars think it was slightly later, around 960 BC; he began work on the Temple in the fourth year of his reign, and the structure took seven and a half years to complete (*I Kings* 6). It is the most famous building in the Bible, and one of the most celebrated in the world. Yet not a stone of it remains, not a trace of all its fabled splendour: it was destined to be wrecked by Nebuchadnezzar in 586 BC when the Jews were carried off into exile in Babylon (see Chapter 11), patched up after the return from exile, totally rebuilt and enlarged by Herod the Great in

The Jerusalem of David and Solomon: in the foreground, the Ophel Hill coming to a point (bottom right) between the Kidron Valley on the right and Hinnom Valley on the left. In the background, the Temple Mount on which Solomon built the First Temple, now dominated by the golden Dome of the Rock.

20 BC (see Chapter 12), razed by the Romans in AD 70, and replaced by a temple dedicated to Jupiter in AD 135. Later, when the great esplanade of the Temple Mount and its buildings had long been abandoned, the magnificent Dome of the Rock was built there by the Moslems in an attempt to make Jerusalem rival Mecca as the chief shrine of Islam.

Our image of Solomon's Temple is wholly derived from extended descriptions in the Bible, particularly in the *First Book of Kings* and the *Second Book of Chronicles*. Neither source is contemporary; *Kings* was written some time after the Babylonian destruction of the Temple, and *Chronicles* considerably later. There have been innumerable attempts to construct elaborate models of the Temple from these descriptions, but the Bible accounts are more fanciful than factual and lack architectual precision even though a wealth of measurements is given. However, archaeological excavations at Canaanite temple sites elsewhere in Palestine and Syria have thrown fresh light on the basic structure of Solomon's Temple, which seems to have been modelled on older Canaanite prototypes.

One such prototype is the temple of Baal-Hadad that Professor Yigael Yadin excavated in the Lower City of Hazor in the 1950s. It dates from the Late Bronze Age (c. 1500-1200 BC), and when excavated it showed tell-tale signs of the

Canaanite temple at Hazor: the Holy of Holies as excavated by Dr Yadin. On the left, the niche in the wall for the altar platform; to the right, the two other chambers.

single-minded violence of the destruction of the city (see Chapter 5): a seated statuette with its head chopped off, broken carved stone slabs, even a headless statue that seems to have been deliberately buried upside down. But it was the ground plan of the temple that persuaded Dr Yadin that it had served as a prototype for the kind of temple Solomon built, based on the indications in the Bible: a much smaller temple than a cursory reading would suggest.

The Hazor temple was built of three elements – a porch, a main hall and a Holy of Holies – situated one behind the other, on a north-south axis. The Holy of Holies lay to the north; it was a large room, measuring about thirteen by nine metres, with a deep niche in its northern wall. In the porch, or vestibule, were found two basalt pillar bases just in front of the entrance to the main hall. They had no structural function, and reminded Dr Yadin of the two enigmatic cultic pillars outside the porch of Solomon's Temple, called 'Jachin' and 'Boaz' in the Bible. Of course there were significant differences, too. Solomon's Temple was orientated east-west, for instance; and Solomon's Temple would not have contained effigies of the gods such as were found at Hazor – only the Ark of the Covenant symbolising the presence of the deity. Nor can we say much about any possible similarities between the decor of the Hazor temple (all of which was

Solomon's Temple: reconstruction from the Howland-Garber model, with the Holy of Holies to the left and the vestibule entrance to the right. In the Holy of Holies, the portable Ark of the Covenant is shown guarded by two cherubim.

destroyed) and the fulsome accounts of the costly ornamentation of Solomon's Temple with its tons of ivory and
bronze and gold; but it is not unlikely that the Hazor temple
may have contained representations of the Biblical cherubim
that guarded the Ark, for cherubs were not the angelic little
winged infants of popular imagination – they were sphinx-
like mythological monsters, part lion, part bird and part
man, which are familiar to us now from the art and religious
symbolism of the ancient Middle East, and which the
Israelites borrowed and adapted for their own religious
iconography.

Solomon's Temple was only one of the major buildings he
erected on the Temple Mount. Next to the Temple he
constructed a magnificent palace of cedars of Lebanon that
took thirteen years to build and served as an armoury and
treasury; he also built a judgment hall, and a palace for one
of his 700 wives, the daughter of the Egyptian Pharaoh.
There was no space for this new palace complex inside the
cramped confines of David's City, so he heaped up an
immense platform on 'Mount Moriah' on which to erect the
buildings, and then joined up David's City with a 300-metre
wall to include it, like some acropolis. This was the start of
the fabled magnificence of Jerusalem that has left such a
profound impression on the world's imagination.

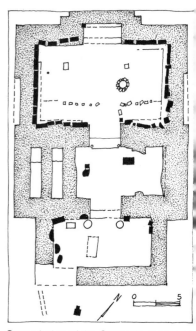

Ground plan of the Canaanite temple at
Hazor that may have served as a model
for Solomon's Temple. The Holy of Holies
is at the top.

It is not surprising that Solomon's buildings should have
been influenced by Canaanite traditions. The Bible reports
that he imported skilled architects, masons and artists from
Phoenicia to build his temple, and it is quite clear that much
of the prosperity and splendour with which the Bible writers
endowed Solomon's reign was ultimately based on the Phoenician Connection.

'Phoenicia' and 'Phoenician' are somewhat artificial terms
which were applied by the classical authors to the city-states
of the narrow coastal strip that corresponds roughly to
modern Lebanon, and the inhabitants who occupied them,
from c.1200 BC onwards. Their chief cities were Tyre,
Sidon and Byblos. The Greek word from which 'Phoenicia'
derived meant 'purple', and was a translation of the name
'Canaan' which may have had some etymological connection
with the purple dye produced from local *murex* shellfish for
which the region was famous.

The Phoenicians did not suddenly arrive upon the historical scene as invaders or immigrants. They were Canaanites,
and cannot be differentiated either ethnically or culturally
from the general mass of Canaanites. They just happened to

The Phoenician Connection: model boat from a Phoenician cemetery at Akhziv.

be the survivors of the havoc that overwhelmed the eastern Mediterranean at the start of the Iron Age around 1200 BC, with the onslaught of the Sea Peoples, the collapse of the Hittite empire, the disintegration of Mycenaean power, and the destruction of the great coastal cities of Ugarit, Aradus and Sidon. The survivors regrouped in the Lebanon and carried on business in the new set of circumstances. They shrewdly exploited the power vacuum that ensued in the twelfth century BC; suddenly the export markets of the Mediterranean were ripe for the taking, with the super-powers quiescent and licking their wounds. The new Phoenicians were already experienced seamen and traders, they had excellent harbours and ships, they had goods to exchange like purple textiles and bronze work and above all the much prized cedar wood of Lebanon; now they seized their chance to develop wide trading interests and built up a great maritime mercantile empire. They founded colonies throughout the western Mediterranean, the greatest of which, Carthage (founded according to Greek tradition by Tyre in 814 BC), eventually grew into a major power strong enough to challenge the might of Rome until she was destroyed in 146 BC.

Tyre was the largest of the Phoenician cities in the Lebanon, half-way between Beirut and Haifa. In ancient times it occupied a small island just off the coast, with two harbours which provided year-round sheltered anchorage whatever the direction of the wind. Today, Tyre is joined to the mainland by a peninsula that formed after Alexander the Great built an artificial causeway to the island for his celebrated seven-month siege and destruction of the city in 332 BC.

Archaeology has so far been unable to recover much of the material culture of the Phoenicians in their home cities, for they are deeply buried under modern settlements and were systematically pillaged for building stone by later occupants. But that they were great craftsmen and artists cannot be doubted, for they were famed throughout the ancient world

Pottery face mask from a Phoenician cemetery at Akhziv.

143

for their skill as metalsmiths and ivory-carvers and cabinet-makers. Surviving examples of their work have all been found outside Phoenicia, where it is not always easy to be certain about their provenance; for the Phoenicians assimilated many cultural and artistic influences, and their workmanship was frequently copied or adapted by others. But their reputation for artistry is reflected in the Biblical account of the furnishing of Solomon's Temple: 'And king Solomon sent and fetched Hiram out of Tyre. He was a widow's son of the tribe of Naphtali, and his father was a man of Tyre, a worker in brass: and he was filled with wisdom, and understanding, and cunning to work all works in brass. And he came to king Solomon, and wrought all his work' (*I Kings* 7: 13-14). In the following verses a list of his works is given – two bronze pillars, two capitals of copper, two ornamental festoons of chain-work, hundreds of ornamental pomegranates, a great 'sea' of cast metal mounted on twelve oxen, ten bronze trolleys with decorations in relief, ten bronze basins, and a variety of ornamental pots, shovels and tossing-bowls.

Another Hiram, King Hiram of Tyre, was the man who provided Solomon with all the materials and craftsmen he required; but where the Phoenician Connection really mattered for Solomon was in the commercial alliance he formed with King Hiram, according to the Biblical accounts: 'King Solomon made a navy of ships in Ezion-geber, which is beside Eloth, on the shore of the Red Sea, in the land of Edom. And Hiram sent in the navy his servants, shipmen that had knowledge of the sea, with the servants of Solomon. And they came to Ophir, and fetched from thence gold, four hundred and twenty talents, and brought it to king Solomon' (*I Kings* 9:26-28).

It reads like a straight economic international deal: Solomon would provide harbourage facilities near Eloth (modern Eilat) at the north of the Gulf of Aqaba giving access to the Red Sea and beyond, and King Hiram of Tyre would provide the naval personnel and expertise – and the ships, according to variant accounts elsewhere in the Bible. The Phoenicians would gain access to the exotic markets and resources of the Far East – spices and gold and other luxury items – while Solomon, by permitting trade transit through his territory, would reap benefit from the trade by means of toll charges.

On the face of it, it was an arrangement of considerable mutual advantage. Palestine was a land-bridge, not only between Egypt and Mesopotamia but also between the Mediterranean and the Red Sea. Solomon seems to have been no

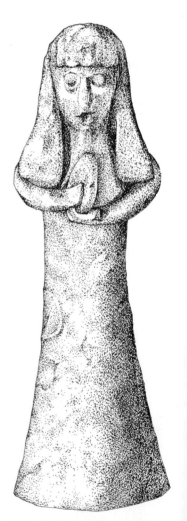

Woman with a tambourine: from a Phoenician cemetery at Akhziv.

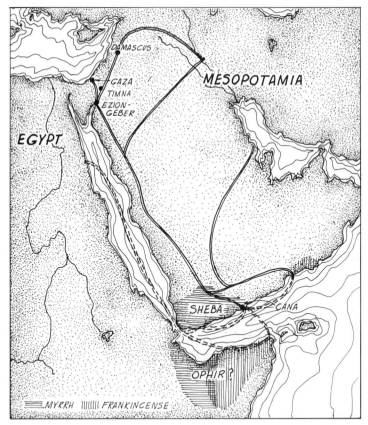

militarist, yet he wanted economic expansion; he could not rely on local agriculture or industry alone, so his only option other than imperial conquest was to get into international trade by exploiting his country's geographical position in partnership with the Phoenicians. They key to this expansion was Ezion-geber: at one inspired stroke, Solomon would be able to bypass the expensive overland caravan routes from the east by using Hiram's ships.

But where exactly was this Ezion-geber? Until recently, it was identified with the small, low mound of Tell el-Kheleifeh not far from Eilat. It was excavated in 1938-40 by an American expedition led by the late Dr Nelson Glueck of the Hebrew Union College of Cincinnati, who in his book *Rivers in the Desert* enthusiastically claimed Tell el-Kheleifeh as Solomon's port of Ezion-geber, which apparently included a huge 'smelter' as well. This identification, not only of the 'smelter' building but also of the site itself, was later abandoned by Dr Glueck.

The site had to be somewhere near the head of the Gulf of Aqaba if the Bible scenario was to make any sense; but the coast there is harbourless and exposed to fierce southerly

Opposite above Tell Dan: the platform High Place probably built by King Ahab originally and greatly enlarged by his successors.

Opposite below Megiddo: the tunnel leading to the spring from the bottom of the great shaft (far distance). On the left, the point at which the gangs of tunnellers met and had to adjust their line fractionally.

145

storms and would wreck any fleet that tried to anchor in the area. Seven miles down the coast, however, there is a picture-postcard island just off the Sinai shore known by the Arab name of Jezirat Fara'un ('Island of the Pharaohs'), now popularly called Coral Island. It is quite small, only about 350 metres by 150. It has three imposing granite hills, the highest surmounted by a conspicuous ruined castle dating from medieval times. On the shoreline right round the island, some 900 metres in length, are the remains of a substantial wall bolstered by square towers at regular intervals. Apart from these man-made features, the island has a small natural lagoon on its west side with an entrance facing the mainland which makes a perfect haven for boats in all weathers.

In 1956-7, Dr Beno Rothenberg of Tel Aviv University, who had been responsible for disproving Dr Glueck's interpretation of the site of Tell el-Kheleifeh, suggested the island of Jezirat Fara'un as a more likely contender for Biblical Ezion-geber, mainly on empirical grounds – he had noticed that it was the one place in the Gulf of Aqaba that ships always ran to for shelter when the south wind rose. Ten years later, his hypothesis was put to the test by an expedition from the Undersea Exploration Society of Israel led by Dr Elisha Linder (now head of the Department for the History of Maritime Civilisations at Haifa University) and architect Alexander Flinder, of the Council for Nautical Archaeology.

Three seasons of underwater exploration by the joint Anglo-Israeli group, from 1968 to 1970, proved inconclusive. They found no wrecks or artefacts or harbour installations that could be dated to the tenth century BC, the Solomonic period. However, Dr Linder remains convinced that further exploration and seabed excavation will confirm that the island had indeed been used as a maritime depot in Solomonic times. It is the sort of site that the Phoenicians favoured – an off-shore island, as at Tyre and elsewhere – which was not unacceptably far from the land-base at Eilat; nor would they have agreed to engage in a major maritime enterprise of this kind without the assurance of a safe anchorage for their fleet. Dr Rothenberg, too, remains confident that evidence will eventually be found; he thinks that the caravan trade that would have ensued from this enterprise helps to explain the constant quarrels between the kings of Judah and Edom reported in the Bible, for the overland trade route would have traversed Palestine either through Jerusalem via Kadesh-Barnea or up the King's Highway through Jordan – and control of the route would have brought lucrative results.

146

The sea routes jointly pioneered by Solomon and Hiram of Tyre from the new base at Ezion-geber would have given the Phoenicians direct access to the profitable markets of Africa and the Orient. And at this precise point in the Biblical narrative (*I Kings* 10) – 'When the Queen of Sheba heard of the fame of Solomon concerning the name of the Lord, she came to prove him with hard questions.' It was a journey that took her straight into the world of romantic legend and folklore, where she survives to this day in a dozen different versions and a dozen different tongues.

The Biblical account, on the face of it, is a factual account of a meeting between two exotic heads of state: the anonymous Queen of Sheba who travelled 2400 kilometres over rugged desert terrain with a caravan of camels laden with precious gifts, to satisfy her curiosity about the fabled wealth and wisdom of her fellow monarch in Jerusalem. Solomon satisfied her curiosity on both counts, answering all her 'hard questions' and dazzling her with the splendour of his court until 'there was no more spirit in her'. In an ecstasy of revelation, she blessed the god of Israel for his good sense in appointing such a peerless king, and then she heaped upon this royal paragon a cornucopia of gifts, four and a half tons of gold, spices and precious stones. Not to be outdone, Solomon

'And when the queen of Sheba heard of the fame of Solomon concerning the name of the Lord, she came to prove him with hard questions' (*I Kings* 10:1). Fifteenth-century Italian marriage salver.

returned the gifts with interest, plus 'all that she desired' as well, and the lady went back home.

Implicit in the wording of the account is a discreet undertone of mutual sexual attraction which is blatantly elaborated in other versions of the encounter. Where the Biblical redactors were content to emphasise the moral and theological superiority of Solomon the Magnificent, others stressed the romantic aspect of the meeting, and depicted the insatiable king as adding to his already formidable list of sexual conquests by seducing the virgin queen by underhand means and making her pregnant. In some versions of the tale she becomes the mother of Nebuchadnezzar of Babylon (which would presuppose a gestation period of at least 300 years); in others she gives birth to the progenitor of the royal dynasty of Ethiopia.

Can there possibly be any kernel of historical truth in this unlikely tale? The Biblical account was not written until at least five centuries after the alleged event, and the writer's motive is unequivocal: he was telling an exemplary tale to glorify Solomon.

The archaeological record is equally unequivocal: nothing has been found at any Solomonic site in Palestine to suggest the kind of ostentatious wealth attributed to Solomon's court. Indeed, the available archaeological evidence indicates a distinctly low material culture in Solomonic times. Even the celebrated gold trade with Ophir (wherever that was), which is attested on the ostracon found at Tell Qasile (see Chapter 6), has left no trace in the Palestine of Solomon's time – and it is worth remembering that the ostracon in question is dated to the eighth century, two centuries later. Everything about Solomon in the Bible sounds wildly exaggerated – his wisdom, his wealth, his wives, his concubines. Even where the building of the Temple is concerned, the same holds true. The Temple was a relatively small structure; yet it apparently required a work force of 30,000 men to hew the timber in Lebanon, 80,000 men to quarry the stone and 70,000 men to haul it home, and 3300 foremen to supervise the work (*I Kings* 5). There is no way in which these extravagant figures can be justified, except in terms of a later romanticisation of the importance of Solomon to Israel's image of its past and the significance of the Temple.

Similarly with Sheba, or Saba as it is called in other sources, which is equated with an area in south-western Arabia roughly equivalent to modern Yemen with its capital at Marib: archaeological expeditions since the Second World War have revealed traces of a sophisticated, wealthy and literate society, but only from periods *later* than the Solomonic period. Almost nothing has been unearthed yet from the Sheba of the tenth century BC, the time of the encounter with Solomon.

Biblical historians like Professor Abraham Malamat nevertheless tend to give the Solomon/Sheba story the benefit of the doubt because they find the political context so plausible: Sheba's economy had been endangered by the new Phoenician trade initiative that bypassed the traditional overland trade routes through Arabia, so Sheba's queen had no option but to travel to Jerusalem on a trade mission to ask Solomon some 'hard questions' – not wisdom riddles as some commentators assume but hard economic questions. For Dr Malamat, it was a matter of political affairs, not romantic *affaires*. But it remains an open question, and the enigmatic Queen of Sheba remains an enigma.

The wealth that is said to have impressed the Queen of Sheba so deeply was always assumed to have been based on Solomon's extensive copper-mining activities. As long ago as 1886, Rider Haggard gave a great boost to this notion with his popular romance *King Solomon's Mines* – although the Bible never explicitly mentions copper-mining as one of Solomon's enterprises.

Until recently, 'King Solomon's Mines' have been associated with some ancient mine-workings in the Timna Valley, some thirty kilometres north of the Gulf of Aqaba. It is a desolate area, searingly hot by day and piercingly cold by night. No one would choose to live there; but man has been

The central massif of Timna. In the foreground, the Nubian sandstone formation known to the tourist guides as 'King Solomon's Pillars' at the entrance to 'Solomon's Mines'.

drawn there intermittently for 6000 years in search of copper.

The area of the ancient mine-workings is superintended by two massive pillars of red sandstone, much scarred and eroded by wind and weather. The guide books dub them 'King Solomon's Pillars', but this has rather more to do with tourist fancy than strict scholarly accuracy. Solomon had nothing to do with the formation of the pillars; that has been the work of Nature, and Nature alone, over the past hundred million years or so. Nevertheless, some of the local guides will tell visitors without a blush that they were shaped by Solomon's slaves gouging into the sandstone cliffs in search of copper nodules.

Recent excavations, however, have proved conclusively

'King Solomon's Mines': prehistoric copper mines at the foot of the Timna cliffs.

that the mines were not in use during Solomon's reign; ironically, it was one of the periods over the past 6000 years when there was no mining activity at Timna at all.

The excavator of Timna is Dr Beno Rothenberg, who had been raised like so many others on Rider Haggard, and who went there in 1959 specifically in search of Solomon. Since then he has excavated a mass of ancient workings which prove that Timna was the largest mining enterprise that has yet been found anywhere in the ancient world, covering an area of sixty square kilometres, with twelve mining camps and at least 5000 tunnels and shafts.

The earliest workings date from c.4000 BC, the Chalcolithic period. After a long period of abandonment, mining

Hathor, the goddess of mining: exquisite faience mask found in the Temple of Hathor at Timna.

operations were restarted on an impressively intensive scale, with a much more sophisticated technology. But who had been responsible for the new Timna enterprise? The clue lay in some Egyptian inscriptions and drawings incised on the rock faces, which looked earlier than the Solomonic period; and the decisive proof came in 1969 with the discovery of a small Egyptian temple under the overhang of 'King Solomon's Pillars'. There Dr Rothenberg unearthed an astonishing hoard of nearly 11,000 votive objects dedicated to the Egyptian cow-eared goddess Hathor, the goddess of abundance and love, but specifically also the goddess of mining, who was represented amongst the finds by an exquisite faience face mask.

But what made the site archaeologically priceless was the presence of inscriptions and cartouches of successive Egyptian Pharaohs of the New Kingdom from Seti I (1308-04 BC) to Ramesses V (1160-56 BC). They gave Dr Rothenberg a means of dating the temple beyond dispute – and showed that the mine-workings had been abandoned two hundred years before the start of Solomon's reign.

This was the catalyst for understanding all the evidence at Timna. It showed that there had been a huge Egyptian royal mining project there from 1300 to 1150 BC, employing skilled metallurgists from Midian (Midianite pottery was found all over the site) and casual Bedouin labour, whose presence was attested by coarse Negev pottery – possibly the Amalekites of the Bible, traditional enemies of the Israelites.

After the Egyptians abandoned the mines during their decline in the twelfth century BC, the Midianites converted the temple into a shrine of their own for a while. The thousands of votive offerings to Hathor were unceremoniously shovelled into a corner. A few standing stones were installed – the *massēbōt* of the Bible. The temple was covered by a large tent, of which substantial traces were found in heaps along the walls. And in the makeshift Holy of Holies of the shrine, the excavators found only one object, perhaps the most intriguing object of all Timna – a tiny, beautifully moulded copper serpent with a gilded head, the ancient fertility symbol of the Middle East. It immediately called to mind the 'serpent of brass' of Moses (*Numbers* 21:9), which later became such an object of veneration.

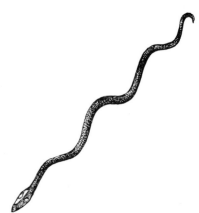

Timna: tiny copper serpent with a gilded head – an echo, perhaps of the 'serpent of brass' of Moses.

For Dr Rothenberg, this was evidence of a significant connection between the Midianites and the Israelite traditions about Moses and the Exodus. Moses had married the daughter of Jethro, the 'priest of Midian', and when Moses returned with the refugee Israelites, it was his father-in-law Jethro who led them in worship and sacrificed 'before Yahweh', and organised their judicial system in the desert (*Exodus* 18). The copper snake from Midianite Timna, and the traces of a tented shrine like a Tabernacle, suggest to Dr Rothenberg that future Biblical studies will have to take cognisance of the possibility that Israel's cultic worship may originally have been of Midianite origins.

Be that as it may, the Solomonic association with Timna has been totally discredited, and the Midianite association has taken its place. Perhaps if the tourist agencies want to give their brochures even a semblance of historical relevance, they should promptly rename 'King Solomon's Pillars' as 'The Pillars of Moses'.

The negative evidence of archaeology has so far tended to diminish the hyperbolic account of Solomon's achievements recorded in the *First Book of Kings* (1-11); but there is another aspect of his building activities which is briefly, almost casually, mentioned in the Bible, to the effect that he also built 'Hazor, and Megiddo, and Gezer' (*I Kings* 9:15), and here archaeology has something much more positive to say.

All three cities were always key strategic centres in ancient Palestine; all three had long histories before the Israelites arrived on the scene; all three have been carefully and extensively excavated. And from all three has come tangible evidence that can be interpreted as having a direct bearing on the Solomonic period and that terse reference in the Bible.

The story reads like a detective novel that could well be entitled 'The Case of the Solomonic Gates', with the redoubtable Professor Yadin cast in the role of an archaeological Hercule Poirot. It starts at Megiddo, in northern Palestine, which was excavated from 1925 to 1939 by a mammoth expedition from the Oriental Institute of the University of Chicago. The archaeologists found that Megiddo had enjoyed a heyday of prosperity in the second millennium BC which came to an abrupt end when it was destroyed by fire c.1100 BC and abandoned for a time; but in the tenth century it was rebuilt, and fortified by a stout solid wall pierced by a gate of distinctive design. It was a triple gate, in effect, with a square tower on each side of the entrance and three chambers set between four piers jutting out from either side of a long passageway, through which any assailants would have had to run a gauntlet of defenders in the guard-rooms to left and right – as well as breaking their way through four sets of doors. From pottery and other suggestive evidence, the excavators attributed the building of this triple gate to the Solomonic period.

Many years later, in 1955, Dr Yadin was excavating the site of Hazor (see Chapter 5) and trying to make sense of the twenty-one city levels through which he was digging. He found that some two centuries after the catastrophic destruction of c.1250 BC which he ascribed to Joshua and the Israelites, a tenth-century city, labelled Stratum X, came to occupy the site. This city had been fortified, not by a solid wall but by what is called a casemate wall – a double wall divided into chambers by right-angled partition walls. Following the line of this casemate wall, he came across the edge of a structure that looked familiar: it was a city gate of distinctive design that reminded him of Megiddo. So sure was he of his hunch that he traced out the plan of the Megiddo triple gate on the ground, and told his workmen exactly what they would find, and where. Sure enough, it turned out to be an identical 'Solomonic' triple gate.

Remembering that the Bible had mentioned that Solomon

had built the city of Gezer as well as Megiddo and Hazor, Dr Yadin now checked the excavation reports from Gezer. Gezer had been rather inexpertly dug between 1902 and 1909 by an enthusiastic young Irish archaeologist called R.A.S.Macalister. He excavated part of the fortifications and a section of the city gate, and came to the conclusion that it was what he called a 'Maccabean Castle' – that is to say, a fortification of the second century BC associated with the Maccabean nationalist rebellion and the last independent Jewish state (see Chapter 12). Dr Yadin studied Macalister's ground plan closely; although Macalister had only excavated part of one side of the gate, Dr Yadin was sure that he could detect the buried plan of a Solomonic triple gate, and published an article to say so. A few years later, an archaeological expedition from the Hebrew Union College of America set to work at Gezer and excavated there between 1965 and 1971. They quickly found that Yadin had been right: it was indeed a triple gate, providing access through a casemate wall.

Gezer: Yadin's extrapolation of the Solomonic gate and casemate wall that fresh excavation would reveal at Macalister's 'Maccabean Castle'.

But Dr Yadin was not yet satisfied. He was concerned about the fact that although Gezer and Hazor had had casemate walls, the excavators of Megiddo had apparently found a solid wall associated with the triple gate there. So he made a series of short exploratory digs at Megiddo, just to check – a series of post mortems in effect, in 1960, 1965, 1967 and 1971-2. Finally he was satisfied: he proved that the solid wall at Megiddo had in fact been erected on *top* of a casemate wall by a later builder. The archaeological features of the three important cities of Megiddo, Hazor and Gezer had thus been identical, and the Bible account had been vindicated.

Dr Yadin's bold conclusion that all three fortifications had been built by Solomon's engineers, working from the same blueprint, has not been accepted unquestioningly by all scholars; there are rumbling arguments about his interpretation of the evidence. But this is an occupational hazard for all archaeologists, and his vindication of the Biblical record has not been effectively challenged yet.

The Bible does not say whether Solomon's building activities at the three named cities were carried out by Phoenician experts from Tyre, like the Temple in Jerusalem. But ultimately the most significant contribution that Phoenicia made to Israel, and indeed the world as a whole, was the invention, or at least the development and diffusion, of our modern alphabetic script. The earliest known example of it is in the inscription carved along the lid of the decorated stone sarcophagus of King Ahiram of Byblos, around 1000 BC. It was a linear script of twenty-two letters, which the Phoenicians passed on to the Greeks and the Hebrews alike, and through them to us. It was an easy alphabet to master, as is shown by the celebrated Calendar found at Gezer, dating from the tenth century BC, a chip of soft limestone incised with a brief listing in Hebrew of the months of the year by the agricultural tasks associated with them. From that, it has been assumed that literacy became widespread in Palestine in the tenth century, particularly in court circles, and that it is to this period that we should look for the earliest palace archives and historical writings that underlie the Bible in the form we have it today.

Professor Malamat is in no doubt about it. He points to Biblical references to 'royal scribes' in the cabinets of both David and Solomon, and infers that they were employed to supervise government and temple archives that became the sources for later Biblical writers to draw upon. In his view, the accounts of the reigns of David and Solomon were based on contemporary annals. Indeed, the disappointingly brief account of Solomon's reign in the *First Book of Kings* (1-11) specifically refers to an unknown source-book: 'And the rest of the acts of Solomon, and all that he did, and his wisdom, are they not written in the book of the acts of Solomon?' (*I Kings* 11:41). Many scholars are convinced that the account of Solomon's accession to the throne is based on a lost 'Succession Document' that had summarised official court annals of the time.

Unfortunately, not a scrap of all this presumed official literature has survived; indeed, the Gezer Calendar is the only example of Hebrew writing from the time of Solomon that has yet been found. This possible objection to the theory is countered by the argument that all the court archives must have been written on papyrus, which is perishable, rather than clay tablets, and that the only writing likely to have survived are on fragments of pottery (ostraca) which were used only for messages and memoranda and the like.

Even more disconcerting is the fact that there is not a single contemporary reference to David or Solomon in the many neighbouring countries which certainly were keeping written records during the tenth century. At a time when the Bible tells us that Solomon created a major empire in the Middle East, none of his contemporaries, not even the Phoenicians, apparently noticed the fact. Without the Biblical accounts, history would be totally unaware of the very existence of the twin founders of the tenth-century expansion of Israel/Judah

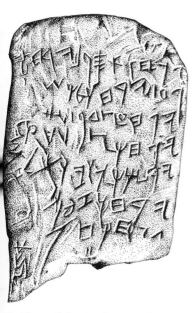

The Gezer Calendar: limestone fragment, probably a school exercise-tablet, with a mnemonic of the months of the year. Dating from the tenth century BC, it is the only known Hebrew inscription from the Solomonic age.

155

into a major power, and archaeology would have been able to do little to indicate that it had ever taken place. As far as archaeology is concerned, it was a paper (or papyrus) empire only.

Many radical scholars believe, on literary grounds, that the picture of the greatness of the period of the United Monarchy under David and Solomon was a late populist creation from the time of the Exile in the sixth century, transmuting whatever traditions or court annals may have existed into an image of cosmopolitan royal splendour (including a huge royal harem) modelled on the history of other major powers, like Egypt or Babylon. But Professor Malamat is sure that, despite the lack of material evidence and despite some manifest exaggerations, the Biblical picture is essentially an accurate one. He sees Solomon not as a 'hawk' or a 'dove' in terms of international politics, but as an octopus, stretching out his commercial and diplomatic tentacles in all directions. Jerusalem was the centre from which he exercised influence throughout the whole of the known world of the time; and this was only possible because of a temporary decline of the superpowers during the tenth century. To Dr Malamat, it is a measure of Solomon's greatness that he seized the opportunity of exploiting the relative weakness of his neighbours to create a commercial empire and fill the political vacuum.

We may never know the truth for certain. We simply know that the later Bible chroniclers who wrote up the reign of Solomon portrayed it as a Golden Age such as Jerusalem and Israel had never known before and would never know again. But behind the brilliant facade there were deep political and religious divisions that were undermining the semblance of national unity that Solomon and his father David had achieved. Although the southern kingdom of Judah had accepted the principle of a centralised monarchy, it seems that the northern kingdom of Israel had never become reconciled to the House of David, or to the loss of their tribal independence. In particular, they bitterly resented the penal taxation and forced labour that Solomon imposed on them in order to carry out his grandiose schemes. By the end of his reign, Solomon the Wise had become Solomon the Tyrant in many people's eyes. When he eventually died around 920 BC after forty years on the throne, this pent-up resentment boiled over, the United Monarchy fell apart, and the empire disintegrated. The Golden Age was well and truly over.

9
A House Divided

I have never quite known why a jumbo-sized bottle of champagne, a jeroboam, should be named after a king of Israel. It is named after King Jeroboam I, who is described in the Bible as 'a mighty man of valour' (*I Kings* 11:28) – and was therefore, conceivably, a mighty tippler as well. Whatever else he may have been, however, he is chiefly remembered in the Bible as the separatist leader who led Israel out of the union with Judah within months, even weeks, of Solomon's death around 920 BC.

The disruption happened at a place called Shechem, about forty kilometres north of Jerusalem in the eastern suburbs of the modern city of Nablus. Shechem was always a highly strategic centre throughout the history of Palestine, lying athwart the entrance to the narrow valley between Mount Ebal and Mount Gerizim where important trade routes from Egypt and Jerusalem converged. The site has been extensively excavated throughout this century, and today it presents a somewhat confusing but formidable picture of monumental walls and gates and ancient ruined temples, charting the turbulent history of Palestine in the second millennium BC.

It was always a significant cult centre in Hebrew tradition, too. It was at Shechem that the Patriarch Abraham was said to have stopped when he first arrived in Canaan, and where he 'builded an altar unto the Lord' (*Genesis* 12:6-7). And it was at the sacred temple precinct in the centre of the site, with its massive *massēbāh* (standing stone) re-erected by the excavators, that Joshua was said to have assembled the victorious tribes after his conquest of Canaan, and where he reaffirmed the covenant with Yahweh and set up a great stone 'under an oak, that was by the sanctuary of the Lord' (*Joshua* 24:26).

More to our present purpose, however, it was to that same temple precinct, the community centre of Shechem, that Solomon's successor, his son Rehoboam (after whom an even larger bottle of champagne is named), came to seek confirmation as king of Israel as well as of Judah. But the northerners, the Israelites proper, were in an unaccommodating mood. They demanded that the penal taxation of Solomon's latter years should be removed. The young Rehoboam, however, disregarding the counsel of his elders, threatened them instead with even heavier impositions: 'My father hath chastised you with whips,' he said, 'but I will chastise you with scorpions' (*I Kings* 12:11). Infuriated by this intransigence, the Israelites promptly repudiated the union and declared themselves a separate state with the immortal slogan, 'To your tents, O Israel!' They lynched the chief tax-collector, and sent Rehoboam scurrying back ignominiously in his chariot to the safety of Jerusalem. In his place they appointed as the first king of a separatist Israel that mighty man of valour, Jeroboam. But with Jeroboam and Rehoboam, alas, the champagne days of Solomonic splendour were over. It was the start of two hundred troubled years for the kingdom of Israel, which would end with its annihilation c.720 BC by the Assyrians (see Chapter 10).

Jeroboam fortified Shechem as the new capital of Israel; one can still see remains of the formidable gateway facing towards Judah. But the real enemy was not Judah, but Egypt. In 918 BC, the Egyptian army swept through Palestine under a resurgent new Pharaoh, Sheshonk I (Biblical 'Shishak'), the founder of the Twenty-second Dynasty, who no doubt scented easy pickings as the Solomonic union disintegrated. In the temple of Ammon at Karnak, Sheshonk's triumphal

Shechem: the re-erected standing stone in the sanctuary area of the ancient site. In the background, the modern suburbs of Nablus.

inscription depicts the Pharaoh smiting groups of cowering Semitic prisoners with a club, and records a list of the cities he ravaged. The Bible account of Sheshonk's campaign suggests that Jerusalem, and Jerusalem alone, was his target: 'And it came to pass in the fifth year of king Rehoboam, that Shishak king of Egypt came up against Jerusalem; and he took away the treasures of the house of the Lord...' (*I Kings* 14:25-6); but the Egyptian lists make it clear that both Judah and Israel were devastated by the blow.

In order to consolidate his position as king, Jeroboam realised that he would have to establish an official religious cult to rival that of Jerusalem: 'If this people go up to do sacrifice in the house of the Lord at Jerusalem, then shall the heart of this people turn again unto their lord, even unto Rehoboam king of Judah, and they shall kill me, and go again to Rehoboam king of Judah' (*I Kings* 12:27). And so, as a counterattraction to the Jerusalem Temple, he gave official royal status to two ancient cult sanctuaries at opposite ends of the realm, the one at Bethel near the southern border and only sixteen kilometres north of Jerusalem, and the other at Dan at the extreme northern edge of the country hard up against the present frontier with Lebanon (Phoenicia).

The Biblical city of Dan is generally identified with Tell Dan (Tell el-Qadi in Arabic), a large and lushly foliaged mound of some fifty acres at the foot of Mount Hermon. Since 1966 it has been under excavation by a team of Israeli archaeologists led by Professor Avraham Biran, Director of the Nelson Glueck School of Biblical Archaeology in Jerusalem. In ten seasons, Professor Biran has come across spectacular evidence of the religious revolution instituted by Jeroboam at Dan; and being a born optimist, he lives in hope that he will one day find something even more spectacular, in the shape of a golden calf! For the new religion that Jeroboam established at Dan and Bethel was a throwback to the early days of the Exodus: 'Whereupon the king took counsel, and made two calves of gold, and said unto [the people], It is too much for you to go up to Jerusalem: behold thy gods, O Israel, which brought thee up out of the land of Egypt. And he set the one in Bethel, and the other put he in Dan' (*I Kings* 12:28-9).

At the entrance to the site, Professor Biran has uncovered a massive gate complex consisting of two towers and four guard-rooms with a paved processional route leading through it and winding up the slope of the mound. Within the complex was a stone-paved square, with a limestone dais flanked by four decorated column bases that may have supported a canopy over a throne, and a long stone bench where the elders of the city may have sat in judgment – those 'that sit in the gate', in the words of Psalm 69:12. Professor Biran dates the gate complex to the end of the tenth century BC, and attributes its building to King Jeroboam I.

Higher up on the *tell* there is a copious spring whose waters feed the Dan River, one of the headwaters of the River Jordan. The fact that it was one of the sources of the Jordan must have given the place a special religious significance throughout antiquity, and Professor Biran found an ancient flight of hewn steps leading down towards the spring.

Near the spring, in the north-western part of the *tell*, Professor Biran has excavated an imposing structure of monumental masonry which he interprets as a High Place (*bāmāh*), forming a wide, flat platform that was the focal point of a paved open-air sanctuary. This, too, he believes, was the work of Jeroboam I, later enlarged by his successors. Nearby, in 1974, he found an Israelite horned altar, 35 centimetres high and 40 centimetres square, cut from a single block of limestone, its surface still scorched from the burning of incense. Horned altars are frequently mentioned in the Bible but only a very few have been found in Palestine; the four horns at the corners may have symbolised miniature stelae, and were considered the holiest part of the altar. Blood of the sacrifice was sprinkled on them, and any refugee who 'caught hold on the horns of the altar' obtained the right of asylum (*I Kings* 1:50).

The Bible writers never forgave Jeroboam for what he did. He is portrayed as one of the most evil of kings. But it must

Tell Dan: the horned altar in the process of excavation.

be remembered that the Bible was written by Jerusalem-orientated priests to whom Jeroboam, even posthumously, was both a rebel and a heretic, and the degree of their hostility to his memory is a measure of his success. Few scholars now believe that Jeroboam actually introduced idol worship; the golden calves were probably the equivalent of the cherubim in the Jerusalem Temple – providing a throne or pedestal for the invisible deity. But Jeroboam undoubtedly touched a deeply responsive chord in his people; 'deviant' cult practices seem to have been much more widespread than the Bible would have us believe.

The High Place at Dan was later greatly enlarged – one can see a new kind of masonry being used for this second stage, embossed stones characteristic of classical Israelite architecture. According to Professor Biran, this was the work of one of the greatest, yet most maligned, of the kings of Israel: Ahab, the son of Omri, and husband of that notorious Phoenician princess, Jezebel, the daughter of the King of Tyre.

It was under Omri (876-69 BC) and his son Ahab (869-50 BC) that the kingdom of Israel reached its peak of strength and political importance, although to read the prejudiced accounts in the Bible you would think that they had dragged Israel down to the lowest depths of degradation.

Omri was a military strong-man who was proclaimed king by the army after years of unstable rule. In his brief reign he restored firm government and stabilised his borders; he patched up relations with Jerusalem by marrying his daughter (or perhaps his granddaughter) Athaliah to the King of Judah, and he sealed an important commercial alliance with Phoenicia by arranging the marriage of his son Ahab to Jezebel. It was almost a return to the days of the United Monarchy.

Omri also has the distinction of being the first king of either Israel or Judah to be mentioned by name in the contemporary records of other states; and it came about directly because of his policy of gaining control of the caravan trade route along the King's Highway through Jordan. This involved subjugating the kingdom of Moab, east of the Dead Sea; and there is a reference to this fact in the famous Moabite Stela of King Mesha.

The Moabite Stela is a large slab of black basalt inscribed with an account of Mesha's struggle against Israel. It was found in 1868 by a Prussian missionary, the Reverend F.A.Klein, in the Arab village of Dhiban (Biblical Dibon),

The Moabite Stela: basalt slab recording the victory of King Mesha of Moab against the kings of Israel.

north of the River Arnon about halfway along the east side of the Dead Sea. It was subsequently smashed by the villagers, but the surviving fragments were collected and the restored stela is now in the Louvre in Paris. The text is (or was) thirty-four lines long, and was written around 830 BC to commemorate King Mesha's victory over the Israelites in his fight for freedom: '...As for Omri, king of Israel, he humbled Moab many years...And his son followed him and he also said "I will humble Moab". In my time he spoke thus, but I have triumphed over him and over his house, while Israel hath perished for ever!' (Translation from *Ancient Near Eastern Texts*.)

In the last year of his reign, Omri embarked on his most ambitious project: he built himself a new capital at a place called Samaria, ten kilometres north-west of Shechem. The site he purchased for two talents of silver (*I Kings* 16:24) was on a conspicuous hill, easily defensible and dominating the surrounding countryside. Here Omri, and after him his son Ahab, built a magnificent palace complex on the summit of the hill protected by a wall of carefully squared stone blocks, with massive fortifications surrounding the outer city farther down the slopes. The new capital of Israel gradually lent its name to the whole region, and its inhabitants would become known as Samaritans.

Samaria has been excavated on two occasions, latterly in the 1930s. It is an impressive site to visit, studded with imposing monuments from Roman times, including a colonnaded basilica and a fine amphitheatre. But it is on the summit of the site, where the excavators uncovered the solid remains of the Israelite royal palace, that we find ourselves transported vividly into the presence of King Ahab and his imperious consort, Jezebel.

Ivory sphinx from the king's palace at Samaria: an echo of Ahab's 'ivory house'.

Ahab and Jezebel were treated with ferocious severity by the Bible writers – so much so that Ahab's name is seldom quoted, and that of Jezebel has become synonymous with brazen immorality. The men of Jerusalem hated her for introducing from her native Tyre the worship of her Phoenician god, Baal; and they hated her husband for allowing her to do it. The great Solomon himself had allowed and even encouraged his countless foreign wives to practise their own pagan religions, but Solomon, of course, could do no wrong. Solomon was Jerusalem. Ahab and Jezebel, unfortunately for them, were Israel.

Jezebel had always seemed to me one of the most repellently fascinating characters in the Bible saga, a seductive

Ivory plaque from Samaria: Phoenician carving in Egyptian style from Ahab's palace.

blend of Delilah and Lady Macbeth. Yet when one walks the ancient corridors where Jezebel herself once trod, it is easy to feel much more in sympathy with her. I see her now as being rather beautiful and regal, bringing to the somewhat provincial court of Ahab a new Phoenician elegance and style and sophistication which was epitomised in the only achievement that the Bible grudgingly admits to Ahab's credit – the building of an 'ivory house' at Samaria (*I Kings* 22:39). Previously, this casual Biblical reference was thought to have been a fable – nobody actually builds houses out of ivory. But when the archaeologists started unearthing hundreds of fragments of carved ivory plaques on the site of Ahab's palace, it quickly became obvious that Ahab's 'ivory house' had not been a figment of someone's imagination.

The ivories from Samaria were Phoenician in style – another indication of the Phoenician Connection that Solomon and Omri had cultivated so assiduously, and of the growing affluence of Ahab's court. They were used as inlays for walls and furniture, and show a high standard of delicate workmanship. The decorative motifs are cosmopolitan and varied: elaborate floral arrangements, themes of Egyptian gods and animals, cherubim, sphinxes, human figures. Perhaps the most intriguing is the 'woman in the window' theme, for it reminds one irresistibly of the cruel fate that awaited Jezebel herself...

Recent excavations elsewhere have revealed that Ahab did not limit himself to beautifying his palace; he was a builder on a heroic scale, on a par with Solomon himself. His main construction projects were the rebuilding and refortification of two of Solomon's so-called 'chariot cities' – Hazor and Megiddo.

Megiddo, the ancient city site dominating the Plain of Jezreel, is the future site of Armageddon. In the appalling revelation of the Apocalypse which St John the Divine saw in a trance, the last battle on the Day of Judgment would be fought at 'a place called in the Hebrew tongue Armageddon' (*Revelation* 16:14-16); and Armageddon in the Hebrew tongue means 'Hill of Megiddo'. It has been called the most important archaeological site in all Palestine, and the fact that St John should fasten upon that particular name is a measure of its significance throughout history as a scene of fateful battles. The Egyptian Pharaoh Tuthmosis III had smashed a confederacy of Hyksos rulers there in the fifteenth century, and left us a detailed account in one of the earliest military histories that has survived (see Chapter 3). Sheshonk

Megiddo: model of the ancient city. Centre foreground, the main gate. The blocks of elongated buildings are the so-called 'Solomon's Stables'. Top right is the great shaft of the water system dug by Ahab's engineers.

I destroyed it again in 918 BC. Ahab now refortified it with massive solid walls which replaced the Solomonic casemate walls, and rebuilt the citadel and other ruined public buildings. He also erected three large complexes of long buildings that have become famous as 'Solomon's Stables'. They were all designed according to a single plan: a long central aisle with two parallel lines of columns on either side to support the roof, with what appeared to be limestone feeding-troughs between the columns. Some of the columns had a hole drilled through them, apparently to take a rope. If the buildings were stables, they could have accommodated 492 animals. Originally, this particular building level was ascribed to the time of Solomon, and it was assumed that they had been built by him to stable the chariot-horses which the Bible claims he kept in great numbers; but after Professor Yadin's re-excavation of Megiddo, they have been reassigned to the time of Ahab. However, the exotic label of 'Solomon's Stables' dies hard, and they are still labelled as such on the tourist route round the site. But were they stables at all? Some scholars now feel that they were more likely to have been ordinary store-houses, although Dr Yadin stoutly disputes this.

The most striking achievement of Ahab's engineers and builders, however, was the massive and complex water system they devised at the western side of the *tell*. The city's water supply came from a spring at the foot of the slope outside the city wall, which rendered it highly vulnerable in times of siege; the problem was how to bring the water safely into the city itself. Ahab's engineers solved it by sinking a deep vertical shaft just inside the walls down to the water level twenty-five metres below. The upper part of the shaft was driven through the debris of earlier occupation levels and lined with stone; the lower half was gouged out of the bedrock. Access was by steps hewn out of the side of the shaft. At the bottom of the shaft a horizontal tunnel about seventy metres long and three metres high was bored right through to the source of the water, the spring itself, passing underneath the city walls. The tunnel was bored simultaneously from both ends; and where the tunnelling gangs met, they had to make a correction of only about one metre to straighten out the course – a remarkable feat of engineering without sophisticated precision instruments.

Megiddo: map detail that emphasises its strategic importance on the *Via Maris*.

The source of the water was a comparatively small spring. Constant use of it for centuries beforehand by generations of Canaanites had deepened and enlarged it into an artificial cavern in the side of the *tell*. The entrance to this cavern seems to have been guarded by a sentry; certainly, a guard was on duty when Sheshonk's army attacked, for the burnt skeleton of a man was found just inside the entrance under the debris associated with the sack of the city in 918 BC. It was presumably the realisation of the vulnerability of the water supply that made Ahab undertake this massive project; and when he had completed the shaft and the tunnel he blocked off the old entrance with a wall of rock so massive that nobody could ever use it from the outside again.

After finishing the Megiddo water system, Ahab turned his attention to Hazor – and so did Dr Yadin. Yadin's work at Megiddo, where he had identified the Ahab level, made him sure that Ahab would not have left such a strategic city as Hazor without a safe water supply. So in 1968 he returned to Hazor with a somewhat sceptical squad of excavators. There was no surface indication of where a great water-shaft might have been sunk; it must have filled up to the brim with debris and become buried. But find it he did, by a combination of patience and shrewd intuition. It turned out to be as sophisticated an engineering project as the one at Megiddo. Today, the visitor who clambers down to the ancient water source deep below the surface of the *tell* can only wonder at the amazing skill and ingenuity of Ahab's engineers.

The Bible mentions neither of these feats. Its attention is focused almost exclusively on the paganism and apostasy from Yahwism of the court, with especial reference to Jezebel and her worship of Baal in the temple dedicated to him in Samaria. Dr James Pritchard points out that the entire Bible was edited in Jerusalem, which was a cultic centre. Samaria was a rival cult, and to the priests and prophets of Judah Jerusalem was the sole legitimate sanctuary of the Hebrews.

In the latter part of the reign of Ahab and Jezebel, opposition to their liberal religious policy was embodied, in the Biblical tradition, in the weird and alarming figure of the prophet Elijah, though I have always thought that the word 'prophet' was rather a misnomer for this particular class of declamatory sage. These early prophets did not look forward and foretell the future, they looked back with hindsight. They represented the primitive desert conscience of the Children of Israel. Often they went about in bands, uttering their oracular pronouncements in an ecstasy of singing and dancing, sometimes induced by drugs or alcohol. A lot of people thought they were mad. They claimed to be mediators in the service of Yahweh, stating his absolute will for the proper governance of state and society. Fiercely Yahwist to a man, fiercely critical of kings and commoners alike at the first hint of religious backsliding, they were not so much prophets as priestly magicians.

'The Woman at the Window': a favourite motif in Phoenician ivories, for romantics to associate with the story of Jezebel's death.

Elijah, erupting out of the desert in his goat's hair shirt and leather loincloth, is depicted as perpetually haunting the conscience of the king and court. He was the implacable enemy of Jezebel and her Phoenician religion. On one celebrated occasion, up on Mount Carmel, he challenged all the pagan priests of Baal from Jezebel's court to a great tournament of wizardry, a magic jousting to prove that Yahweh was a greater god than Baal. Baal lost the bout: he failed to make a sacrifice catch fire by magic. Yahweh duly obliged, however, and Elijah had the priests of Baal seized and done to death (*I Kings* 18).

Ahab died in battle in 850 BC, and soon afterwards Elijah himself died. But he did not just die, like other men: in a fitting end to his career, he disappeared in a puff of smoke – or rather, according to the Bible, he ascended to heaven in a whirlwind and a fiery chariot (*II Kings* 2). His hatred of Jezebel was perpetuated through his disciple and successor, Elisha. Two of Ahab's sons reigned briefly as kings of Israel, one after the other, but the real power behind the throne seems to have been the Queen Mother, Jezebel.

In the year 842, the religious opposition to her exploded in a military coup. Elisha sent word to the army commander, that furious charioteer Jehu, appointing him as king in the name of the Lord. It signalled the start of a palace revolution and purge of a ferocity unequalled in Biblical history. Jehu drove like the wind to Jezreel, where Jezebel was staying with her son King Jehoram of Israel and his cousin King Ahaziah of Judah. When the kings came out to parley, they were ruthlessly shot down by arrows.

Jezebel was waiting in her quarters upstairs. Proud and defiant, she had painted her face and groomed her hair – how ironic that in popular parlance this dignified gesture in the face of death should be scorned in the taunt of 'a painted Jezebel'. As Jehu approached in his chariot, she came to the window, so reminiscent of the ivory plaques that had adorned her palace in Samaria. Jehu ordered her attendant eunuchs to throw her out of the window, which they did, and Jehu trampled her body with his chariot (*II Kings* 9).

But that was just the start of it. The whole of the royal family and court of Israel was exterminated, root and stock, some seventy people in all. Then Jehu raced off to the capital, Samaria. He enticed all the chief priests and worshippers of Baal into their temple on the pretence that he was offering a great sacrifice there. He did, but not in the way they had expected. As soon as they were inside, he had them all butchered to a man, and the temple razed to the ground: 'Thus Jehu destroyed Baal out of Israel' (*II Kings* 10:28).

Jehu's usurpation inaugurated a period of perilous weakness for Israel that lasted for fifty years. The southern kingdom of Judah was also undergoing a period of weak and unstable government. In the eighth century, however, both kingdoms enjoyed a remarkable resurgence of power and prosperity under two extremely able and long-lived rulers – King Jeroboam II in Israel (786-46) and King Uzziah in Judah (783-42). The two states were at peace with one another, external enemies were quiescent for a while, and trade flowed.

This period of growth and expansion has been illustrated by recent archaeological discoveries in Jerusalem by Professor Nachman Avigad of the Hebrew University of Jerusalem. Since 1968 he has been excavating in the Jewish Quarter of what is called the Old City of Jerusalem, on the western ridge overlooking the Temple Mount. Large areas of this quarter were destroyed during the War of Independence in 1948; when the city was partitioned, the Jordanian author-

'And Ahab had seventy sons in Samaria. And Jehu wrote letters, and sent to Samaria, unto the rulers of Jezreel...And it came to pass, when the letter came to them, that they took the king's sons, and slew seventy persons, and put their heads in baskets, and sent him them to Jezreel' (*II Kings* 10:1-7). German eleventh-century Bible illumination.

ities did little rebuilding in the area, so after the two parts of Jerusalem were reunited as a result of the Six Day War in 1967, reconstruction work began with the clearance of the modern ruins in the formerly densely populated Jewish Quarter. Thus, for the first time, archaeologists were able to get at a part of the city over which scholarly argument had raged: when had Jerusalem started expanding out of the cramped confines of the city of David and Solomon on the ridge of the Ophel Hill and the Temple Mount?

It is not the sort of area that will ever become a showpiece archaeological site, for there is redevelopment taking place everywhere. The archaeologists have to dodge about, working all the year round just ahead of the bulldozers, excavating and recording what are in effect bomb-sites before new buildings are erected there. There is little to show for their efforts except a growing mass of careful documentation of what they found at the lowest occupation levels, although some of the more significant remains may eventually be incorporated into the basements of the new buildings on the site.

In her now classic excavations in Jerusalem in the 1960s (see Chapter 7), Dame Kathleen Kenyon had made some trial soundings on the western ridge wherever sites were available, but her limited soundings had produced no evidence of occupation before the time of Herod the Great in the first century BC, when it was well known that Jerusalem had been greatly expanded. Trial soundings, however, can be misleading. Israeli archaeologists claim that the only way to be certain is by digging large areas, rather than doing sample borings at random. When Professor Avigad started clearing building sites down to bedrock, he quickly found evidence that there had, indeed, been a settlement on the western ridge, under the present Jewish Quarter, and that it started in the eighth century BC. He found widespread traces of walls and floors, and a lot of Iron Age pottery. Amongst the debris he also found several pottery figurines, which can only be interpreted as fertility symbols – especially pillar-figurines of women holding their breasts. It seems that pagan cults or pagan thinking did not flourish exclusively in Israel during this period: Judah, too, had its backsliders.

The decisive find came in 1970, however, when Professor Avigad came across the foundations of a substantial city wall, some seven metres thick and still standing to a height of three metres. He was able to follow and expose this wall for a length of fifty metres; it ran north-south, roughly parallel to the line

The early wall of Jerusalem: angled section of the massive city wall foundations found by Professor Avigad in the Jewish Quarter of Jerusalem in 1970.

Jerusalem in the eighth century BC: the dotted lines represent the putative city walls, based on Professor Avigad's discovery of an angled section of the early wall (marked in heavy black).

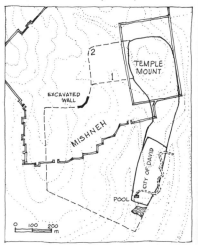

169

of the Temple Mount, and then curved outwards to the west. This wall is dated to the late eighth century BC, the time of King Hezekiah (see Chapter 10). From this, Professor Avigad concludes that during the reign of Uzziah a settlement started forming on the western ridge above the Temple Mount; it was an unwalled quarter at first, but was later included within the city limits when the new wall was built. In 1975, Professor Avigad came across another stretch of wall, of much later date, but which had incorporated a massive defensive tower still preserved to a height of seven metres, which had formed part of the eighth-century Israelite wall. Both of these crucial sections of wall have now been covered over again, to protect them, but will eventually become part of the permanent landscape of the Jewish Quarter.

Just how large an area this Hezekiah Wall, as we might call it, encompassed is still a matter of speculation and disagreement; but whatever the outcome of further excavations, it has at least been established that Jerusalem in the time of the Divided Monarchy (920-586 BC) was considerably larger than the pocket-handkerchief village it had previously been assumed to be.

Another indication of life, or rather death, in Jerusalem during this period is the unique monumental necropolis in the rock cliffs on the eastern wall of the Kidron Valley, in the area of the Arab Silwan village. The village is as densely packed as a colony of nesting sea-birds; the street winds up along ledges of rock, and in amongst the huddled houses are a number of handsome rock-cut burial chambers whose entrances are hewn in the vertical cliffs. Some of the tombs, indeed, have been converted into houses or store sheds by the villagers.

Rock tombs in Jerusalem have always been of particular interest to Christian scholars, of course, who have scoured the city looking for the Tomb of Jesus (and finding it, to their own satisfaction at least, in several different locations). The Silwan necropolis, however, should not be confused with that exercise in piety. It is situated right opposite the original City of David on Ophel Hill, the core of Biblical Jerusalem, and as such made a distinguished location for a cemetery for the Jerusalem nobility in the early days of the monarchy.

One of the leading authorities on these tombs is Gabriel Barkai of the Institute of Archaeology of Tel Aviv University, who has been taking part in a far-reaching survey of all the Iron Age tombs in Jerusalem. As a result of this study,

'Tomb of Pharaoh's Daughter': freestanding Iron Age tomb in Silwan Village in Jerusalem. The pyramid which originally surmounted the roof has been demolished.

scholars have been able to refine the dating of the Silwan tombs and key them more precisely into the historical framework of Jerusalem.

The tombs on the lowest levels, nine in number and not all of them finished, represent a time of foreign influence in the royal court, and Barkai attributes this to the presence of Queen Athaliah, Omri's daughter (or granddaughter), wife of King Jehoram (849-42). Like her sister-in-law (or mother) Jezebel, Athaliah was a Baal-worshipper and introduced the cult to Jerusalem. She usurped the throne after her husband's death, but according to the Biblical narrative she ran into the same sort of religious opposition as Jezebel did in Judah, and was done to death in 837 (*II Kings* 11:16). The fact that these tombs were in use for only a short time, occasionally unfinished, and designed in a foreign style, makes Barkai sure that they were made for Athaliah's Phoenician courtiers and friends.

At the northern end of the village are two famous monuments known familiarly as the 'Tomb of Pharaoh's Daughter' and the 'Tomb of the Royal Steward'. The former is the best preserved of all the tombs; once the cave had been made, the surrounding rock was cut away, leaving it a freestanding

171

The main street of Silwan Village: on the left-hand wall, low down, the entrance to a newly discovered tomb. The 'Tomb of the Royal Steward' is behind the staircase.

monolith. Inside, it has a gabled roof which is reminiscent of Egyptian architecture, and originally it was surmounted by a pyramid – hence the name. The inscription that had been incised above the entrance was defaced in Christian times by hermits who had a horror of 'magical' inscriptions.

The entrance of the 'Tomb of the Royal Steward' is on the main street of Silwan village. It had an inscription in archaic Hebrew above the door, which was removed and sent to the British Museum a hundred years ago. This inscription was eventually deciphered only a few years ago by Professor Avigad: 'This (is the burial) of ...-yahu who is over the house. There is no silver and gold here but (his bones) and the bones of his slave-wife with him. Cursed be the one who opens this tomb.' Inside the tomb, the dead were laid in stone troughs with a stone head-rest, and a shelf above for their grave-goods. The archaic script, and the royal title 'Who is over the house' (see *Isaiah* 22:15), both match the period of the Judean monarchy in the eighth century BC, and could well date from the time of King Uzziah, a time when Judah was more prosperous and cosmopolitan than usual.

One last echo of this resurgence of Judah in the eighth century BC has recently been detected in the ruins of a remote building in the northern Sinai desert at a place called Kuntilet Ajrud, some fifty kilometres south of Kadesh-Barnea. It stands on a small hillock overlooking the main caravan route from Kadesh-Barnea to Eilat on the Gulf of Aqaba, at a junction where a route branches west across the desert to Gaza. The presence of water in a series of wells below the hill made it a natural staging post for travellers.

In the winter and spring of 1975-6, this ruin was excavated by Dr Ze'ev Meshel of Tel Aviv University. It was a single, large rectangular structure, measuring twenty-five metres by fifteen, with an open courtyard in the centre, with large storerooms built against two of the outer walls. Originally Dr Meshel thought it was a Judean border fortress, but now he thinks it was a very special caravan station with important cultic associations; in the debris he found fragments of painted frescoes – and much more important, a great number of ancient votive inscriptions, some on pottery sherds, some on wall plaster, some on storage jars, some on stone vessels. The inscriptions have not all been deciphered or published yet; but the preliminary reports indicate that they were not only in Hebrew but also in Phoenician, and that they invoked the blessing of several gods, not just Yahweh but Baal and the Egyptian god Bes as well. It seems to have been the equivalent of a modern ecumenical wayside chapel.

From the pottery finds and other associated evidence, Dr Meshel has provisionally dated the building to a relatively short period in the first half of the eighth century BC. Now this is particularly interesting, because the Biblical narrative says specifically that King Uzziah (or Azariah as he is sometimes called) 'built Elath, and restored it to Judah' (*II Kings* 14:22). This can only be a reference to some refortification of Ezion-geber and a reopening of the Phoenician Connection, the Solomonic trade route from Eilat through Judah and Israel to Tyre. The presence of so many cosmopolitan inscriptions from Judah, Israel and Phoenicia at Kuntilet Ajrud certainly seems to support this interpretation. It is also clear that the revived Phoenician Connection did not last very long.

King Uzziah himself, according to the Bible, was stricken with leprosy towards the end of his reign, around 750 BC, and had to spend his last years in an isolated house outside the city. In the Russian church on the Mount of Olives, an inscribed stone slab was found which is now in the Israel Museum; the inscription reads: 'Hither were brought the bones of Uzziah king of Judah. Do not open.'

Under those able kings, Jeroboam II and Uzziah, Israel and Judah lived in peace with one another and flourished until the middle of the eighth century BC. But however vigorous or prosperous they might become, individually they were much too small ever to become major powers. It would only take the emergence of a super-power somewhere for their inherent vulnerability and disunity to be exposed – and that is precisely what happened. In the middle of the eighth century such a super-power would emerge, and within a few years the power vacuum in which Israel and Judah had been allowed to survive would come to an end. The kingdom of Israel would be erased from the map of history for ever, and the cities of Judah would be laid waste by the most violent and ruthless conquerors the Middle East had ever seen – the Assyrians.

Inscribed tomb plaque of King Uzziah.

174

10
The Wolf on the Fold

'Nineveh has perished. No trace of it remains. No one can say where once it existed.' Thus, nearly 2000 years ago, a traveller in the Roman world, one Lucian of Samosata in Syria, wrote the epitaph of an empire. The Nineveh of Sennacherib, Sennacherib the Terrible, from which he had descended on Judah 'like the wolf on the fold' in Byron's memorable phrase – Nineveh and all the might of the Assyrian empire that once made the whole Middle East tremble had vanished. The exultant declamation of the prophet Nahum seemed to have been fulfilled: 'Woe to the bloody city!...Nineveh is laid waste: who will bemoan her?' (*Nahum* 3:1-7).

And then in one spectacular decade in the middle of the nineteenth century, British and French excavators like Sir Austen Henry Layard and Paul Emile Botta rediscovered in northern Iraq the ancient remains of three Assyrian cities – Khorsabad, Nimrud and Nineveh – and evidence of the military panoply that had crushed all resistance from the Tigris to the Nile. The Assyrian empire (or the neo-Assyrian empire, as historians call it) in all its awesome power had been resurrected through archaeology.

These and later discoveries have done much to illuminate, and temper, the image of the Assyrians, those formidable empire-builders who were the first people to subjugate the whole of the Fertile Crescent from Mesopotamia to Egypt. But the shock of the impact on the Bible of their war-machine still remains, for it was the Assyrians who brought the kingdom of Israel to an end for ever, around 720 BC.

The importance of Assyriology to our particular line of inquiry is that as a result of these momentous discoveries, as Dr James Pritchard has pointed out, we have gained for the first time independent and contemporary historical sources that throw direct light on events related in the Bible; they give us the picture from the other side of the series of conflicts that ultimately decided the fate of Israel. At Nineveh and elsewhere, archaeologists have unearthed inscriptions that mention half a dozen kings in Palestine whose names were already familiar from the Bible – names like Omri, Ahab and Jehu, for instance. There are references to battles and campaigns which are *not* recorded in the Bible; but on the whole, where specific events are mentioned in both sources, the picture meshes rather well – although naturally the Assyrians tend to exaggerate their victories and the amount of tribute exacted, while the Bible tends to minimise them. Generally speaking, it is only in the neo-Assyrian period that the previously isolated and privileged 'history' of the Children of Israel is brought fully into the framework of the history of the Middle East.

As a bonus, Assyriology has also given us the first and only portrait of an Israelite king – and the first graphic impression of what it must have felt like to be on the receiving end of an Assyrian visitation.

The heartland of Assyria was always a surprisingly short stretch of the upper valley of the Tigris, from Nineveh (modern Mosul) south to Ashur – a distance of scarcely more than a hundred kilometres. Ashur was the first capital of the ancient kingdom of Assyria. It stood on a spur of hilly land on the western bank of the Tigris, nudging the river into a gentle curve of startling blue in the dun and dusty landscape. It was named after the god Ashur, chief god of the Assyrian pantheon, from whom the Assyrians in turn took their names. Although it was founded in the third millennium BC, during the supremacy of Sumer and Akkad, it was not until early in the second millennium that the first (or Old) Assyrian empire arose, when a king in Ashur briefly ruled the whole of northern Mesopotamia and titled himself 'Legitimate king, king of the world'.

But Ashur was ill-sited, strategically, to be the capital. It

lay on the southern fringe of the main concentration of population, and the land available for cultivation, even with the help of irrigation, was severely limited. But it had potent religious associations, so that even after the centre of power was moved farther north, Assyrian kings continued dutifully to

The site of Nineveh in the 1840s, where Layard started excavating there.

rebuild and embellish its temples. Today, after excavation by a German expedition in the early years of this century, it is still an impressive site, dominated by the stumpy ruin of its ancient mud-brick ziggurat.

There was a resurgence of Assyrian power in the fourteenth century BC – the so-called Middle Assyrian period – and for a time Assyria controlled the whole of northern Iraq. Then this empire was swamped by an invasion or infiltration of West Semitic nomads known as Aramaeans, who took over the whole countryside, leaving the Assyrian cities apparently islanded. The incomers spoke a West Semitic language, Aramaic, which was to become the *lingua franca* of the neo-Assyrian empire – and, incidentally, the language that Jesus would speak.

Round about 880 BC, forty years after the United Monarchy of David and Solomon had broken into the separate kingdoms of Israel and Judah, there came a decisive change in the fortunes of the Assyrians. A dynamic and aggressive king, Ashurnasirpal II (c.883-59), moved the capital from Ashur farther north to the city of Nimrud (Biblical Calah, Assyrian Kalhu), whose name was apparently related to Nimrod, that 'mighty hunter before the Lord' (*Genesis* 10:9), and also to the god Ninurta or Nimurta, whom Ashurnasirpal installed as the patron diety of his new capital. It lay some thirty kilometres south of Mosul. When Layard started to excavate the site in 1845, the Tigris flowed some three kilometres to the west, but in antiquity the river ran right past the city walls. It was excellently sited, with good agricultural land available and a ford across the Tigris that gave Nimrud command of an important trade route.

It was the start of ominous times for Israel. Throughout the tenth century Assyrian power had been at a low ebb, and David and Solomon had been able to enjoy their own little empires relatively unmolested by the super-powers in Egypt or Mesopotamia. Ashurnasirpal II changed all that. He spent the first five years building his capital, which he hanselled with a ten-day banquet for 69,574 guests – and then he swept westwards through upper Mesopotamia right across to the Mediterranean, where he 'washed his weapons in the sea', as he boasted in his inscriptions. He returned to Nimrud laden with tribute and treasure from the city-states he said he had crushed, and recorded his heroic exploits by decorating the state rooms of his palace with a series of magnificent carved bas-reliefs and huge stone statues of menacing creatures, now in the British Museum in London.

Ashurnasirpal II, king of Assyria (left), from Nimrud: it was Ashurnasirpal who moved the Assyrian capital to Nimrud.

177

Ashurnasirpal spared no detail of the ferocity and brutality with which he conducted his campaigns. Prisoners were hanged from poles or impaled on stakes at the walls of besieged cities as a grim warning to the defenders; young men and maidens were flayed alive. Victorian England, which had a curiously morbid fascination for horror stories, was both shocked and thrilled by the savagery depicted on Layard's sensational discoveries at Nimrud in the 1850s, and the image of the Assyrian 'reign of terror' was born. But how justified is their reputation for cruelty?

It is noticeable that in the Bible itself the Assyrians are not castigated for being abnormally cruel or barbarous – after all, Joshua had behaved just as mercilessly at the Lord's behest; prophets like Nahum were more concerned with their religious abominations. Nicholas Postgate, the young Director of the British Archaeological Expedition to Iraq in Baghdad, thinks there is no evidence to suggest that the Assyrians were more cruel in their methods of warfare than any of their contemporaries were; the difference is that the Assyrians thought fit to record their acts of cruelty in the goriest detail. Ashurnasirpal seems to have been particularly sadistic in his palace reliefs; but later Assyrian kings were comparatively merciful, executing only the ring-leaders of revolts. They preferred rather to deport dissident populations than massacre them, for sound practical and economic reasons. Postgate feels that the practice of recording scenes of cruel punishment in the royal state rooms was intended as a warning to potential trouble-makers. In effect, it was propaganda as much as anything else.

It was obvious to everyone that a formidable and ruthless power was rising in the east – and the warning did not go unheeded by the lesser states. Ashurnasirpal's campaign across Syria to the Lebanon did not directly affect the kingdom of Israel, where Omri had come to the throne for his brief reign (876-69 BC). But Ashurnasirpal's son and successor, Shalmaneser III (c.859-24 BC) had even wider ambitions. In the first year of his reign, he repeated the drive to the Mediterranean. In the sixth year (c.853) he did it again; this time he planned to drive south through Syria to Palestine – and this time, realising that they were in mortal danger, a number of kings of the smaller states sank their chronic differences and formed a coalition. Among them, according to Shalmaneser's own account (now in the British Museum), were King Ahab of Israel, and Ahab's arch-enemy, Ben-Hadad of Damascus, the greatest of the Aramaean kings. There is no mention of

Assyrian 'atrocities': prisoners being flayed alive outside the walls of a besieged city.

The Black Obelisk of Shalmaneser III: a record of the Assyrian king's conquests in twenty panels, with pictures and inscriptions on all four sides.

this episode in the Bible; but Ahab, according to Shalmaneser, contributed 2000 chariots and 10,000 foot-soldiers.

Battle was engaged at a place called Qarqar, in the valley of the River Orontes in northern Syria. In his inscription, Shalmaneser boasted of a great victory: 'They rose against me for a decisive battle...I slew 14,000 of their soldiers with the sword, descending upon them like Adad [Baal] when he makes a rainstorm pour down. I spread their corpses, filling the entire plain with their widely scattered soldiers...With their corpses I spanned the Orontes before there was a bridge.' (Translation from *Ancient Near Eastern Texts*.)

In spite of Shalmaneser's claims, he must at least have been checked, because the Assyrian forces withdrew for the time being. Israel was safe – but not for long. In 841, the year after Jehu had seized the throne following his bloody purge

The Black Obelisk: the panel shows King Jehu of Israel bowing in homage before Shalmaneser III, who holds a bowl in his raised hand. The inscription lists tribute of silver and golden objects.

of Jezebel and the House of Omri, Shalmaneser III raged through Syria again and into the northern reaches of Israel. His inscriptions say that he destroyed innumerable towns and exacted tribute from Tyre and Sidon – and 'Jehu, son of Omri' (i.e. of the House of Omri). The famous Black Obelisk of Shalmaneser III, now in the British Museum, depicts Jehu kneeling abjectly in homage before the Assyrian king and kissing the ground at his feet – the only known portrait we have of an Israelite king, albeit in rather humiliating circumstances.

On this occasion, Shalmaneser was content with taking tribute. He went back to Nimrud, and for the next hundred years the Assyrians were preoccupied with campaigns elsewhere and scarcely troubled Israel. But in the middle of the eighth century, the Assyrians came again, under the formidable king Tiglath-Pileser III (known as 'Pul' in the Bible).

Tiglath-Pileser came to the throne in 745, the year after the death of King Jeroboam II of Israel. Israel now plunged into anarchy in a succession of murderous palace coups.

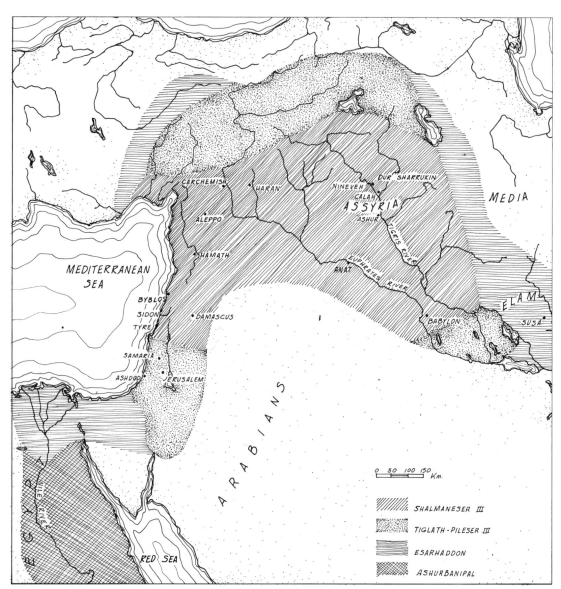

The growth of the neo-Assyrian empire, from the ninth century BC to the seventh.

Assyria, on the other hand, had just emerged victorious from a long struggle against rival powers, and now Tiglath-Pileser launched a new era of empire building; instead of merely collecting tribute from defeated states, he installed Assyrian governors. He is therefore counted as the true founder of the neo-Assyrian empire. Within a very few years he had extended Assyrian power over all Syria and the Lebanon, and was exacting tribute from Israel under King Menahem (745-38 BC). Menahem's son Pekahiah (738-37) was assassinated soon after he succeeded his father, and one of the army commanders, Pekah, seized the throne (737-32 BC). Tiglath-Pileser came again in 734 BC, pushing down

180

the Philistine coast as far as Gaza, which he garrisoned. Alarmed by this ominous flanking movement, Pekah formed an anti-Assyrian coalition of neighbouring states – Damascus, Ammon, Moab, Edom and some of the old Philistine city-states; but Judah, under King Ahaz (735-15 BC), refused to join the alliance. The allies responded by invading Judah from all sides, and laid siege to Jerusalem; whereupon, in despair, Ahaz appealed for help to the only power that could help him – Assyria. He sent messengers to Tiglath-Pileser with a huge gift of silver and gold taken from the Temple: 'I am thy servant and thy son: come up, and save me out of the hand of the king of Syria, and out of the hand of the king of Israel, which rise up against me' (*II Kings* 16:7).

Nothing loath, Tiglath-Pileser came sweeping down through Syria and burst into Israel. Both the Bible and his own inscriptions, and the archaeological record, confirm that he destroyed key fortified cities like Hazor and Megiddo. The capital, Samaria, was only spared because Pekah was assassinated and Tiglath-Pileser placed a vassal king, Hoshea ben Elah, on the throne. But the rest of Israel was overrun and organised into three Assyrian provinces, and large numbers of the inhabitants were deported to other parts of the Assyrian empire.

Because Judah had placed herself under Assyrian protection she was allowed to remain intact, at the price of a huge tribute that King Ahaz looted from the Temple and took to Tiglath-Pileser. But even now, Israel had not learned the lesson. As soon as Tiglath-Pileser died in 727 BC, King Hoshea (732-24 BC) attempted a revolt. Tiglath-Pileser's successor, his son Shalmaneser V (727-22 BC) responded by invading Israel in 724 BC. Hoshea appeared before him to make peace, but was taken captive. The city of Samaria, however, refused to yield, and Shalmaneser laid siege to it. For over two agonising years the city held out, and then in the autumn of 722-1 it fell. Shalmaneser died just before or just after Samaria was captured, and it was left to his successor, Sargon II (721-05), to boast of the success and its grim aftermath.

Sargon claimed that he deported 27,290 of the inhabitants. The Bible says that he 'carried Israel away into Assyria' (*II Kings* 17:6). It was the end of the northern kingdom of Israel. It was the end of the Israelites proper. The Lost Tribes went into the Assyrian melting-pot and disappeared from history. Samaria was reorganised as a new Assyrian province and repopulated with foreign deportees from Syria, Babylon and

Sargon II of Assyria: he completed the capture of Samaria and deported the inhabitants of Israel in 720 BC.

Arabia; out of this *mélange* evolved the Samaritans.

Wholesale deportation of this kind was central to Assyrian imperial policy, and had been so for centuries. Nicholas Postgate points out that there was nothing uniquely terrible about the fate of the Israelites; the Assyrians had always needed manpower in their homelands, to serve as farmers and labourers and soldiers, and had solved the problem by forced population recruitment. One result of this policy was that instead of ruling large areas through vassal kings of disparate and individual local kingdoms, the Assyrians found themselves assimilating the conquered lands into a homogeneous empire. The subject states, repopulated by foreigners, lost their independent entities and were incorporated into a single massive unit, without local identity or patriotism or cohesion. It was an entirely new conception of empire, and it helps to explain why it was that when the Assyrian capital eventually fell, the conquerors could simply take over the whole empire as a going concern.

Once again, Judah escaped the ultimate fate of deportation by acquiescing to Assyrian 'protection'. King Ahaz became to all intents and purposes a vassal king, having signed away his nation's freedom. Naturally, he was berated by the later Bible writers for apostasy, for recognising the gods of his masters in Assyria. His son, Hezekiah (715-687 BC), one of the most notable kings of Judah, played a much shrewder game. While maintaining a submissive posture towards the Assyrians, he set about building up the internal strength of the kingdom and the morale of the people. In particular, he launched a major religious reform, to sweep away the creeping paganism that had been tolerated in his father's reign and to strengthen the central Temple cult: 'And he did that which was right in the sight of the Lord... He removed the high places, and brake the images, and cut down the groves...' (*II Kings* 18:3-4).

A recent archaeological excavation has revealed what may be graphic evidence of Hezekiah's religious reforms at an important site in the south of Judah, the Biblical city of Beersheba. It was always a significant centre, capital of a highly sensitive border area at the edge of the Negev desert, and one of the frontier-markers of the Israelite occupation: 'From Dan to Beer-sheba.'

The ancient city is identified with Tell es-Seba, some five kilometres to the east of the modern city. It is an exceptionally impressive *tell*, massive and sandy brown, with an inviting oasis at the foot which houses the excavation quarters

The *tell* of Beer-sheba: massive three-dimensional archaeology. The three long store-houses or 'stables' are on the right of the picture. In the background, the extensive headquarters of the excavation team.

erected by the late Professor Yohanan Aharoni of Tel Aviv University when he started digging there in 1969.

In Biblical terms, communities have congregated there since Patriarchal times, just as the Bedouin nomads do to this day. Abraham was said to have dug a well and made a pact over water rights, and planted a sacred grove of tamarisk there (*Genesis* 21:25-33). His son Isaac dug wells there, too (*Genesis* 26:32-3).

On top of the *tell*, the royal fortress is being restored with specially made mud-bricks to give visitors an idea of what it was like in its heyday: it is an experiment in what can be called three-dimensional archaeology. Professor Aharoni died in 1976 before his work was complete, but it is being enthusiastically continued by his closest associates, including Professor Anson Rainey of Tel Aviv University and the American Institute of Holy Land Studies in Jerusalem. Beer-sheba is peculiarly suitable for this restoration project; when the Biblical city was destroyed by fire, the essential shape of the town plan was marvellously preserved under the collapsed mud-brick walls, and it was possible to gain a very exact idea of the layout of the city – its streets, its houses, its government quarters, its store-houses, its gates. One complete section of it, showing the distinctive circular street or ring-road that encircled the city just inside the walls, will eventually be permanently restored.

In many ways, it has turned out to be a highly controversial excavation. Near the gate, three big store-houses were uncovered which closely resemble the 'stables' at Megiddo – the same arrangement of aisles and 'stalls' and 'tethering-holes' in some of the pillars; but they were found to be full of storage jars and cooking pots. They were obviously the garrison's stores, and this has made the Aharoni men openly sceptical of Dr Yadin's identification of the Megiddo buildings as stables (see Chapter 9). Dr Rainey reckons that the central aisle with its stone mangers at either side were for the use of tethered donkeys while they were being unloaded. Dr Yadin retorts that they may well have been converted for use as storage at some later stage, but insists that they were originally built as stables. The argument continues.

But the most controversial find that was made in the store-house complex was a very large and impressive horned altar. It came to light in 1973, but it was not found whole. Its smoothed ashlar blocks had been dismantled and deliberately reused in a repaired section of the entrance of one of the store-houses; three of the four altar horns had been arranged one beside the other in the wall. When it was reassembled, the altar stood 157 centimetres high. The excavators assumed that the altar had stood in a temple which had been pulled down on the orders of Hezekiah, who wanted to centralise all worship at the Jerusalem Temple and therefore banned all local shrines.

But when was the altar dismantled? That depends on when the city of which the store-houses formed a part had been destroyed by fire. Aharoni was convinced that it was destroyed during the invasion of Judah by Sennacherib the Terrible in 701 BC, which we shall be dealing with shortly;

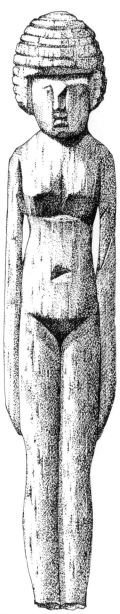

Beer-sheba: figurine of a goddess from the Israelite level.

Beer-sheba: the horned altar, after reconstruction.

Yadin, on the other hand, argues that it was destroyed during the Babylonian invasion in the following century (see Chapter 11), in which case the altar would have been buried in the wall during the reign of a second notable religious reformer, King Josiah (640-09 BC). It is a complex argument that depends on the dating of certain pottery styles and the sequence of town walls, and at present it is still unresolved.

From Judah's point of view, an Assyrian assault was always a fearful possibility during Hezekiah's reign. His religious reforms, powerfully supported by the most formidable of the classical Hebrew prophets, Isaiah, released a tide of nationalism that was nudging the country closer and closer to rebellion, although Isaiah railed repeatedly against the folly of such a suicidal policy. Sargon II of Assyria seemed content to leave Judah alone. He was occupied, among other things, with building himself a magnificent new capital at Khorsabad, a little to the east of Mosul. Deportees from Samaria worked on the building of the palace, we are told. The city was completed in 706 BC, and Sargon took up residence; in the following year, however, he was killed on a campaign in distant lands, and for some reason the capital was abandoned by his successor, Sennacherib (704-681 BC), who moved instead to nearby Nineveh. Nineveh is a huge site, just across the river from central Mosul; it had a

Beer-sheba: excavating the long storehouses. In the centre of picture, the central aisle, flanked by stones which scholars at Megiddo interpreted as tethering posts for stalled horses.

185

surrounding wall twelve kilometres long, with no fewer than fifteen gateways. Today it is being restored by the Iraqi authorities, to try to revive some of the glories of its past.

When a ruler died, revolts would break out all over the empire while the new ruler was struggling to establish himself. Now Hezekiah showed his hand, and joined in the insurrection, despite Isaiah's prophecies of doom. It took Sennacherib three years to consolidate his position in Mesopotamia, and then he struck.

> 'The Assyrian came down like the wolf on the fold
> And his cohorts were gleaming in purple and gold.'

The Bible puts it all in one bleak verse: 'Now in the fourteenth year of king Hezekiah did Sennacherib king of Assyria come up against all the fenced cities of Judah, and took them' (*II Kings* 18:13). Sennacherib's own annals are fuller: 'As to Hezekiah the Jew, he did not submit to my yoke, I laid siege to forty-six of his strong cities, walled forts and to countless small villages in their vicinity, and conquered by means of well-stamped ramps, and battering-rams brought near, attack by foot soldiers, mines, breeches as well as sapper work...Himself I made a prisoner in Jerusalem, his royal residence, like a bird in a cage.' (Translation from *Ancient Near Eastern Texts*.)

The crucial battle took place at the heavily fortified city of Lachish, one of the strategic centres in the plain of Shephelah in southern Palestine, halfway between Hebron and Ashkelon. For Sennacherib, the siege and sack of Lachish was the climax of the campaign; he chose it as the subject of a magnificent series of carved wall reliefs for the most important room in his palace at Nineveh. They were excavated by Layard, and are now handsomely displayed in the British Museum. They are quite extraordinarily vivid: we see all the well-stamped ramps, the battering-rams, the assaults by foot soldiers, executed captives hanging from the walls, defenders pleading for mercy, and finally the inhabitants being led off to slavery and exile. There, too, we see Sennacherib himself, sitting on his ivory throne and watching from a safe distance as the city goes up in flames. The accompanying inscription says: 'Sennacherib, king of the world, king of Assyria, sat upon an ivory throne and passed in review the booty from Lachish.' It is the most graphic war documentary ever found in the ancient world.

What makes it doubly valuable is that archaeological excavations at Lachish have revealed in vivid detail the ground

The Sennacherib prism: hexagonal clay column from Nineveh describing Sennacherib's victorious campaigns. It includes an account of the siege of Hezekiah in Jerusalem.

The siege of Lachish, from Nineveh: battering-rams supported by archers trundle up the siege-ramps.

plan of the city defences; and it matches in every detail the fortifications depicted by Sennacherib's war artist. We can stand where the great king sat on his throne, three hundred metres away, just out of bowshot – it is now the site of a turkey farm. We can stand at the point where the artist made his perspective, and see still the outline on the side of the *tell* of the earthen ramp that the Assyrians threw up against the walls.

The site, known as Tell ed-Duweir, was first excavated in the 1930s by the British archaeologist James L. Starkey, but that project came to an abrupt end when he was murdered in 1938 by armed bandits when he was on his way to Jerusalem. The excavations were not resumed until 1973, when Dr David Ussishkin of Tel Aviv University started a large-scale dig that will take many years to complete. A number of areas are being tackled, to achieve an overall picture of the many stages of the city's chequered history, and eventually it is

The siege of Lachish: Sennacherib on his ivory throne, watching the battle and receiving booty.

hoped that the site will become an archaeological laboratory and model showpiece. But the major archaeological interest at present is focused on the city gate complex, in order to identify beyond question the precise level of the city that was destroyed by Sennacherib. Starkey's excavation had left that point undecided, and much now depends on getting the sequence right; for if the level can be identified beyond any

The siege of Lachish: the inhabitants start the long trek to exile in Assyria.

question, it will give an absolute date to that style of fortification and the pottery associated with it, which can then be used to elucidate other sites with complete certainty. There is a final destruction level of the Biblical city which everyone agrees should be ascribed to the Babylonian invasion in 586 BC (see Chapter 11); underneath that, there are the remains of an even larger and mightier city, which was destroyed by a fire of such intensity that the mud-bricks of the city towers were baked as hard as cement. Was that the Sennacherib level? Or was it, as some scholars would like to believe, the result of some preliminary Babylonian campaign a few years before the final destruction? If so, there must be another destruction level underneath it, marking the Sennacherib roasting. So far, no sign of it has appeared, and it looks very much as if the question has been resolved. But it is so important for the dating sequences of other sites that Dr Ussishkin is not saying anything about it until he is absolutely sure beyond any possible doubt.

As Sennacherib was besieging Lachish, all Judah trembled; and those who could, and those who had no other option, fled to Jerusalem for safety.

This is the conclusion being drawn from the present excavations on Mount Zion that are being conducted by Dr Magen

Lachish (Tell ed-Duweir): excavation in progress at the gate area, showing the foundations of the typical Solomonic three-chambered gate, and the underground sewer curving sharply to run out of the gate.

Broshi, Curator of the Shrine of the Book at the Israel Museum. He has been digging in the courtyard of the Armenian Monastery at St Saviour, which was built around the house ascribed to the High Priest Caiaphas, just outside the Zion Gate of Jerusalem. Everywhere he has dug, he has come across remains of Israelite houses at bedrock level, dating to round 700 BC; he believes that about that time the population and size of Jerusalem trebled practically overnight, from a city of about fifty acres to a city of about 150 acres, spilling out beyond the confines of the old city walls into sprawling new suburbs. He thinks it can only be explained by sudden waves of refugees, first from the kingdom of Israel when it fell to the Assyrians in the 720s, and then from the provinces and cities of Judah that were annexed or smashed by the Assyrians. The old City of David could not accommodate such a massive influx without bursting at the seams.

These findings by Dr Broshi have greatly strengthened the arguments of the 'maximalists' (chiefly Israeli scholars) who believe that Jerusalem became a sizeable city during the Monarchy. It would also help to explain why King Hezekiah found it necessary to build a new and greatly expanded perimeter wall, as Professor Avigad suggests (see previous chapter). The Biblical accounts say that Hezekiah repaired and strengthened the city walls, mending breaches and erecting towers, and apparently adding an outer wall somewhere as well, and that he pulled down houses to provide materials for the fortifications (*Isaiah* 22:10). Certainly, if Hezekiah had a refugee problem to cope with as well, as the archaeological evidence suggests, it was the only prudent thing to do.

But that was not all, apparently. It was at this critical moment in the city's history, when the fate of Jerusalem hung in the balance, that Hezekiah is credited with carrying out his most spectacular engineering project – the construction of the celebrated Siloam Tunnel. A scatter of Biblical references imply that Hezekiah safeguarded the city's water supply by blocking up the old Gihon spring through which David's commandos had originally captured the city, and diverting the water-flow to a reservoir inside the city walls: 'He made a pool, and a conduit, and brought water into the city' (*II Kings* 20:20); 'This same Hezekiah also stopped the upper watercourse of Gihon, and brought it straight down to the west side of the city of David' (*II Chronicles* 32:30); 'Ye gathered together the waters of the lower pool...Ye made also a ditch between the two walls for the water of the old pool' (*Isaiah* 22:9-11).

Nearly 150 years ago, the American orientalist Edward Robinson noticed and explored a long underground tunnel leading from the Gihon spring, which has been associated with Hezekiah's waterworks ever since. It was about 530 metres long, quite narrow but above head height (except when choked with silt, as it was in Robinson's day), and it snaked in an exaggerated S-curve through the solid rock of the Ophel Hill before it reached an open pool – apparently the Pool of Siloam, with whose waters Jesus was said to have healed a blind man (*John* 9:1-12). It was a quite extraordinary piece of tunnelling: despite the waywardness of the line (which may, of course, have been following some geological fault in the rock), two gangs of tunnellers working from opposite ends managed to meet up, almost dead plumb. They commemorated their achievement by incising an inscription in classical Hebrew on the rock wall of the tunnel, which was accidentally spotted in 1888 by a truant Arab boy who slipped and fell as he was wading through the tunnel. The inscription, which was first stolen and then recovered and placed in the Istanbul Museum, had this to say (the first part seems to be missing): '...when the tunnel was driven through. And this was the way in which it was cut through:

The Siloam Tunnel: half-way along, the roof is well above head height.

The Siloam Tunnel: the Hebrew inscription at the point where the gangs of tunnellers met.

While...were still...axes, each man towards his fellow, and while there were still three cubits to be cut through, there was heard the voice of a man calling to his fellow, for there was an overlap in the rock on the right and on the left. And when the tunnel was driven through, the quarrymen hewed the rock, each man toward his fellow, axe against axe; and the water flowed from the spring towards the reservoir for 1200 cubits, and the height of the rock above the heads of the quarrymen was a hundred cubits.' (Translation from *Ancient Near Eastern Texts*.)

The only snag about this splendid inscription is that it was only about forty metres from the present outlet of the tunnel; and if it marked the precise spot where the two gangs of tunnellers met, it creates a problem, because it is nowhere near the centre point of the tunnel. The original tunnel must therefore have been considerably longer.

The rather unlovely pool of water at the present outlet is confidently marked in all the Guide Books as the 'Pool of Siloam', although it bears singularly little resemblance to 'cool Siloam's shady rill', in the words of the hymn. In fact, it certainly is not the original Siloam Pool; it was constructed in the fifth century AD.

Dr David Ussishkin has recently published a fresh study on the original length of the Siloam Tunnel; he concludes that the 'cubit' mentioned in the inscription was not the common cubit, but the longer 'royal' cubit of about 52.5 centimetres. This would mean that the original tunnel had been about 630 metres. Beyond the present pool, there is an escarpment which had been quarried away in antiquity, to expose a further length of tunnel; and by adding the lengths

of various ancillary tunnels further down the valley, Dr Ussishkin came up with the overall figure of about 640 metres for the original tunnel.

But if the original Siloam Pool was farther down the Kidron Valley, it creates an even greater problem; because then it would apparently have lain *outside* the city walls!

I have heard a rather ingenious suggestion from one scholar to the effect that the tunnel had nothing at all to do with the city's defensive preparations to meet an Assyrian siege – that was just a gloss put on it by later Biblical commentators based on popular legend. In actual fact it was a conduit designed to lead water from the Gihon spring to an ornamental pool in a royal park, or even a royal zoo, outside the walls of the City of David – the King's Garden which later

The present-day 'Siloam Pool', at the exit from the Tunnel. In fact it was constructed in the fifth century AD.

Opposite above The Lion of Babylon: monumental sculpture from the time of Nebuchadnezzar, depicting a lion standing on top of a man.

Opposite below Babylon: foundation buildings that may have provided the base for the fabled Hanging Gardens. One of these cellars contained the administrative archive relating to the exile of King Jehoiachin of Judah.

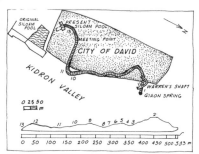

Plan of the Siloam Tunnel.

commentators referred to. It was an example of keeping up with the royal Jones's, for Sennacherib of Assyria had expended huge efforts to beautify his city and construct immense viaducts to lead water into it.

It is an entertaining notion, certainly; but most archaeologists in this field still tend to believe that the Pool of Siloam must have lain inside the city walls. No trace of the wall at this point has been found, and Dame Kathleen Kenyon, who excavated the area, is convinced that the wall was destroyed by the quarrying of the escarpment. However, the inexorable logic of the position inclines scholars like Dr Magen Broshi to assume that the walls must have lain farther down the valley, somewhere; all he can hope is that some day, somehow, they will be found by archaeology.

Whatever the truth of the matter, 'Hezekiah's Tunnel' was never put to the test. Sennacherib never laid siege to Jerusalem. Hezekiah, according to the Bible accounts, tried to bribe him off by a huge tribute of gold and silver which drained the Treasury and stripped the Temple of its remaining gold and silver. It failed to satisfy Sennacherib, who demanded unconditional surrender. Now urged on by Isaiah, Hezekiah refused to yield; and when Sennacherib left Lachish to deal with him, 'the angel of the Lord went out, and smote in the camp of the Assyrians 185,000: and when they arose early in the morning, behold, they were all dead corpses' (*II Kings* 19:35). So Sennacherib went home.

The reason for his departure as given in the Bible sounds suspiciously like a legend. Be that as it may, he returned to Nineveh and Jerusalem was saved. But the Assyrian grip on Palestine did not slacken. After Sennacherib's death (he was assassinated in 680 BC by two of his sons while at prayer in his temple at Nineveh), he was succeeded by a younger son, the dynamic Esarhaddon (680-69 BC). Esarhaddon was determined to extend the Assyrian empire further than it had ever reached before – and that meant the conquest of Egypt. In 671 BC, Esarhaddon realised his ambition, and Lower Egypt fell to the Assyrians.

As part of the build-up for his invasion he captured 'Arsa near the Brook of Egypt', according to his inscriptions. This Arsa, the ancient Canaanite city of Yurza that is mentioned in Egyptian sources, has been identified with the site of Tell Jemmeh, about ten kilometres south of Gaza on the southern bank of the Besor River, one of the frontier posts between Palestine and Egypt.

Tell Jemmeh has been under excavation since 1970 by an

Opposite 'Belshazzar the king made a great feast to a thousand of his lords...In the same hour came forth fingers of a man's hand, and wrote over against the candlestick upon the plaister of the wall of the king's palace...' (*Daniel* 5:1-5). *Belshazzar's Feast*, by the Victorian artist John Martin.

193

American expedition directed by Dr Gus Van Beek, Curator of Old World Archaeology at the Smithsonian Institution in Washington, which has revealed with startling clarity that in the first quarter of the seventh century BC it was an extremely important Assyrian military and administrative centre, a forward base for the conquest of Egypt. It is a splendid dig, and Dr Van Beek has been amply rewarded for his exemplary care; under fifteen metres of occupation debris he has found a major building of at least six rooms, with mud-brick barrel vaulting still in position in four of the rooms.

This architectural technique had been discovered earlier in archaeological sites in Assyria, but it is a unique find in Israel, and despite its fragility, Dr Van Beek has managed to save it for permanent conservation on site. The chambers probably formed a cellarage of the military governor's residence, for in the rooms he found copious quantities of delicate off-white Assyrian Palace Ware, as it is called – a palace dinner service in effect, the kind of plates that were used on the royal tables of Nineveh and Nimrud. Tell Jemmeh must have housed an army commander of the very highest rank.

At this point in history, the power of the neo-Assyrian empire was at its zenith: a massive empire stretching all the way from Mesopotamia to Egypt, hated and feared by its subject peoples. The state of Israel had been obliterated. The state of Judah had been filleted, its provinces under Assyrian rule, its kings vassals to the Assyrian throne. Assyrian gods once again shared pride of place with Yahweh in the Jerusalem Temple.

And yet, within a mere fifty years, that seemingly invincible Assyrian empire would collapse and vanish almost overnight. Judah would find a brief respite of independence. But the new super-power that would destroy Assyria, the neo-Babylonian empire, would bring yet more terrible disasters on the Children of Israel than even the Assyrians had managed to inflict – the destruction of Jerusalem and its Temple, and the years of exile by the rivers of Babylon.

11
By the Rivers of Babylon

'By the rivers of Babylon, there we sat down, yea, we wept, when we remembered Zion. We hanged our harps upon the willows in the midst thereof. For there they that carried us away captive required of us a song; and they that wasted us required of us mirth, saying, Sing us one of the songs of Zion' (*Psalms* 137:1-3).

I have always found that one of the most affecting of all the Psalms: the image of a people in exile, forced by their captors to sing cheerful songs of their homeland, but all the while in tears as they remembered the Jerusalem they had lost. Not that Jerusalem with its cramped quarters and narrow alleyways compared in any way with the dazzling opulence of Babylon in the sixth century BC. Babylon at this time was the greatest and most magnificent metropolis in the world. But that, too, was something which the Hebrew scribes could never forgive or forget, and Babylon in their eyes was transformed into a byword for luxury and voluptuous vice: 'Babylon the Great, the mother of harlots and abominations of the earth,' as St John would condemn it in his *Revelation*.

The impact of the Babylonian Exile on the Hebrews, brief though it was – less than half a century, in fact, from 586 to 538 BC – probably had a more traumatic and decisive effect on Judaism than any other event in the history of its people. For it was by the rivers of Babylon that they were forced to come to terms with certain harsh realities about their status as a 'Chosen People' with a privileged relationship with God. It was there that a new philosophy and theology had to be hammered out, there that a new understanding of their place in history had to be reached; for it was by the rivers of Babylon that much of the Bible seems to have been written or at least inspired.

Babylon and Babylonia had already had a much longer and more eventful history than the Children of Israel who arrived there in despair in 586 BC. Ancient Babylon lies near the town of Hilla, some 115 kilometres south of Baghdad in Iraq, in the middle reaches of the Euphrates river. In earliest times, during the heyday of Sumer and Akkad in the fourth and third millennia BC, Babylon was an undistinguished village nestling on the east bank of the Euphrates. It remained a place of no importance until the start of the second millennium BC when, after the collapse of the Third Dynasty of Ur (see Chapter 2), northern Mesopotamia was overrun by Semitic invaders from the west, from Amurru (Biblical Amorites); these newcomers established their capital at Babylon. Under a succession of war-lords, Babylon tried to make its presence felt by its neighbouring city-states, but it was not until the sixth king in this new dynasty, Hammurabi (c.1750 BC, or perhaps a little later), that Babylon was able to bring the whole of Mesopotamia under its rule. This was the real start of the Old Babylonian empire.

Under Hammurabi, Babylon enjoyed a remarkable flowering of culture and prosperity. Strong central administration was vested in the temple cult under the tutelage of the city god, Marduk (the equivalent of Baal, the storm god). Literature and all forms of learning flourished as never before – astronomy, mathematics, algebra, astrology, magic. From this period came the Babylonian versions of ancient mythological epics like the Creation and the Flood. But perhaps the most significant achievement of his reign, and certainly the most celebrated, was Hammurabi's Law Code, which he evidently promulgated early in his reign. The original has survived on a great slab of black diorite stone, over two metres high, inscribed front and back with thirty-four horizontal columns of cuneiform script. The stela had been carried off from Babylon as a trophy of war by raiders in the days of its decline, and was unearthed in three large fragments at the ancient site of Susa (Biblical Shushan) in Iran by the French archaeologist Jacques de Morgan in 1902; it is now in the Louvre in Paris.

A sculpture at the top of the stela depicts Hammurabi receiving his commission as a law-giver from the sun god Shamash, the great god of justice; this is precisely how the later Bible writers would visualise Moses receiving the tablets of law from Yahweh on Mount Sinai. It is not the earliest law code known to us, nor was it new and revolutionary; it was a fresh formulation of traditions of law and justice reaching far back into the third millennium. Three earlier law codes with many similar laws to those of Hammurabi have been discovered in the last thirty years, of which that of Ur-Nammu, the founder of the Third Dynasty of Ur (see Chapter 2), is the earliest in date.

Hammurabi's Code contains more than 250 laws, sandwiched between a lengthy prologue and epilogue, dealing

Hammurabi of Babylon: the king is on the left, receiving his commission as a law-giver from the sun-god Shamash. Detail from the Hammurabi Law Code from Susa.

with a broad variety of subjects of social and ethical importance: the administration of justice, false testimony, commercial transactions, offences against property, offences against the person, security of tenure, feudal obligations, marriage, adultery, incest, divorce, murder, inheritance, slander, wages, slavery. What excited Biblical scholars most keenly when the Law Code was first translated was the parallelism with some of the laws of Moses. There are many resemblances, and many differences too, and scholars have debated endlessly the question of the extent to which Mosaic law was influenced or shaped by the legal tenets found in the ancient Mesopotamian law codes such as that of Hammurabi; but perhaps the most vivid parallel is echoed in the Biblical phrase of 'an eye for an eye'. Hammurabi wrote (*Laws* 196, 197): 'If a seignior has destroyed the eye of a member of the aristocracy, they shall destroy his eye. If he has broken a seignior's bone, they shall break his bone.' The thunderous Mosaic law of *lex talionis*, the law of retaliation, seems to be based directly upon this concept: 'Life shall go for life, eye for eye, tooth for tooth, hand for hand, foot for foot' (*Deuteronomy* 19:21).

It was also in the time of Hammurabi that Babylon got its first ziggurat, or stepped tower, in the southern part of Hammurabi's city. Practically nothing of that city remains for the archaeologist's spade, because the water-table has risen in the intervening centuries and limited the chances of deep excavation. And not much remains of the ziggurat, either. It was destroyed more than once, and rebuilt and restored more than once by later kings – the latest attempt was by Alexander the Great, who found the task too great even for a man of his boundless energy and resources. Today, only a low rectangular stump remains, islanded by an artificial ditch.

The Babylonians called it Etemenanki, the 'House of the Foundations of Heaven and Earth'. It had originally been a huge construction, one hundred metres square at the base, rising to a height of about a hundred metres in seven great stages, with a chapel on the summit; it was a cosmic mountain, in effect, with a rest-house on top for the deity, the paramount city god, Marduk. And it was the ziggurat at Babylon, it is believed, that lay behind the fable in *Genesis* of the Tower of Babel that was built by the descendants of Noah: 'And the whole earth was of one language, and of one speech...And they said, Go to, let us build us a city and a tower, whose top may reach unto heaven; and let us make us a name, lest we be scattered abroad upon the face of the whole earth…And the Lord said, Behold, the people is one, and they have all one language; and this they begin to do: and now nothing will be restrained from them, which they have imagined to do. Go to, let us go down, and there confound their language, that they may not understand one another's speech. So the Lord scattered them abroad from thence upon the face of all the earth: and they left off to build the city. Therefore is the name of it called Babel; because the Lord did there confound the language of all the earth: and from thence did the Lord scatter them abroad upon the face of all the earth' (*Genesis* 11:1-9).

It is a very curious story, because there seem to be two quite distinct stories blended together in it. The word 'Babel' simply means 'Gate of God' – Bab-El – and at one level the story

'And they said one to another, Go to, let us make brick, and burn them throughly. And they had brick for stone, and slime had they for mortar. And they said, Go to, let us build us a city and a tower, whose top may reach unto heaven...' (*Genesis II*:3-4). The Tower of Babel from a French Book of Hours of 1423.

198

is clearly an aetiological one, to explain the presence in Mesopotamian cities of these strange ziggurat structures which were alien to Palestine: people built them simply to try to reach the heights of heaven. God had thereupon punished the builders for their presumptuousness by scatter-mankind all over the face of the earth. The other part of the story is an attempt to explain the confusion of languages in the world, and it seems oddly unrelated to the Babel story, except that the Hebrew word for 'confusion' is *balal*. Curiously enough, in the Old Babylonian myth about the Flood the reason why the gods sent the universal deluge was said to be because they grew tired of all the noise that mankind was making – an intriguing adumbration of the Babel story in the Bible. But there is another intriguing aspect of the story that should be borne in mind when we discuss the question of where and when the Bible was written, and that is: why, out of all the ziggurats in Mesopotamia, did the redactors or compilers of *Genesis* choose this particular one, the ziggurat at Babylon, to illustrate the fable? Could it be because the inspiration for *Genesis* and the other books of the Pentateuch came during the Babylonian Exile?

It is tempting to think so, if only because between the Hammurabi period and the Babylonian Exile, Babylon itself meant little on the world stage. The Old Babylonian empire went into decline after Hammurabi's death (perhaps around 1700 BC), and collapsed around 1530 BC when Babylon was sacked by a far-ranging army of Hittites from Anatolia. For nearly a thousand years it lay under the heel of more powerful neighbours, particularly Assyria. There were fitful attempts to reassert Babylonian independence; but after a series of insurrections against Sargon II of Assyria and his son Sennacherib at the end of the eighth century BC, Babylon was savagely destroyed by Sennacherib in 689 BC: 'I hit it harder than a flood,' he boasted in his inscriptions, having butchered its inhabitants and levelled its temples. The city and its great Temple of Marduk were restored by Sennacherib's successors, the energetic Esarhaddon and Ashurbanipal (668-627 BC), and by the middle of the seventh century BC, Babylon began to emerge as a growing power in its own right.

Ashurbanipal turned out to be the last great king of the neo-Assyrian empire. With the conquest of Egypt, Assyria's resources were stretched to the limit; overstretched, in fact. Ashurbanipal just managed to hold most of his empire together during his long reign by dint of relentless campaigning against enemies on his borders; but as soon as he died,

Ashurbanipal, king of Assyria: a stone stela from Babylon, showing the king ceremonially starting work on the rebuilding of a temple.

the massive edifice began to totter and crumble.

As Assyrian control weakened, the kingdom of Judah regained its independence, almost by default. The king of Judah at this time was Josiah (640-609 BC), fondly remembered in the Bible as a notable religious reformer in the mould of his great-grandfather Hezekiah. His reign ushered in a last interlude of greatness before the end of the kingdom; there are indications that he even managed to extend some sort of

The Holy of Holies from the Israelite temple at Arad, with two incense altars flanking the steps: it has been reassembled in the Israel Museum in Jerusalem.

sway over the Assyrian province of Samaria, the rump of the old kingdom of Israel. Material evidence of Josiah's religious reforms has been claimed at the Biblical citadel of Arad, in southern Judah, about thirty kilometres north-east of Beer-sheba and guarding the main route towards Edom. It was excavated by Professor Yohanan Aharoni in the 1960s. In the north-western corner of the citadel he uncovered what he interpreted as a large Israelite temple – the earliest Israelite temple yet discovered by archaeology. It was built during the Solomonic period in the tenth century BC, and was clearly a place of considerable importance, for it took up a large pro-portion of space in the compact, heavily fortified citadel.

Many of the features of the sanctuary were reminiscent of the Jerusalem Temple. The Holy of Holies, to the west, was approached by three steps, on which stood two stone incense altars; inside, there was a paved platform (*bāmāh*) and a standing stone (*massēbāh*) about one metre high and painted red. In the courtyard there was a large altar for burnt offer-ings, built of earth and unhewn stone, measuring about 2.5 metres square. This temple was deliberately built over, late in the seventh century, during the final phase of Israelite occupation on the citadel; a heavy wall was laid right through the main room of the temple, and this has been interpreted as an example of the way in which provincial shrines and cultic centres were closed down on Josiah's orders, and worship confined exclusively to the Jerusalem Temple.

Ostracon from Arad: this letter contains a reference to the temple as the 'House of God'.

Some two hundred ostraca (inscribed pottery fragments) from different periods from the tenth century to the seventh were found on this site; and one of the latest is an urgent mil-itary instruction that reflects the anxieties of the time. The Edomites, traditional southern enemies of Judah, were on the move, prowling the frontiers, waiting to pounce if Judah went under. The writer of the letter smelled danger in the air: 'Behold, I have sent to warn you today: get the men to Elisha at Ramoth-Negeb, lest anything should happen to the town, lest Edom should come thither.'

As it happened, Judah's freedom was soon to be snuffed out in the battle of the super-powers as the Assyrian empire went into its death-throes. In 626 BC Babylonia revolted and resumed its independence, while on the eastern borders of the empire a formidable new enemy was massing, the Medes in Iran. In 614 BC, the Medes stormed the ancient Assyrian capital of Ashur, and together the Medes and the Babylonians advanced north up the Tigris against Nineveh. In 612 BC Nineveh fell and was utterly destroyed, and the subject peoples rejoiced. Within three years the last remnants of opposition had been wiped out, and Assyria was finished for ever. Tragedy struck Judah in that year of 609 BC, too, when King Josiah tried to stop an Egyptian army marching north through Palestine to the aid of the last beleaguered Assyrians. He met the Egyptians at Megiddo, scene of so many fateful battles, but was defeated and killed. It was the end of Judah's independence.

In 604 BC King Nabopolassar of Babylon, the founder of the neo-Babylonian empire, was succeeded on the throne by his celebrated son, Nebuchadnezzar – or Nebuchadrezzar, to give him his correct name according to the latest scholarly fashion. Nebuchadnezzar was an outstanding warrior, scion of a new Semitic dynasty in Mesopotamia called the Chaldaeans (hence the Biblical name for 'Ur of the Chaldees'), and he quickly drove the occupying Egyptian forces out of Syria. Then he set about beautifying Babylon to make it the most magnificent city in the world.

Nebuchadnezzar's city was very large, covering an area of about a square mile. Originally the Euphrates ran through the centre of it, but the river has shifted westwards since then and now skirts the ruins of the city. The site was extensively excavated from 1899 to 1917 by a German expedition from the Deutsche Orient Gesellschaft led by the architect Robert Koldewey, and various areas were cleared. To this day, however, ancient Babylon looks for all the world like a bomb-site, a chaos of mounds and ruins studded with occasional showpiece monuments; but the Iraqi authorities have now embarked on a long-term programme of restoration which should pay rich dividends for visitors in the years to come.

Nebuchadnezzar laid out broad thoroughfares and avenues paved with bricks and bitumen and lined with imposing buildings. Most impressive of all was the great Processional Way which passed through the Ishtar Gate with its two pairs of towers faced with alternate rows of bulls and dragons in brick relief against a background of blue glazed enamel. This gate was dismantled by Koldewey and re-erected in Berlin, but at Babylon one can still admire the lower stages of the gateway which have since been excavated and left *in situ*.

The Hanging Gardens of Babylon, one of the Seven Wonders of the ancient world, were also Nebuchadnezzar's doing – allegedly in order to help his mountain-bred wife to feel more at home in the city. Near the Ishtar Gate, Koldewey excavated a curious and complex structure that was clearly a series of basement or foundation cellars; and he interpreted it as the vaulting for the sub-structure of the Hanging Gardens, for which a well at the bottom provided irrigation. No one is quite sure how the Hanging Gardens were constructed, whether on built-up verandahs or on a miniature ziggurat to give an impression of suspended foliage; but whether or not these were their foundations, a much more certain and significant historical find was made amongst the ruins by the German excavators. It was a small administrative archive lying in one of the basements, dating from the time of Nebuchadnezzar. There were only about two hundred tablets in all; but four of them referred directly to the rations of grain and high-quality sesame oil supplied to one Jehoiachin, the king of Judah: 'Ten sila of oil [about eight litres] to Jehoiachin, King of the land of Judah. Two and a half sila of oil to the sons of the King of Judah. Four sila to eight men from Judah,' and so on.

Suddenly we are back in the Bible saga, because we know from the Biblical account, supplemented by contemporary Babylonian sources, that in the year 597 BC Nebuchadnezzar made a token assault on Judah, a lazy flick of the lion's paw, during which he removed the young king, Jehoiachin, from Jerusalem and carried him off captive to Babylon, together with 'his mother, and his servants, and his princes, and his officers...and all the mighty men of valour, even ten thousand captives, and all the craftsmen and smiths' (*II Kings* 24:12-14). Those clay requisition slips from the quartermaster's stores were direct confirmation of his exile in the palace of Nebuchadnezzar, an exile that would last forty-seven years.

This was the first deportation from Judah. But it was only a foretaste. Ten years later, irritated by continuing intransigence and rebelliousness in Judah, Nebuchadnezzar moved again – and this time he moved in earnest.

In Jerusalem the king whom Nebuchadnezzar had placed on the throne as his puppet, Jehoiachin's uncle Zedekiah, had been finding vassalage irksome. On one side his nationalistic courtiers urged rebellion; but on the other side stood the gaunt and dramatic figure of the prophet Jeremiah, preaching doom and damnation and the righteous wrath of God, and warning that any resistance against the Babylonians was tantamount to rebellion against God's will. The Babylonian yoke, said Jeremiah, had been placed on Judah by God as a punishment for sin – and he went about Jerusalem wearing a yoke to prove his point.

But Zedekiah did rebel; and the Babylonian army marched. Nebuchadnezzar's strategy was to blockade Jerusalem and then pick off the other fortified cities of Judah one by one, leaving Jerusalem to the last. One by one they fell, until only two were left – Lachish and Azekah, eleven kilometres to the north-east; and from Lachish has come vivid written evidence of the mood of the times, the mood of Jeremiah one might say, as the Babylonian army raged through Judah.

In 1935, James Starkey, the excavator of Lachish (see Chapter 10), discovered in the debris of a guard-room at the city gate of Lachish the first of eighteen ostraca, written in early cursive Hebrew script, and dating from this period. They were letters that had been received by the military commander of Lachish from a subordinate officer, one Hoshaiah, who was in charge of an outpost to the north. They form a fascinating and tantalising correspondence, rather like listening to only one side of a critical telephone conversation. It is clear that morale was at a low ebb, and that stories of political intrigue and sedition in Jerusalem were rife: 'And behold the words of the princes are not good, but to weaken our hands and to slacken the hands of the men who are informed about them...truly since your servant read the letters there has been no peace for your servant...' Another of the letters ends with a poignant observation that suggests that Azekah had just fallen and that the turn of Lachish

'We are watching for the fire-beacons of Lachish': one of the ostraca found at Lachish, dating from the eve of the Babylonian invasion.

Dr David Ussishkin, the present excavator of Lachish, standing by some of the monumental masonry of the Israelite period.

was not far off: 'And let my lord know that we are watching for the fire-beacons of Lachish, according to all the indications which my lord hath given; for we cannot see Azekah.'

The end for Lachish must have come soon. At the site of the ancient city, a tell-tale destruction layer (Layer II, as it is labelled) records the evidence of a violent conflagration that swept through Lachish, barely a century after Sennacherib the Assyrian had razed it to the ground.

Jerusalem itself was now doomed. But its walls were stout, and it held out for a desperate eighteen months, slowly starving to death. Professor Avigad's discovery in 1975 of part of the Israelite fortifications (see Chapter 9) tells a whole story in itself: at the base of the massive tower that had been incorporated into a later wall, he found four Babylonian arrow-heads buried in a heap of ashes. The arrows had obviously fallen short of their mark and hit the outside wall of the tower before the city went up in flames.

And so Jerusalem fell, in the summer of 586, or 587 as some scholars opine. This time Nebuchadnezzar showed no mercy. The city was burned to the ground. The walls were torn down, leaving only the stumps of the foundations of the towers, such as the one that Professor Avigad has found; and the Temple with its sacred Ark of the Covenant was looted

Lachish: the city walls. To the right, the outer layer is the foundation of the city wall destroyed by the Assyrians: the upper level is the foundation of the city wall destroyed by the Babylonians.

and utterly destroyed. And thus the First Temple, Solomon's Temple, came to an end. King Zedekiah managed to escape from the city, but was captured near Jericho. He was forced to watch the execution of his sons, then he was blinded and taken to Babylon in chains, where he died.

And now a second great deportation took place, leaving Judah a shambles. No one can estimate exactly how many people died or were taken into captivity, though the numbers of those deported probably did not exceed twenty thousand. But these represented the cream of the nation's intellectual, political and religious leadership. They became internees of the Babylonians; and now, by the rivers of Babylon, they sat down and wept.

Dr James Pritchard of Pennsylvania University believes that the sack of Jerusalem by the Babylonians was the most important and determinative event in all Israel's history, because of the stamp it left on Judaism and the subsequent history of the Israelites. It is known that the population who were deported to Babylonia produced certain Hebrew writings: the latter part of *Isaiah* for certain, and probably much else. The literary and historical traditions were re-shaped in Babylon in the light of their experience there; they tended to write the history of the past in terms of the present, to construct a pattern of history which was formulated by their experience of exile away from Jerusalem. The Babylonian Hebrews had an enormous influence on the formation of Israelite tradition, since it was they who put it into literary form during the Captivity.

It was a period when the Babylonians themselves were showing an intense interest in history. Nebuchadnezzar had his scribes copy archives in Old Babylonian. His successor, Nabonidus, had ruined shrines and temples excavated; he restored the ziggurat at Ur and translated the inscriptions that told him who had built it. John van Seters points out that this antiquarianism seems to have rubbed off onto the Bible writers: when they wrote up their prehistory, they used archaic terms which were becoming fashionable again amongst the historians of Babylon, mixed with contemporary terms like 'Chaldaeans', who did not appear in Mesopotamia until the seventh century BC.

Despite the elegiac cadences of that beautiful Psalm 137, with its images of weeping Israelites softly remembering the songs of Zion, there is no evidence that the captivity in Babylon was physically disagreeable. Many of the internees seem to have taken Jeremiah's advice: 'Build ye houses, and dwell

Nabonidus, the last king of the neo-Babylonian empire: his son Belshazzar acted as regent in Babylon for much of his reign.

in them; and plant gardens, and eat the fruit of them...and seek the peace of the city whither I have caused you to be carried away captives, and pray unto the Lord for it...' (*Jeremiah* 29:5-7). When the release came, most were reluctant to return to the Jerusalem they had lost, and at first stayed where they were.

The release came through the most unlikely Messiah in the Bible – Cyrus the Persian, who is hailed as the Lord's anointed (*Isaiah* 45:1). Cyrus was to be the unwitting instrument of Yahweh's purpose for the Jews, for after their punishment there must come redemption. Cyrus had a meteoric rise to power in the middle of the sixth century, and by 550 BC he was ruler of the empire of the Medes; and with that the days of the neo-Babylonian empire were numbered. Nebuchadnezzar had died in 562 BC, and with his departure from the scene Babylonian power rapidly declined. The last ruler, Nabonidus (556-39 BC), spent most of his reign in the Arabian desert south-east of Edom, leaving his son Belshazzar as regent in Babylon, and during his absence the Babylonian empire began to fall apart as Cyrus the Persian seized control of most of Asia Minor, leaving Babylon increasingly isolated and friendless.

Considering how close they were to the events, the Bible writers signally fail to provide us with a clear or coherent account of the drama leading up to their release from captivity through the agency of Cyrus. All we have, instead, is one amazing scene so bizarre that it has gripped the world's imagination ever since – Belshazzar's Feast (*Daniel* 5). The setting was the banqueting court of one of the great palaces of Babylon; Belshazzar, 'king of Babylon', flown with insolence and wine, dared to use the gold and silver vessels of the Jerusalem Temple for a banquet, whereupon a man's hand appeared from thin air and wrote some mysterious words on the plaster of the wall, much to Belshazzar's discomfiture. None of his soothsayers could interpret the miraculous writing, so the 'king' summoned the legendary Jewish magician Daniel – he who would later be cast into a den of lions and emerge unscathed. Daniel read the writing for him, the four enigmatic words, '*Mene, mene, tekel, upharsin*,' which roughly translated meant 'Numbered, numbered, weighed, divided'.

Now, the *Book of Daniel* is known to be a very late composition, at least four centuries after the Exile, and it has no historical value whatsoever; in fact it gets its details rather muddled, in that Belshazzar was not the son of Nebuchadnezzar (as it suggests) but the son of Nabonidus; nor was he king, only viceroy, and so on. But what a powerful image of dark magic it conjures up. And certainly, for Belshazzar and the Babylonians, the writing really *was* on the wall: the Persians were at the gates.

So enfeebled had the Babylonian empire become by then that Cyrus and his army walked into the city of Babylon unopposed, as he recorded on the 'Cyrus Cylinder' of baked clay in the British Museum. The city was spared any damage, and Cyrus was welcomed as a liberator. Cyrus quickly showed his theological liberality; he adopted the chief god of Babylon, Marduk, as his paramount god (much to the chagrin, no doubt, of the Jewish prophets, who had confidently expected him to acknowledge Yahweh as the one true God), and restored other gods to their former sanctuaries. He also resettled Babylonian captives in their homelands: 'I gathered all their former inhabitants and restored to them their habitations' (Cyrus Cylinder); and it was in line with this policy of religious and social tolerance that he issued a decree in 538 BC ordaining the restoration of the community and cult in Jerusalem, according to the Biblical account: 'In the first year of Cyrus the king the same Cyrus the king made a decree concerning the house of God at Jerusalem, Let the house be builded, the place where they offered sacrifices, and let the foundations thereof be strongly laid...and let the expenses be given out of the king's house' (*Ezra* 6:3-4). The

The Cyrus Cylinder: a clay cylinder found at Babylon, in which Cyrus recorded his defeat of King Nabonidus and his capture of Babylon. He also tells how he returned captives and their gods to their homelands.

sacred vessels removed from the temple by Nebuchadnezzar (and desecrated by Belshazzar during his feast, presumably) were also to be restored to their rightful place, and all at the king's expense.

It seems as if only a very small party of pioneers took advantage of the edict in the first instance. Nor was the return to Jerusalem the triumphal homecoming they had dreamed about. Work on the foundations of the Temple dragged, and it seems that it was not until about 515 BC – more than twenty years after the initial return from exile – that the project was completed. The restored Temple seems to have been rather a modest affair compared with the dimly remembered glories of Solomon's Temple; but at least it provided a focus for the new community in Jerusalem – a community that evidently had to struggle against economic hardship and hostility from the existing population of Judah.

Archaeology does not give us much help for this difficult period, except possibly at one point at the eastern wall of the Temple Mount, the retaining wall of the platform on which the Temple was built. Some thirty metres from the southeast corner of this massive construction, most of which dates from the time of Herod, 500 years later, there is a distinct and unmistakable break, a change in the style of the masonry – a seam that is called in technical terms a 'straight joint'. On the south side of this seam, we find handsome blocks of beautifully-dressed stone that are distinctively Herodian; but on the north side the style is very different: the blocks have heavy, irregular bosses with a large and lumpy central area. There is still some disagreement about this, but some scholars, particularly Dame Kathleen Kenyon, feel that the style of this rather lumpy masonry is distinctly Persian, and should be attributed to the period of the rebuilding of the Temple platform under Persian influence and impetus; so that at that point, and that point alone, one can see and touch the only surviving evidence of the rebuilding of the Temple by the returned Babylonian exiles.

One enduring by-product of the return from the Babylonian exile was the enmity that sprang up between the returning Jews and their northern neighbours in Samaria, the Samaritans. The Samaritans, although they viewed the resettlement of the Babylonian Jews with a wary suspicion, had offered to help to rebuild the Temple in Jerusalem. But the fiercely Yahwist priesthood, buoyed up by their hopes of an imminent coming of the Kingdom of God, had spurned the offer on the ground that the Samaritans were no longer ethnically or

Opposite Petra: 'rose-red city half as old as time'.

209

theologically pure enough; and this was the origin of the mutual hatred and contempt that is evident in the pages of the Old Testament. It was to be a full five centuries before they would be rehabilitated in the parable of the Good Samaritan. During those five centuries, the Samaritans went their own separate way. They built themselves a rival temple of their own on the summit of Mount Gerizim, overlooking Shechem (modern Nablus), which they made their main religious centre. Mount Gerizim was already famous as the 'Mountain of Blessing', where Joshua had assembled the tribes after the Conquest of Canaan to hear the curses and the blessings connected with the observance of the Law: while the blessings were cried out from the summit of Mount Gerizim, the curses rained down from the twin mountain on the other side of the valley, Mount Ebal. The Samaritans also believed that the rock on which Abraham had been prepared to sacrifice his son Isaac was not on the Temple Mount in Jerusalem, but a broad stony outcrop on the summit of Mount Gerizim. The rival cult centre at Shechem was a constant irritant to the Jerusalem priesthood, and in 128 BC both the Samaritan temple and the Shechem settlement were destroyed during a Jewish insurrection. To this day the Samaritans are still a people apart, strictly speaking considered neither Jew nor Gentile, a people who claim to be the true descendants of Israel, with their own archaic version of

Shechem (modern Nablus): view from Mount Gerizim, where the Samaritans built their temple in rivalry with that of Jerusalem.

210

Debris on the slopes of Ophel Hill: from Dame Kathleen Kenyon's excavations in the 1960s. It recalls the state of ruin in which Nehemiah found Jerusalem's walls, when his donkey could not climb the slope.

the Pentateuch and their own uncompromising observance of the laws of Moses – including a particularly gory celebration of the Passover on top of Mount Gerizim every year, complete with animal sacrifices.

Although the Jerusalem Temple had been restored by 515 BC, Jerusalem itself remained a beleaguered community, an insignificant part of an insignificant Persian province. No reconstruction of the ruined city walls was allowed – the officials of Samaria saw to that. But in 445 BC the position changed dramatically with the arrival in Jerusalem of a special governor for Judah, a man called Nehemiah.

Nehemiah was a high-ranking Jewish official in the court of the Persian king, Artaxerxes I. Recognising the plight of his Jewish kinsmen in Jerusalem, he persuaded the king to allow the rebuilding of the walls, and was sent to Jerusalem with special powers to get the work done.

The story told by Nehemiah in the so-called 'Nehemiah Memoir' (the *Book of Nehemiah*) is remarkably vivid; parts of it read like a piece of first-hand documentary journalism, but that is probably due to the style of presentation of some later redactor. It seems that his first task when he arrived in Jerusalem was to do a rapid three-day survey of the state of the walls and the gates; apparently it had to be done in the greatest secrecy, because he went out by night on a donkey, with only two companions. But when he reached the lower slopes of the Ophel Hill above the Gihon spring, he found the ancient terraces of David's city in such tumbled ruin that 'there was no place for the beast that was under me to pass' (*Nehemiah* 2:14). And so he turned back.

Dame Kathleen Kenyon's excavation of the slope in the 1960s (see Chapter 7) showed what a terrible state of ruin these terraces had fallen into after the destruction of the city by Nebuchadnezzar. It took her several years to dig and shore up her deep trench down the hill. But for Nehemiah, the one commodity he did not have was time. He had to work fast, extremely fast, for there were growling neighbours on every side who did not want to see Jerusalem refortified. Yet with extraordinary single-mindedness and by involving the whole community, Nehemiah completed the tremendous project of rebuilding the walls of Jerusalem in only fifty-two days. He had to abandon the old eastern line of the wall half-way down the slope towards the Gihon spring, but that did not matter so much, for Jerusalem had other and better water supplies by then. Instead he chose a new line for the eastern wall along the crest of the ridge, linking directly to the corner of the Temple Mount. The remains that stand there now, including the erroneously named 'David's Tower', are later versions of Nehemiah's wall; but the line is the same, and within these new city walls there was ensconced a population of some 10,000 people, it is thought – most of them descendants of exiles returned from Babylon. Jerusalem itself, as a community, was rebuilt at last; and on the day of the dedication of the new walls, 'the joy of Jerusalem was heard even afar off '. The Exile, at last, was really over.

12
The End of the Old

It started a long time ago with 'In the beginning'; now we are
very nearly at the end. In fact, as far as the Old Testament is
concerned we are going beyond the end, into the realms of
the Apocrypha. In the Old Testament, history ended with
the return to Jerusalem under Persian patronage after the
Babylonian Exile. But history went on its own way nonetheless, and would bring Jerusalem to a zenith of greatness
during the Roman period under Herod, and then to the
eventual and final destruction of the Temple.

History was still to have a major impact on the Middle
East, starting with one of the most remarkable young men
who ever lived – Alexander the Great of Macedonia. In ten
brief years, from 334 to 323 BC, he conquered the known
world. He destroyed the Persians and took over their empire
– and that meant he took over the whole Middle East.

This was the first time that Europe, Western civilisation
as such, had ever annexed the Near and Middle East, and the
effect was massive and enduring. It introduced to the ancient
Orient a new way of living and thinking called Hellenism,
a new intellectual ideal, symbolised by the great cities that
Alexander and his successors built – cities like Afamia
(Apamea) and Palmyra in Syria. Suddenly, in the middle of
nowhere, the traveller comes upon great porticoed avenues
of elegant colonnades, ruined but not derelict, reminders of
the ideals of grace and beauty that so informed Hellenistic
thought. Not much is left of the cities now, for most of them
were absorbed and adapted and rebuilt by the successor
Roman empire; but those occasional glimpses of an airy
splendour, seemingly so out of place in the harsh environment of sand and rock, remind us of the tremendous changes
that took place when the traditional political and cultural
boundaries between East and West were swept aside. Hellenism affected the whole fabric of Middle Eastern society
and Middle Eastern thought – and the traffic was by no
means one way, either. Alexander himself became more
Mesopotamian than Macedonian.

Our interest in Hellenism must be confined to the impact
of Western ideas: new concepts of citizenship, in which

every free citizen had a responsibility for the governance of his community; of education, in which young citizens were trained in gymnasia in physical culture as well as poetry, philosophy and music; of religion and science and learning. It must be remembered that Alexander had been tutored by Aristotle, so that through him and his circle there was a direct channel to the classical masters like Socrates and Plato.

The impact of Hellenism on Judaism is hard to assess. During and after the Babylonian Exile, the theocrats of Jerusalem had to deal with a philosophical crisis of faith; they had to reforge a covenant that had apparently been broken when Yahweh allowed the inviolable rights of the Chosen People to be violated by the Babylonians. One can detect a siege mentality developing, a retreat into legalistic moralism, which came to be challenged by the moral individualism of the Hellenistic way of thinking. Professor John Gray thinks that this conflict is reflected in some of the most famous of the post-Exilic works, like the *Book of Job* and the *Book of Jonah*. There is no general agreement on when these books were written, but most scholars tend to think of them as post-Hellenistic rather than earlier.

The story of Jonah is celebrated mainly because of his unlikely adventure in the stomach of a great fish – not a whale. One tends to forget how it was that he got there: it was because Yahweh wanted to send him on a mission to save Nineveh from destruction, by warning its inhabitants of their sins. Jonah refused, and tried to run away to sea; he was cast overboard as a scapegoat for a storm, and swallowed by the fish so that Yahweh could concentrate his mind on the task he had been set. Jonah eventually went to Nineveh as ordered, carried out his missionary duties, and the wrath of God was averted from Nineveh; but Jonah then failed to see the point of the whole exercise. The moral of this parable, however, is that it expresses an anonymous author's protest against the pernicious exclusiveness of narrow Judaism, claiming the grace of God for themselves and themselves alone. It is the first indication in the Old Testament that Yahweh was the god not just of a select few of mankind, but of all mankind; the story of Jonah has been called the Old Testament equivalent of 'God so loved the world'.

The story of Job seems to be another example of an anti-establishment composition, a reaction against the mechanical and rigid view of suffering as a punishment for sin, with its converse that absolute conformity to the will of Yahweh as interpreted by the priesthood was the only path to prosperity.

If a good man suffered misfortune, that simply proved he could not have been a good man after all! The *Book of Job* is saying that theological systems cannot have the last word in the dealings of god and man; the essential thing is the living encounter and the response to that encounter. Many scholars argue that it was Hellenism which liberated this attitude of mind, the capacity to contemplate the profoundly difficult problems of the relationship between suffering and the concept of a just and benevolent god; and Job has been called the Hebrew philosophical genius.

The intellectual upheavals that Hellenism inspired were matched by the political upheavals that ensued in the Middle East. After Alexander's death at Babylon in 323 BC, his empire was divided up by three rival dynasties: Egypt under the Ptolemies, Mesopotamia under the Seleucids, and Asia Minor under Antigonus. As usual, Palestine and Syria became the cockpit of competing empires. For a century Judah belonged to the Ptolemies; but in 198 BC the Seleucids threw out the Egyptians and took over in their stead.

While this tug of war was taking place in central Palestine, a large shift of power was taking place farther south in Edom, in Jordan. With Judah at her lowest ebb during and after the Exile, her traditional enemies started moving into the southlands, where they would become known as Idumeans; the warning on the Arad ostracon had been right after all (see Chapter 11). Their place in Edom was taken – perhaps forcibly – by a vigorous race of desert Arabs known as Nabataeans, who set about creating one of the most dramatic and beautiful cities in the world, known in the Bible as Rekem, and known to us as Petra.

A nineteenth-century English cleric, John William Burgon, later Dean of Winchester, immortalised himself and the site with a couple of lines he penned in his long winning poem on Petra for the Newdigate Prize at Oxford:

> 'Match me such a marvel save in Eastern clime,
> A rose-red city half as old as time.'

He had not actually visited Petra before he wrote the poem, and when he eventually did go, he complained that there was nothing rosy about it! But somehow he had managed to catch the essential spirit of the place; for Petra is, quite literally, breath-taking. Rose-red it is not, except in patches, half as old as time it is not, for its monuments date from around 200 BC onwards; but a marvel it certainly is, and a unique marvel at that.

The city lies hidden in great folds of mountain overlooking the Wadi Arabah, about half-way between the Dead Sea and the Gulf of Aqaba. The approach to it is down the so-called Siq, a fantastic chasm of towering cliffs, their rock faces chiselled smooth into billowing shapes by the funnelled wind, marbled in colour like the endpapers of old leather-bound books. And then suddenly you turn a last bend, and straight ahead you catch a glimpse of what seems to be a perfectly formed classical temple in the heart of the mountain – and for once the colour *is* rose-red. Then the ravine opens out, and you are standing in front of the beautifully sculpted facade of a temple, every detail crisp and clean as if it had been made yesterday. This is the so-called 'Treasury of Pharaoh', carved from the rock face, its cavernous chambers gouged from the rock inside.

Petra: first glimpse of the 'Treasury' at the end of the narrow winding Siq.

It is only the first of countless such marvels: temples, tombs, villas, a whole city in the rock, large enough to accommodate a population of 30,000 of the most sophisticated troglodytes the world has ever known. Here at Petra, their capital, the Nabataeans grew enormously rich on the trade which flowed up the King's Highway to the booming new markets of the Hellenistic cities, and invested their fortunes not in bricks and mortar but in living rock.

It is a site that no one should miss. Even staying in the government rest-house is a peculiar delight, for it is a converted tomb. The stone walls of the dining-room are lined with niches to receive the bodies of the dead.

A stiff climb from 'street level' takes you breathlessly up a soaring eminence above the city of the High Place of Sacrifice, more than 1000 metres above sea level. The summit has been levelled to form a shallow courtyard, with an altar complex to one side. The altars have basins and runnels gouged out of the rock, presumably run-offs for the blood of sacrifices. This was the royal High Place, with a marvellous panoramic view over the sea of mountain ridges all round. Here the Nabataeans, and no doubt also the Edomites before them, worshipped the gods of their cult.

What one finds most striking about this sacred area of Petra is the way in which it embodies the insistent motif of the High Place in so many of the various religions of the Bible lands: a constant reaching upwards for the fullest communication with the god, like the High Places of the Canaanites with their standing stones, or the ziggurats of Mesopotamia. Jacob's dream of a ladder with angels descending and ascending expresses the same concept of a sort of instant lightning-conductor from Heaven. And of course it was at a High Place on Mount Sinai that Moses was portrayed as making the covenant with Yahweh. Nor would the god of the Hebrews have felt out of place up there above Petra, for Yahweh was also said to be 'He of Seir' – Seir being the Biblical name for the mountain range all around, modern Shara. Mountains and rocks and stones – they were at once the abode and the embodiment of the god, formalised in the concept of the stone altar: a block of stone, on a High Place at Petra, 'the Rock' – it seems to communicate most directly and uncompromisingly the quintessence of the Semitic religions.

From their capital at Petra, the Nabataeans spread their commercial empire far and wide. In the face of all the political and military turmoil of the times, they stubbornly defended their independence against all comers. But in the end they succumbed to the most powerful and far-flung empire that the ancient world had yet seen – the empire of Rome.

The best preserved Roman city in the Middle East is the city of Jerash, in northern Jordan. More than a thousand years ago it was shattered by a disastrous earthquake and abandoned for ever; and that, paradoxically, is why it is so well preserved today, for no one built on its ruins. Now it is gradually being restored to something of its former glory. The great forum, with its oddly elliptical shape, has been cleared of the accumulated earth and debris that had buried it to the top of its columns. The theatre is being reconstructed. Fallen columns are being re-erected.

Roman Jerash – Gerasa as it was called then – was built in the middle of the first century BC on the site of a Hellenistic city. Throughout the first two centuries AD, the high period of the *Pax Romana* in the Mediterranean, it was constantly being enlarged. Prolonged peace allowed business and trade to flourish unhampered, and provincial cities like Jerash prospered as never before. As an outpost of Western civilisation, Jerash attained a sustained peak of grandeur. The elegant

Jerash: the Roman theatre, which has been largely reconstructed by the Jordanian authorities.

temple of Artemis, towering over the remains of a fourth-century cathedral – the first church to be built in Jerash – reflects the high provincial civilisation of the Roman empire in which early Christianity would struggle to take root.

The building of Jerash and the other provincial Roman centres was the start of a new chapter in the history of the Middle East. Those marching colonnades, all power and self-confidence and administrative rectitude, spelled the end for the time being at least of the fierce tribal squabbles that over and over again had disrupted its past. But it was also the end of a chapter for Palestine – and very nearly the end of the book for Jewish Judea, the old kingdom of Judah.

In 64 BC, the Roman general Pompey the Great had broken the resistance of the last potentates in the Middle East, and annexed Syria for the Roman Empire. Judah had been independent then for a hundred years, after throwing off the yoke of the Seleucids in 167 BC in an insurrection led by the resolute Judas Maccabeus. The Maccabean dynasty, also known as the Hasmonean dynasty, had clung to power through a series of vicissitudes since then; indeed, at one stage the Hasmonean kingdom embraced practically the whole of Palestine, and the cities of Jordan like Jerash had suffered severely from its punitive campaigns. But Pompey's arrival spelled the end for the Hasmoneans; in 63 BC his army entered Jerusalem and after a prolonged struggle cleared the fortified Temple area of its defenders. The Hasmonean dynasty was overthrown, and Palestine became a province of Rome. There was only one final flourish of magnificence left for the kingdom that David and Solomon had founded nearly a thousand years before: the rebuilding of Jerusalem by a client king, Herod the Great.

Herod the Great, 'King of the Jews' under Roman tutelage, was an Idumean. He was appointed King by the Roman Senate in 40 BC, but it was not until 37 BC that he was able to force his way into Jerusalem in the teeth of nationalistic opposition to ascend the throne. His reign lasted thirty-three years, and a lurid, troubled reign it was. He left his mark on history, but he left it even more deeply on Jerusalem. Visitors to the Holyland Hotel in Jerusalem can see a magnificent scale model of Herodian Jerusalem in marble, stone and wood which reproduces in minute and faithful detail what the city was like 2000 years ago. It was then that Jerusalem reached the height of its architectural splendour, for Herod was a builder on a grand scale. He built a new administrative and defensive centre in the shape of a grandiose royal palace

The Wailing Wall in Jerusalem: the great blocks of hewn masonry are from the time of Herod the Great. The wall forms part of the Temple Platform, not the Second Temple itself, which was destroyed in AD 70.

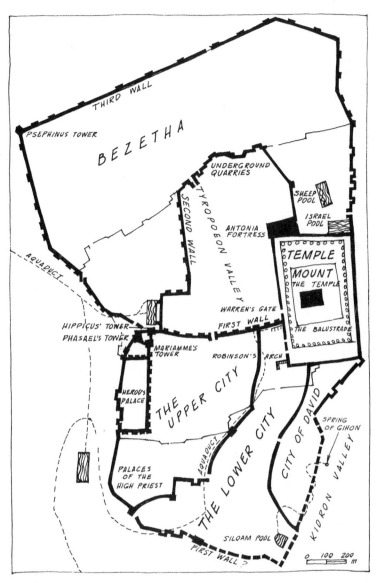

Jerusalem at the time of Herod the Great. The Third Wall was built to defend the city's vulnerable northern approaches.

THIRD WALL

PSEPHINUS TOWER

BEZETHA

UNDERGROUND QUARRIES

SHEEP POOL

ISRAEL POOL

TYROPOEON VALLEY

SECOND WALL

ANTONIA FORTRESS

TEMPLE MOUNT

THE TEMPLE

AQUADUCT

WARREN'S GATE

FIRST WALL

THE BALUSTRADE

HIPPICUS' TOWER
PHASAEL'S TOWER

MARIAMME'S TOWER

ROBINSON'S ARCH

THE UPPER CITY

HEROD'S PALACE

CITY OF DAVID

SPRING OF GIHON

THE LOWER CITY

AQUADUCT

PALACES OF THE HIGH PRIEST

KIDRON VALLEY

SILOAM POOL

FIRST WALL?

0 100 200
m

at the north-western corner of the Upper City. His courtiers and noblemen built themselves luxurious private residences nearby. But Herod's major project was the total reconstruction of the Temple and a massive enlargement of the Temple Mount. Not a stone of the Temple, the Second Temple as it is called, now remains; but the base of the enlarged Temple Mount is still there, with its formidable blocks of superbly hewn masonry. Herodian architecture is unmistakable. The celebrated Wailing Wall, on the west side of the Temple Mount, is part of this platform, and not, of course, part of the original Temple.

Today, intensive archaeological activity since the Six Day

War of 1967 round the base of the Temple Mount at its south-western corner is revealing more and more clearly Herod's overall design for the Temple area. The grandeur of the lay-out was not due to megalomania; it was a realistic develop-ment to accommodate the hundreds of thousands of visitors and pilgrims who flocked to the Temple every year. Once he had completed the massive new platform for his Temple, making it the largest structure in antiquity (almost 500 metres square), he had to decide what to do with the approaches to it. The front of the Temple precinct faced south overlooking David's original city on the Ophel Hill; and what Herod did was to create a great sweep of stairs about sixty-five metres wide running down the slope to the south, with a plaza halfway down. Not a hint of this monumental stairway was visible in 1968 when the Israeli excavation began; it lay buried under the many metres of debris that had piled up against the sides of the Temple Mount over the cen-turies. It is a most impressive approach; but what intrigued the archaeologists as much as anything else was the way in which Herod's architects had designed the stairs themselves. Throughout antiquity architects wrestled with the problem of how to make people approach a temple in the right spirit of reverence; at the Parthenon in Athens, for instance, they built steps of more than half a metre high to force visitors practically to climb into the temple. Herod's solution, it turned out, was much more elegant: he forced people to break step and thus slow down, by alternating broad stairs with narrow stairs. Worshippers had to take two paces then one pace, two paces then one pace, so that when they reached the top they were going slowly. They could not take the stairs at a run without great difficulty, and as a result they arrived at the threshold of the Temple precincts in a proper frame of mind to enter the House of the Lord.

Just around the corner, on the west side of the Temple Mount, archaeologists have excavated down to bedrock in places; here they have uncovered a broad thoroughfare, twelve metres wide and paved with huge hewn slabs, skirting the western wall. This was Jerusalem's main north-south street in Herod's time. It was supported on three rows of solid chambers, since it lay on sloping ground.

The excavations in this section have also helped to solve a problem that has puzzled scholars for a long time – the prob-lem of 'Robinson's Arch'. This is the broken-off spring of a massive arch jutting out from the western wall about twelve metres from the corner; it is named after the American scholar Dr Edward Robinson who first drew attention to it in the 1830s. The arch had originally rested on a great pier fifteen metres away, and it now became evident that it spanned this arterial thoroughfare. Earlier scholars had believed that 'Robinson's Arch' was only the first of a series which formed a causeway connecting the Temple Mount to the Upper City, despite the fact that no trace of any other piers had been found. The new excavations have proved conclusively that there were no other piers on the westward side; instead, they revealed the presence of a series of piers running *southwards*, each one shorter than the other. The rubble round about contained broken flights of stairs; it was clear that 'Robinson's Arch' had formed the upper platform of an enormous monumental stairway leading up from the thoroughfare below and crossing it to the Temple Mount. Between the smaller piers there were the remains of four chambers opening onto the street; in them were found stoneware, pottery, weights and coins, so it could be assumed that they had originally been souvenir shops catering for visitors to the Temple.

Finding the solution to architectural problems like this is more than merely an academic exercise. The excavations, which are being directed by Professor Benjamin Mazar on behalf of the Israel Exploration Society and the Hebrew University of Jerusalem, also have a highly practical and functional purpose: it is the long-term intention of the excavators to turn the long-buried area round the foot of the Temple Platform into an archaeological park which will display in graphic cross-section the complete history of Jerusalem from Herod's time to the 1967 War.

The Assistant Director of the excavation, Mr Meir Ben-Dov of the Israel Exploration Society, is enthusiastic about

The Temple Mount at the time of Herod the Great: reconstruction of the south-west corner, showing the monumental stairway on the south wall (right), and the pedestrian stairway across 'Robinson's Arch' (centre). On top of the Temple Mount, the immense colonnades built by Herod to accommodate the hundreds of thousands of worshippers.

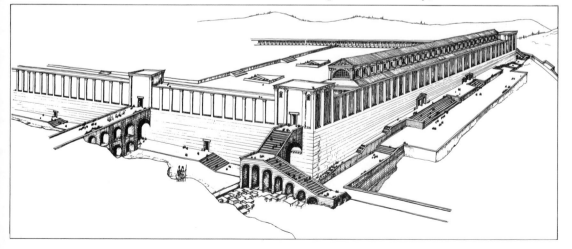

the project. In the cleared area at the south-western end he points out the layers of the building history that have been uncovered and meticulously preserved. Visitors will soon be able, literally, to take a walk through the ages: starting at the top with the city fortifications of the Ottoman sultan, Suleiman the Magnificent, in the sixteenth century AD, then a Crusader tower from the twelfth century AD. Under that tower there is a pavement which is part of a huge palace complex built by the first Moslem dynasty in Jerusalem, the Omayyads of the late seventh century AD, the time of the building of the Dome of the Rock. Underneath that palace there lies a Byzantine building from the end of the sixth century AD, representing Christian Jerusalem. Underneath that are the remains of the camp of the Tenth Roman Legion

Excavations at the south-west corner of the Temple Mount: on the right, the vast complex of the palace built by the Omayyads is beginning to emerge from the ground. On the left, the structures at the foot of 'Robinson's Arch'.

Opposite above Jerusalem: excavations at the south-west corner of the Temple Mount. Half-way up the Herodian wall, on the left, is the broken-off spring of 'Robinson's Arch'.

Opposite below Jerusalem: the magnificent Dome of the Rock in the Haram es-Sherif (Temple Mount).

that was quartered at the Temple Mount, and under the camp lie the streets and plazas of Herodian Jerusalem. It will be history in three dimensions.

It should be stressed that it is by no means the intention of the excavators to obliterate everything from later periods in order to reconstruct the surroundings of the Temple Mount exclusively as they were in Herod's time. The present excavation has been condemned by UNESCO on the ground that it is a wanton destruction of the material remains of the other major religions which venerate Jerusalem as a Holy City. I found no evidence to support such a grave charge against the professional and scientific integrity of the excavators concerned; on the contrary, I am convinced that this major archaeological enterprise will illuminate the history of the Holy City in a way which will bring satisfaction and pleasure to all believers, whatever their particular persuasion.

Herod's Jerusalem, and Herod's Second Temple, represented a new monumentalism not only in architecture but in religious thought as well. However, there were some Jews who never appreciated grandiose buildings and the centralised worship they demanded. Such groups had taken to living in monastic communities in the desert, shunning the cities as being impure and unworthy of inheriting the new Kingdom of God which they were convinced was at hand for Israel.

One such group or sect that we know of from contemporary sources were the Essenes. They lived by the shores of the Dead Sea, a community totally dedicated to godliness and cleanliness, preparing themselves for a new Heaven upon earth, a new Jerusalem: seeing themselves as an elect within the elect. Although they were not mentioned at all in the pages of the New Testament, surprisingly enough, they were one of the three major sects within Judaism in the Second Temple period, the others being the Pharisees and the Sadducees.

Public interest in the Essenes was electrified just after the Second World War by the chance discovery of the celebrated Dead Sea Scrolls in some caves in the limestone hills behind Qumran. This sensational discovery, perhaps the most sensational find of the century, led in turn to the excavation of a ruined site at Khirbet Qumran, as the Arabs call it. All that could be seen above ground was the stump of a ruined watchtower, which people had casually assumed to be the remains of a Roman fort. But when the site was excavated in the 1950s by the late Père Roland de Vaux of the Ecole Biblique in Jerusalem and G. Lankester Harding, then Director of the

Opposite One of the caves in the Qumran area in which the Dead Sea Scrolls were found.

225

Department of Antiquities in Jordan, it turned out that it had actually been a community centre of a sect or group very like the Essenes – so much so, indeed, that most people now tend to identify Qumran with the actual headquarters of the Dead Sea Essenes themselves.

The members of the sect did not live in the buildings. They lived all around the area in tents and booths, and in caves up in the cliffs behind the site, and when they died they were buried in a large cemetery that lies between the community centre and the Dead Sea. There are about 1100 tombs in this cemetery, and in those that have been excavated nearly all the skeletons were those of males. Morality was very high. It was a real monastic community in the popular sense of the term. The sect had established their headquarters there around 150 BC, apparently using the remains of an Iron Age fort from the time of either King Hezekiah or King Josiah. The original building was expanded until it could accommodate some two hundred members of the sect. They survived a disastrous earthquake in 31 BC which shattered the buildings. The date of the earthquake is known, so the archaeologists were able to date the structure accurately at

Qumran, with the Dead Sea in the background. The ruins of the Qumran community centre are just to the right of the tarmac car park (left of picture). In the foreground, the hills where the caves of the Dead Sea Scrolls were found.

the time of its destruction, before it was rebuilt. There was a complex of large public rooms. One was a refectory where the white-clad members of the sect would meet for communal meals. Another was a storage room containing large quantities of pottery which matched exactly the pottery vessels which were used to preserve the scrolls when they were hidden in the caves up in the mountains. There was a kitchen with floor ovens, and a pottery kiln. And there was an elaborate water-storage system – a number of large, carefully plastered cisterns to supply the sect with all the water those fanatical purists required for their endless ritual ablutions.

But most remarkable of all, one of the long narrow rooms there was found to have in it a solid writing table of gypsum that had fallen through the floor from the room above. All around were inkpots of bronze and clay. To write at that table would have meant kneeling, not sitting. Combined with the evidence of the pottery vessels with their distinctive shape, the conclusion was inescapable: Qumran was where most if not all of the scrolls had actually been written and studied. The Dead Sea Scrolls were the library of Qumran, hidden for safety in the surrounding caves when danger threatened, as it did soon after AD 66.

More has probably been written about the Dead Sea Scrolls over the past few years than about any other archaeological find in the world. But what precisely was their importance? Were they a 'new' version of the Old Testament? Do they require us to change all our thinking about the Bible?

The prime importance of the Scrolls, says Dr James Pritchard, is that they have produced copies of major parts of the Old Testament which are a thousand years earlier than the earliest Hebrew copy previously available; before the discovery of the Scrolls, the oldest preserved copy of the Old Testament was a manuscript in Leningrad dated to the tenth century AD. But curiously enough this has not materially altered the readings in the Bible. The principal scroll is a copy of the *Book of Isaiah*, and it has only a very few minor variations; this underlines the essential integrity of the scribal tradition, that a manuscript could be copied over and over again for a thousand years and still preserve an extremely faithful version of the original.

Right across from the Qumran community centre there is a cave, labelled Cave 4, which produced literally thousands of fragments of scrolls in 1952. The Editor-in-Chief who is in charge of co-ordinating and publishing the work on all these fragments by a host of scholars from all over the world is

Père Benoit of the Ecole Biblique in Jerusalem. He has established that the fragments come from about six hundred separate scrolls, which must surely be close to the total number of volumes possessed by the sect. One interesting fact to emerge so far is that the library often owned several copies of the same text: fourteen copies of *Deuteronomy*, for instance, and four or five copies of *Genesis*; and in all of them, the same basic integrity of the scribal tradition is attested.

Qumran: part of the community centre after excavation: centre of picture, the room farthest away was the store-room for the pottery vessels in which the Dead Sea Scrolls were packed before being hidden.

Dr Yigael Yadin has a very special interest in the scrolls, for it was his father, the late Professor Elazar L. Sukenik, Professor of Archaeology at the Hebrew University of Jerusalem, who first recognised their antiquity; and it was Yadin himself who was instrumental in buying the first of them for Israel in 1954 when they had been smuggled out to America. They are now on display in the Shrine of the Book that was specially built to house them at the Israel Museum. Dr Yadin thinks that their prime importance lies not so much in the integrity of the texts of the Old Testament, but in what they tell us about the inter-Testamental period between the Old and the New. Until now we had only known what so-called 'normative' Judaism had thought; now, from this library of the Essenes, we gain an idea of what other Jews were thinking at this time, the time of Jesus.

The great surprise is that there was so much similarity between some of the teachings of these Essenes and some of the teachings found in the New Testament. Dr Yadin believes the Essene library provides a sort of missing link between Judaism and Christianity. The early Christians were Jews, but some Christian teaching did not tally with 'normative' Judaism; now, because of the resemblances not to 'normative' Judaism but sectarian Judaism, he concludes that early Christianity was actually more Jewish than had been thought before. To him, the Dead Sea Scrolls represent a great revelation and revolution in the study of the origins of Christianity.

But what eventually happened to the Essenes, or the Qumranis? The archaeological evidence from the Qumran site shows that the community centre was destroyed in June, AD 68, and thereafter garrisoned by Roman soldiery for a time.

The year AD 66 was a fateful one for the Jews. An insurrection broke out against the Romans, led by a group of fanatical nationalists known as the Zealots. The rebellion was surely doomed to failure from the start, but the Zealots fought every inch of the way, until by the year AD 70 the hard-core survivors of the rebellion were trapped in the desert fortress of Masada, near the Dead Sea. It had been turned into a

Restoration work on one of the Dead Sea Scrolls: a copy of *Genesis* in the Apocryphon scroll, in the Ecole Biblique in Jerusalem.

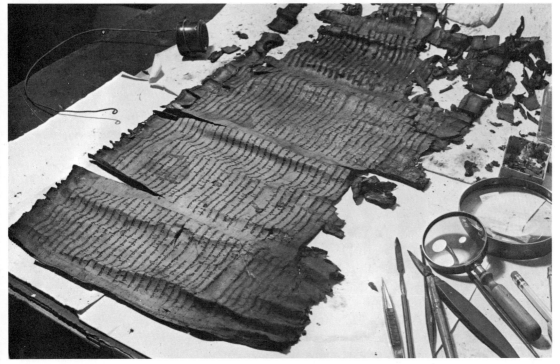

fortified palace by Herod the Great, who was ever fearful of his life – with good reason – and here the Zealots made their last stand.

The Temple Mount in Jerusalem: Herodian pavement and steps at the foot of the south wall, showing the depth below present ground level.

Masada was excavated by Dr Yadin in an epic international excavation in the 1960s. The world's imagination has been caught by the story of the mass suicide whereby the beleaguered Jews cheated their enemy on the eve of the final Roman assault; and most people assume that the only people who took part in the last stand were exclusively the Zealots. But one of the commanders in the fortress was called 'John the Essene'; and Dr Yadin found the remains of several leather scrolls, one of which he could positively identify as a Dead Sea scroll because it dealt with the discipline of the Dead Sea sect. So he concludes that the Essenes were, in fact, partisans as well, and that when the great revolt broke out and they were threatened by the Romans, the Essenes carefully hid their precious library in the mountain caves and went to Masada to join in the last-ditch stand – taking one or two scrolls with them. If he is right, it means that the Qumranis, or the Essenes, died to a man in the mass suicide at Masada. But it also raises the question: if the Essenes were Zealots under the skin, and if there was some connection between the teaching of the Essenes and the teaching of Jesus, was Jesus perhaps a Zealot himself? It is a large question – and much too large for the scope of this present book.

The destruction of Masada in AD 73 was only a footnote to the Jewish Revolt of AD 66 – the First Jewish Revolt, as it is called, because it would not be the last. It simply tidied up the loose ends of tragedy. The real catastrophe had come three years earlier, with the fall of Jerusalem. The nationalist uprising had turned into bloody civil war. Extremist fought extremist, Zealot fought fanatic, while the moderates in between were butchered without compunction. In AD 70, Jerusalem was invested by the Roman legions; after weeks of desperate fighting, the Temple Mount was taken, and Herod's Temple, the Second Temple, went up in flames. Jerusalem was destroyed.

It was the end of a long, long story.

The last century has seen the beginning of another story: the systematic recovery of that past through archaeology. In the last few years, remarkable discoveries have been made all over the Middle East which are helping to clarify the outlines of history. So far, archaeology has really only scratched the surface, metaphorically speaking. But with every month and every year, new archaeological discoveries are lighting up our knowledge and our understanding of the Bible Lands BC.

Time Chart

150,000	Neanderthal Man emerges
35,000	Modern form of Man emerges
10,000	**Neolithic (New Stone) Age**
9500	Jericho (pre-pottery): oldest walled city in the world
7000	Catal Hüyük: first pottery in the Near East
4000	**Chalcolithic (Copper-Stone) Age**
3500	Sumer: first city-states in Mesopotamia
3100	Sumer: pictographic writing starts
	Egypt: unification of Upper and Lower Egypt
3000	**Early Bronze Age**
2800	Britain: earliest stage of Stonehenge begun
2700	Egypt: Old Kingdom starts
2600	Egypt: Great Pyramid built
2500	Sumer: First Dynasty of Ur. Literary texts
2400	Syria: Canaanite empire based on Ebla
2350	Akkad: Sargon the Great subjugates Sumer
2100	Sumer: Third Dynasty of Ur
	Egypt: Middle Kingdom starts
2000	**Middle Bronze Age**
2000-1750	Syria: the 'Mari age', culminating with Zimri-Lim
1900	Assyria: Old Assyrian Empire based on Ashur
1750	Babylon: Old Babylonian Empire under Hammurabi
1700-1550	Egypt: period of Hyksos domination
1600-1200	Greece: period of Mycenaean domination
1550	Egypt: New Kingdom starts
1500	**Late Bronze Age**
1490-36	Egypt: Tuthmosis III, campaigns in Palestine and Syria
1475-1200	Anatolia: Hittite New Kingdom
1450	Crete: Minoan empire destroyed
1400-1200	Canaan: Ugarit palace archives (Ras Shamra)
1290-24	Egypt: Ramesses II (Ramesses the Great)
1280	Syria: Battle of Kadesh between Egyptians and Hittites
1250 (?)	Anatolia: fall of 'Homeric' Troy
1250 (?)	Egypt: traditional date of the Bondage and Exodus
1225-05	Egypt: Pharaoh Merneptah
1225 (?)	Canaan: traditional date of Joshua's conquest
1200	**Iron Age**
1200	The Sea Peoples: Ugarit destroyed, end of Hittite Empire
1190	Egypt: Ramesses III defeats the Sea Peoples
	Palestine: Philistines settle the coastal plain
1150-1025	Palestine: period of the Biblical Judges
1100	Egypt: end of the Egyptian Empire
1050	Palestine: Philistines win the battle of Eben-ezer
1025-1000	Palestine: King Saul
1000-965	Palestine: David takes Jerusalem. The United Monarchy

965-20 Palestine: King Solomon
920 Palestine: the Divided Monarchy – Judah and Israel
883-59 Assyria: Ashurnasirpal II, moves capital to Nimrud
876-69 Israel: King Omri, founder of capital at Samaria
869-50 Israel: King Ahab, husband of Jezebel
859-24 Assyria: Shalmaneser III
853 Syria: Battle of Qarqar, the Assyrians checked
842-15 Israel: King Jehu
786-46 Israel: King Jeroboam II
783-42 Judah: King Uzziah
745-27 Assyria: Tiglath-Pileser III, founds Neo-Assyrian Empire
735-15 Judah: King Ahaz
722-1 Israel: fall of Samaria. Israel deported to Assyria
721-05 Assyria: Sargon II, moves capital to Khorsabad
715-687 Judah: King Hezekiah, fortifies Jerusalem
705-680 Assyria: Sennacherib, moves capital to Nineveh
701 Judah: Assyrian invasion, sack of Lachish
689 Babylon: destruction by Sennacherib
680-69 Assyria: King Esarhaddon
671 Egypt: conquest by Assyria
668-27 Assyria: Ashurbanipal, last effective king of Assyria
640-09 Judah: King Josiah, religious reforms
626-539 Babylon: Neo-Babylonian Empire
614 Assyria: Ashur captured by the Medes
612 Assyria: Nineveh destroyed by Babylonians and Medes
604-562 Babylon: King Nebuchadnezzar
597 Judah: Babylonian invasion. The first deportation
586 Judah: the fall of Jerusalem. Destruction of the Temple
586-38 Babylon: the Hebrew Exile
539 Babylon: Cyrus the Persian takes over the Babylonian Empire
538 Babylon: The Edict of Cyrus, exiles return
520-15 Palestine: the rebuilding of the Temple in Jerusalem
445 Palestine: Nehemiah, the walls of Jerusalem rebuilt
336-23 Macedonia: Alexander the Great conquers the world
323 Egypt: Ptolemy I, Palestine under the Ptolemies
200 Palestine: conquest by the Seleucids
166-63 Palestine: the Maccabean insurrection, the Hasmonean kingdom
63 Palestine: Romans under Pompey capture Jerusalem
37-4 BC Palestine: Herod the Great
AD 66 Palestine: the First Jewish Revolt against the Romans
70 Palestine: Jerusalem falls. Destruction of the Second Temple
73 Palestine: Masada falls

Book List

This list comprises the main books that I consulted and found illuminating but does not include the scores of excavation reports and articles in journals and periodicals which provided the bulk of the information in this book.

Ackroyd, P.R. *Exile and Restoration: A Study of Hebrew Thought in the Sixth Century*, London, SCM Press 1968

Aharoni, Y. *The Land of the Bible: A Historical Geography*, London, Burns & Oates 1967

Albright, W.F. *Archaeology and the Religion of Israel*, New York, Doubleday 1969
From the Stone Age to Christianity, New York, Doubleday 1957

Anati, E. *Palestine Before the Hebrews*, London, Jonathan Cape 1963

Avi-Yonah, M. (ed) *Encyclopaedia of Archaeological Excavations in the Holy Land, vols I & II*, Oxford University Press 1976

Beebe, H.K. *The Old Testament*, London, Dickenson 1970

Bright, J.A. *History of Israel*, London, SCM Press 1972
Cambridge Ancient History, Cambridge University Press 1975

Finegan, J. *Light from the Ancient Past*, vols 1 & II, Princeton University Press 1959

Gardiner, A.H. *Egypt of the Pharaohs*, Oxford University Press 1961

Gray, J. *The Canaanites*, London, Thames & Hudson 1964
Near Eastern Mythology, London, Hamlyn 1969

Harden, D. *The Phoenicians*, London, Thames & Hudson 1962

Harding, G.L. *The Antiquities of Jordan*, London, Lutterworth 1967

Harker, R. *Digging up the Bible Lands*, London, Bodley Head 1972

Heaton, E.W. *Solomon's New Men: The Emergence of Ancient Israel as a National State*, London, Thames & Hudson 1974

James, T.G.H. *The Archaeology of Ancient Egypt*, London, Bodley Head 1972

Jordan, P. *Egypt The Black Land*, London, Phaidon 1976

Kenyon, K.M. *Archaeology in the Holy Land*, London, Ernest Benn 1965
Digging Up Jericho, London, Ernest Benn 1957
Digging Up Jerusalem, London, Ernest Benn 1974

Kitchen, K.A. *Ancient Orient and Old Testament*, London, Tyndale Press 1966

Kramer, S.N. *History Begins at Sumer*, London, Thames & Hudson 1958

May, H.G. (ed) *Oxford Bible Atlas*, Oxford University Press 1974

Mazar, B. *The Mountain of the Lord*, New York, Doubleday 1975

Mellaart, J. *Earliest Civilisations of the Near East*, London, Thames & Hudson 1965

Moorey, P.R.S. *Biblical Lands*, London, Elsevier-Phaidon 1975

Moscati, S. *The World of the Phoenicians*, London, Weidenfeld & Nicolson 1968
The Face of the Ancient Orient, London, Routledge 1960

Negev, A. (ed) *Archaeological Encyclopaedia of the Holy Land*, London, Weidenfeld & Nicolson 1973

Neil, W. (ed) *The Bible Companion*, London, Skeffington 1960

Noth, M. *The History of Israel*, London, A. & C. Black 1960

Oppenheim, A.L. *Ancient Mesopotamia: Portrait of a Dead Civilisation*, Chicago University Press 1969

Pritchard, J.B. *Ancient Near Eastern Texts Relating to the Old Testament*, Princeton University Press 1955
Archaeology and the Old Testament, Princeton University Press 1958
(ed) *Archaeological Discoveries in the Holy Land*, New York, Bonanza Books 1974
Gibeon Where the Sun Stood Still, Princeton University Press 1963

Redford, D.B. *A Study of the Biblical Story of Joseph*, Leiden, E.J.Brill 1970

Rothenberg, B. *Timna: Valley of the Biblical Copper Mines*, London, Thames & Hudson 1972

Seters, J. van *Abraham in History and Tradition*, Yale University Press 1975

Thomas, D.W. (ed) *Archaeology and Old Testament Study*, Oxford University Press 1967
    Documents from Old Testament Times, London, Nelson 1958
Thomson, T.L. *The Historicity of the Patriarchal Narratives*, Berlin & New York, W.De Gruyter 1974
Wright, G.E. *Biblical Archaeology*, London, Duckworth 1962
Yadin, Y. *The Art of War in Biblical Lands*, London, Weidenfeld & Nicolsen 1963
    Hazor: Great Citadel of the Bible, London, Weidenfeld & Nicolson 1975
    The Message of the Scrolls, London, Weidenfeld & Nicolson 1957
    (ed) *Jerusalem Revealed*, Jerusalem, Israel Exploration Society 1975

Acknowledgements

Thanks are due to the following for permission to reproduce black and white photographs: Dame Kathleen Kenyon and the Jericho Excavation Fund, pages 11, 12, 14 (*top*), 92, 93 and 94; the photographs on pages 9, 10, 86, 126, 143 (*top and bottom*) and 204 (*top*) are reproduced by courtesy of the Israel Department of Antiquities and Museums; those on pages 15 (*top and bottom*), 23, 86, 127, 162, 163 and 201 are from the collections of the Israel Department of Museums and Antiquities and that on page 108 is reproduced by the Department's courtesy and that of the Ashdod Expedition; Paul Jordan, pages 13, 58, 60, 69, 73, 125, 158, 178, 187 (*top and bottom*), 188, 210, 218, 226 and 228; Antonia Benedek, pages 20, 26, 28, 36, 81, 83, 85, 166, 179 and 207; Hirmer Verlag, Munchen, pages 19, 21, 31 and 34; Dr H.J.Franken, page 24; the Trustees of the British Museum, pages 32 (*top*), 33, 48, 177, 178, 186, 199 and 208; Musées Nationaux, Paris, pages 37 and 161; the Trustees of the National Gallery, pages 39 and 121; John Ross, page 45; the Egyptian Tourist Office, page 47; the Wallace Collection, page 50; Peter Clayton, pages 53 and 63; Dr Labib Habachi, page 54; Centre of Documentation and Studies on Egypt, Cairo, pages 55 and 56; Crown Copyright, the Victoria and Albert Museum (Prints and Drawings Department) for 'The Destruction of Pharaoh's Hosts' by John Martin, page 70; the British School of Archaeology in Jerusalem, page 74; Professor L.Geraty and Andrews University, Berrien Springs, pages 75 and 77; Professor Yigael Yadin from *Hazor* published by Weidenfeld & Nicolson, pages 84, 87, 88 and 140; Dr Joseph A.Callaway and Richard Cleave, page 90; Tel Aviv University Institute of Archaeology, Professor Rainey and Avraham Hay (photographer), pages 96, 183, 185 (*top and bottom*); the Oriental Institute, University of Chicago, pages 99, 102 and 104; the Mansell Collection, page 111; Dr A.Mazar, pages 112 and 113; Dr M. Kochavi, pages 115 and 116; Kunsthistorisches Museum, Vienna, page 124; Professor James B.Pritchard, pages 128, 129 and 130; Dame Kathleen Kenyon and the Jerusalem Excavation Fund, pages 133, 134, 190, 192 and 211; the Israel Exploration Society for photographs from their publication *Jerusalem Revealed*, pages 139, 191, 220, 224 and 230; Dr Paul Garber and Southeastern Films, Atlanta, Georgia, for the Howland-Garber Reconstruction of Solomon's Temple, page 141 (*bottom*); Museum of Fine Arts, Boston, page 147; Dr Beno Rothenberg, pages 149, 150 and 151; Professor A.Biran, Director of the Tell Dan Archaeological Expedition, page 160; Palphot Ltd., Israel, page 164; Osterreichische Nationalbibliotek, page 167; Professor N.Avigad, the Hebrew University, Jerusalem, page 169; David Harris, pages 171, 174 and 200; Dr David Ussishkin, pages 172 (David Harris, photographer), 189 (Avraham Hay, photographer), 204 (*bottom*) and 205; Radio Times Hulton Picture Library, page 176; Alia, Royal Jordanian Airlines, page 216; Meir Ben Dov, page 223; the British Library Board, Additional MS. 18850, f. 15v., page 198; the Shrine of the Book, Jerusalem, page 229.

Thanks are due to the following for permission to reproduce colour photographs: Paul Jordan, jacket (2), facing pages 8 (*top*), 32 (*top and bottom*), 49 (*bottom*), 64 (*top and bottom*), 65 (*top and bottom*), 80 (*bottom*), 81, 96 (*top*), 97 (*bottom*), 112, 113 (*top and bottom*), 129 (*top and bottom*), 144, 145 (*top and bottom*), 160, 161 (*top and bottom*), 208 (*bottom*) and 224 (*top and bottom*); Hirmer Verlag, Munchen, facing pages 8 (*bottom*) and 17; Gillian Cleeve, facing page 33 (*top*); Palphot Ltd., Israel, facing pages 33 (*bottom*), 96 (*top*) and 225; Antonia Benedek, facing pages 16 (*top and bottom*), 49 (*top*), 128, 176 (*top and bottom*), 192 (*top and bottom*) and 208 (*top*); Peter Clayton, facing page 48 (*top*); John Ross, facing page 48 (*bottom*); Edgar Asher, facing page 80 (*top*); Dr A.Mazar, facing page 97 (*top*); The Smithsonian Institution, facing page 177 (*top and bottom*); the Corporation of Newcastle, facing page 193; Alia, Royal Jordanian Airline, facing page 209.

The map on page 17 is based on one in Dr Svend Helm's *Jawa: A Preliminary Report, 1973*, published by the Institute of Archaeology, London; the maps on pages 35 and 66 and those facing pages 8 and 9 are based on maps in the *Oxford Bible Atlas*, Second Edition 1974, edited by Herbert G.May, G.N.S.Hunt and R.W.Hamilton, published by the Oxford University Press; the drawing on page 71 is based on a photograph in *The Tabernacle* by Moses Levine, published by the Soncino Press, Tel Aviv; the drawings on pages 140 (*top*) and 165 are based on plans from *Hazor* by Yigael Yadin, published by Weidenfeld & Nicolson, and that on page 154 on a plan by Professor Yadin first published in the *Biblical Archaeology Review*; the drawing on page 107 is based on one from *Ancient Pottery of the Holy Land* by Professor R.Amiran, published by the Masada Press; the drawings on page 131 are based on two from *Gibeon Where the Sun Stood Still* by Professor James B.Pritchard, published by Princeton University Press. Thanks are due to Dame Kathleen Kenyon and the Jerusalem Excavation Fund for permission to base the drawings on pages 132 and 136 on ones from *Digging Up Jerusalem* published by Ernest Benn. The maps on pages 168, 193 and 221 are based on ones appearing in *Jerusalem Revealed*, published by the Israel Exploration Society; the map on page 145 is based on one from *Solomon and Sheba* edited by Dr James B.Pritchard, published by Phaidon; the map on page 180 is based on one in *The Macmillan Bible Atlas* by Yohanan Aharoni and Michael Avi-Yonah, published by Macmillan Publishing Co., New York, (Copyright 1964, 1966, 1968 by Carta, Jerusalem).

Extracts used from the Authorised Version of the Holy Bible, which is Crown copyright, are with permission.

Index

237